Engraved by W.H. Mote from a Photograph by Nichols

*Your humble Servant
John Brown*

SIXTY YEARS' GLEANINGS FROM LIFE'S HARVEST.

A GENUINE AUTOBIOGRAPHY.

BY JOHN BROWN,
PROPRIETOR OF THE UNIVERSITY BILLIARD ROOMS, CAMBRIDGE.

"All the world's a stage,
And all the men and women merely players:
They have their exits and their entrances;
And one man in his time plays many parts."
SHAKSPEARE.

Printed for the Author, by
J. PALMER, 58, SIDNEY STREET, CAMBRIDGE.
WILLIS & SOTHERAN, 136, STRAND, LONDON.
1858.

TO

The Authorities of this Ancient University,

WHOSE FAVOR

I HAVE LARGELY EXPERIENCED,

AND TO THE

Municipal Corporation of my Native Town,

IN WHOSE COUNCILS

I HAVE HAD THE HONOR TO SHARE,

THESE HUMBLE RECORDS OF AN ACTIVE LIFE

ARE MOST

GRATEFULLY AND RESPECTFULLY

Dedicated

BY THEIR OBLIGED AND FAITHFUL SERVANT,

John Brown.

CAMBRIDGE,
10th October, 1858.

THE OLD CASTLE, CAMBRIDGE.

THE AUTHOR'S APOLOGY FOR HIS UNDERTAKING.

It has been my lot to figure in curious and stirring scenes, and to acquire practical experience of various phases in human existence. But it is only within the last few years that I have been permitted to enjoy occasional hours of unalloyed leisure. Thus, although the idea had often occurred to me that sundry passages of my life might be so embodied in a pen-and-ink sketch, as to be presentable to the public,—it was not until lately that I attempted to realise my thought. Neither was I, even then, so enamoured of my own conceptions as to have prosecuted the task seriously,—had I not received unexpected encouragement to do so. I refer to the kind approbation bestowed upon my earliest efforts, by several friends,—far more accustomed than myself to judging of such matters,—to whom certain portions of my MS. were from time to time submitted. Their opinion confirmed my own belief that many of the incidents I should have to relate, possessed a natural and inherent interest,—which the narrator's shortcomings could not altogether neutralise. But to affect the style and title of a 'contributor to literature' would be, indeed, a foolish ambition in me; for these memoirs will sufficiently indicate that all regular instruction ceased, in my case, at ten years old. Whatever knowledge I have since gained, was picked up hastily in the many highways and byways which I have since trodden.

I have yet another and perhaps better excuse for rushing into print: an excuse which is based upon the hope that, throughout my otherwise unpretending volume, there will be found traces of an uniform design to inculcate a definite moral. Some slight allusion to such a purpose is hazarded at the close of the work.

The age in which I have lived has been an age of progress, such as is wholly unexampled in the world's annals. But by far the most material advances (whether in science or civilisation) of which the period can boast, were made during the *latter* half of my sixty years' experience. Thus it happens, that many of the earlier scenes described by me are but stray records of a state of things that has for ever passed away, and truly thankful am I that such is the case. Had it been otherwise, I might have hesitated about printing even the mitigated details of much that I have witnessed, and attempted to narrate in the following pages. It is my trust however, that sufficient discretion has been exercised to avoid offending even the most fastidious reader.

Lastly, as it is quite impossible that any man (situated as I have been) should have lived to my years, and kept clear of "parish squabbles," I am happy to state, that these Memoirs are, to the best of my knowledge and intention, absolutely free from any offensive reference to local questions, upon which it may have been my fate at times to differ from men as good, as, or better than, myself.

J. B.

PARISH CHURCH, AND BURIAL PLACE OF THE AUTHOR'S MOTHER.

CONTENTS.

PART I.

CHILDHOOD AND EARLY STRUGGLES.

CHAPTER I.

My Birth—Family Reverses—'The Drove' 1

CHAPTER II.

My Apprenticeship—Sparrows and Spectres—I become a 'Juvenile Offender', and am sent to Prison—The Indentures Cancelled . 7

CHAPTER III.

I throw myself on the world—London—The 'Trade' Quarter—My Lodging, and new Associate—I make a very poor beginning 23

CHAPTER IV.

I grow desperate—But 'all's well that ends well'—My circumstances improve—The 'Strike'—The Recruiting Sergeant . 36

PART II.

THE VAGABOND ASHORE AND AFLOAT.

CHAPTER I.

My military career; rather brief than glorious . . . 47

CHAPTER II.

The Strollers—I become an Actor—Our way of life . . . 51

CHAPTER III.

I am compelled to refuse a most noble offer—Change of Quarters and change of Business—The Clown—The Inundation—Close of the Season, and break-up of the Company 61

CHAPTER IV.

A Resolution—The 'Tender'—Scene on Board—At Chatham again—French Prisoners—I sail in the 'Tigris'—The Irish Station—'Over-land' Waghorn—Life on board-ship . . 72

CHAPTER V.

Ship's 'Idlers'—Floating Theatre—Bantry Bay, and Kinsale—Dealings with the Natives—A Sailor's accomplishments—State of discipline during the war—Frightful use of the 'Cat', and other arbitrary inflictions—An unjust punishment, and its melancholy results 85

CHAPTER VI.

Chase of the 'Peacock'—Christmas eve in Harbour—A Quarrel—I come to grief and to the Gratings—My subsequent feelings, and resolve—A sullen Crew—An attempt at Escape—It is frustrated, but not discovered 101

CHAPTER VII.

A Gale in the Bay of Biscay—Gibraltar—Our Ship plague-stricken—Awful Mortality—Quarantine—The Irish Widows—Plymouth Sound—Napoleon I. on board the Bellerophon—Paying off—A lark with the Israelites—A Plucked Pigeon 114

CHAPTER VIII.

Haslar Hospital—A Relapse and Convalescence—Singular Meeting with an old Acquaintance—I am discharged, and obtain a free passage round to Chatham 128

PART III.

I RECOMMENCE LIFE AT HOME: AND MEET WITH VARIOUS 'UPS' AND 'DOWNS'.

CHAPTER I.

I refit at Chatham—A disputed Identity—An agreeable Fellow-traveller—Arrival in London—My 'bottle-green-black' coat—A Day in Town—Miss O'Neill—I bid adieu to my travelling Companion 139

CHAPTER II.

Bird the Waggoner—My Mother's Retreat—A Family reunion—Leadenhall lingo—The Prize Ring—I determine to resume my old Trade 151

CHAPTER III.

I re-commence work—A slippery Tutor—My Rescue by Archie M'Gill—The Biter Bit—Circumstances improve—Amusements of the period—A Set-to with 'Barney Aaron'—The Jews' Quarter—Rag Fair—Anecdotes 166

CHAPTER IV.

A Lark with an Israelite—'Tippy Bobby's' Courtship—The Labour market overstocked—'Old Biddles'—I complete my Professional Education, and resolve to leave town for a season . . . 181

CHAPTER V.

I return to Cambridge—'Hobson's Conduit' and 'Hobson's Choice'—I encounter my old enemy—Meeting with my Grandmother—Barnwell—The College walks 197

CHAPTER VI.

My Progress at Cambridge—I win Honours, and others wear them—The Dean of St. John's—I get disgusted—Though not for want of good Friends—A 'Mill' in Jesus-lane 209

CHAPTER VII.

Bound for London—A facetious Jehu, and an extortionate Publican—Sydenham as it was—Heroes of the Ring—I astonish my new employer—The Snobs' Feast—Adrift again 224

CHAPTER VIII.

The Two Stutterers—The 'Fuddlers'—'Trying the Boot'—The Rival 'Rooks'—The Dog Stealers—'King Hobdel'—Skittles—Female Pugilists—The Stourbridge Fair Catastrophe 240

CHAPTER IX.

Sketches in London Streets—Sadler's Wells—Brown the Costermonger—Old Friends—Billiards—A Set-to with Paddy—The Two Weddings—A romance in real Life 255

CHAPTER X.

I renew an old Acquaintance—Bartholomew's Hospital—Abernethy—The Cato-street Gang—'De Mishner'—Real Charity—'The Lord's People'—The end of honest Archie McGill—Barber-ous Practices—A Ball in Cateaton-street—Gallery of Select Portraits 273

CHAPTER XI.

Working Double Tides—The Irish 'Cock and Hen' Club—Rouse's Concerts—The 'Wake'—I figure as a Witness at Guildhall—The Result—An Entertainment—The Boot-Club . . . 292

CHAPTER XII.

A Distressing Incident—Dog-Fighting—'Jacko Makakko'—A visit to the 'Crown and Anchor' Booth at Stepney—Encounter with a 'Bargee' 312

PART IV.

I MARRY, AND EXPERIENCE FURTHER VICISSITUDES IN LIFE: BUT, AS I HOPE, FINALLY COME TO A SAFE ANCHORAGE.

CHAPTER I.

I think of 'Settling Down'—And go a Courting—Edmonton Fair—An uncivil Driver—My Intended and her Family—Unfortunate Circumstances—A Wedding-Feast, and no Wedding—The exertions of a young Married Couple—The old 'Cobourg' Theatre—'Little Coley' and 'Long Dick'—I give 'Jack Holloway' a lesson 325

CHAPTER II.

Serious illness of my Brother—We bring him home from Margate—Poor 'Tom'—I resolve on settling in Cambridge—My Difficulties—A Friend in Need—My old Employer—I engage with his Son—Adventure with a Drowning Man—My difference with 'The Marquis' 337

CHAPTER III.

I rebel against injustice, and set up my standard at Fort St. George—My Brother's death—The Bowling-Green Theatre—My first appearance on the Barnwell Stage—A Change for the Worse—The Garrick Club—My 'Accepted' Address—University Dramatic Club—The Theatre in Jesus-lane—Cambridge Theatrical Anecdotes 353

CHAPTER IV.

I am beggared again by an act of robbery—The friendly Host, and the honest Usurer—Stanzas—A merry Christmas—The 'Odd Fellows'—My honourable discharge under the Insolvent Act—I accept an Engagement—The divided Inheritance—Six weeks of Slavery 373

CHAPTER V.

I resolve on trying the London Stage—I delight the 'Peoples' in Sheva, at the Pavilion—'Governor Davidge' at the Surrey—Othello at a discount—A trans-pontine row—Virginius and his Daughter—'One for his nob'—I return to Cambridge—Try Billiards—My Slate Table—Tom Egan's Stroke—I begin to go ahead once more 383

CHAPTER VI.

Fresh Difficulties—A dreadfully zealous Official—My appearance before the 'Heads,' who decide in my favour—From which event my steady turn of fortune appears to date—'That' Carriage is bought—I do a bit of Good Samaritan, and get my reward—Sowing Gold—Coach versus Rail . . . 396

CHAPTER VII.

'I shall lick you!'—Thunder and Lightning—Putting on the screw—I become a Town Councillor—My robe of office—A few hints upon Brewing 411

CHAPTER VIII.

Some details of my Establishment—Re-appearance of an old Friend—His account of himself—I begin to feel myself tolerably comfortable—My mother is brought to end her days in our family circle—Practical suggestions and anecdotes connected with the game of Billiards—A rare chance at Cribbage . 420

CHAPTER IX.

I begin upon these Memoirs—Another ancient ally returns in good season—Withers's Poems—My address to the Author, and our subsequent meeting—Sir John Patteson's Arbitration between Town and Gown 434

CHAPTER X.

The Manchester Exhibition—My troublesome, but successful search after a long lost relative—The Atlas Iron Works, and other Manchester marvels—My manœuvres as chief of a Fire-brigade—Grandeur of the Exhibition—Death of Chatterton—Song of the Moon—Return to London—My Illness—I reach home again—A serious accident—Conclusion 443

BIRTH-PLACE OF THE AUTHOR.

PART I.

CHILDHOOD AND EARLY STRUGGLES.

CHAPTER I.

MY BIRTH—FAMILY REVERSES—"THE DROVE."

IN the year 1796, on the 4th of August, in the notorious village of Barnwell,[1] near Cambridge, I was ushered into the world with the usual bustle and noise attending such events. My father was what is called a respect-

[1] Barnwell is at the present day an integral portion of Cambridge, and constitutes by far the larger part of the Parish of 'St. Andrew the Less.'

able tradesman, doing a large business as a butcher both for home consumption and for the London market. Like other children, when I grew old enough I was sent to the village school, and made such progress as gave tolerable satisfaction to my parents and others who felt some little interest in my future welfare. As I advanced in years, it was observed that I evinced a headstrong and determined will of my own: nor was it possible to prevent the accomplishment of anything that I had once made up my mind to do. At the age of seven years I was sent to a school in Cambridge, where most of the boys were older than myself. Here we received what is termed a plain education; and plain enough it was. However, it was quite enough with reference to the times and to the circumstances in which I was placed. My daily attendance at school continued for about three years; at the end of which time I was thought ahead of the boys of my own age, whether in book-learning or mischief; and was rewarded accordingly. Indeed, at ten years old I was tolerably proficient in all sorts of knowledge of which boys of that age are capable. About this period my father died of consumption, leaving my mother with six of us,—the youngest in arms, and the eldest about fourteen. Even now I can very well remember the darkened windows and the house of mourning. My mother sat sorrowing by herself: and cause enough she had, for never did woman pass through greater troubles. After my father's death the business was managed, or rather mismanaged, by his youngest brother whom he had brought up from boyhood. My uncle was a weak-minded, idle fellow, fond of his pipe, cards, drinking, anything rather than business. So by degrees, in about two years, he brought us to poverty; and we were scattered to the winds. After having so nobly performed a brother's and an uncle's part, our worthless relative went off to sea, leaving my mother bankrupt, with her young family, to struggle on as best as she could.

In consideration of our misfortunes, the butchers of the town gave us 'the drove.' The duties connected with this our new occupation were very laborious and fatiguing. The stock-market being held at St. Ives, a distance of thirteen miles from Cambridge, we had to rise at three o'clock on Monday morning to be there, ready to mark the sheep purchased by the butchers, some with red-ochre and others with tar; as each person had a peculiar mark by which his sheep were known. After having done this, we took them from the pens and drove them to a paddock outside the town, lot after lot, until we had collected the entire drove. Occasionally, when the waters were out, we had to take them a considerable distance in boats; which was attended with great risk and trouble, as the sheep would sometimes jump into the water, although it is a thing they are not very fond of. When this happened, we had to follow and lead them through, till we arrived on the high road. After completing this part of the business, which took up our time till twelve o'clock, we started with the drove, amounting to three or four hundred, more or less; for I cannot now remember the average number. Saturated with water above the waist, I have often toiled along the dreary road at the rate of less than two miles an hour; not a house was to be met with on many parts of the journey; and frequently we did not reach our destination till nine o'clock at night, perfectly benumbed with cold. Then, after securing our charge in a spacious place boarded round for the purpose, we had to walk nearly two miles to our own home, weary and jaded almost beyond nature's bearing; having been eighteen hours employed in the most miserable and sickening work that either boy or man was ever engaged in. Our usual supper was a mess of boiled milk; this was soon dispatched; then, after having our feet washed in warm water, we retired to rest, requiring neither rocking nor opiates to win soft sleep to our spent frames. Although on these occasions we were allowed to sleep till nine the next morning, that morn always arrived too soon.

The next day our first business was to draw off the sheep belonging to the different butchers in the town, and to send them in separate lots to their destinations; then to drive small lots to different villages two or three miles round, and on Wednesday or Thursday to Saffron Walden, a distance of fifteen miles. This was another crawling or tedious day's work. But if this was miserable drudgery in the winter, it was ten times worse in the hot summer months, when we toiled beneath a burning sun, choked with dust, and not a drop of water on the road for ten miles; the poor sheep lying down in agony, panting for their lives. Such as were unable to travel we were compelled to leave by the roadside, to be taken up by the butchers in their carts as they returned from market; others of a lighter breed would run into the young wheats, causing us and our dogs incessant trouble. Of all the vexatious things I ever met with, this was the very worst. Those racer-bred southdowns would leap over our heads like deer, and sometimes hit us on the face and lay us sprawling on our backs. If one bolts the rest are sure to follow, jumping one after the other like boys playing at leap-frog. How often I have cried over this heart-breaking task! What added to our misery was the unfeelingness of the farmers, who frequently beat us for not keeping the sheep off the corn; which was an impossibility, as at this time the land lay open, the Inclosure Act not having yet come into operation.

For two years we thus dragged through a miserable state of existence. Towards the conclusion of this never-to-be-forgotten part of my life, as we were one day moving slowly along the road some of the sheep started from the rest, and ran into the growing corn. The more we tried to bring them back the further they went, bounding away towards the village of Fen Drayton; and whilst we chased the runaways, the drove got amongst the green corn, and were making a most delicious feast. At this juncture there appeared a fat-headed farmer on horseback, who riding up to us, dismounted, and without ceremony began to lay into my brother with an ash-plant. Hereon my young blood boiled; for I knew we had done our best to prevent any damage occurring to the crops: so seeing my brother down, and his thick-headed assailant cutting at him with his stick, I rushed at the latter while in a stooping posture, caught him under the ear, and sent him rolling over my brother, where he measured his length; making a comfortable bed of his own property, to which we did not desire to dispute his right. As he tumbled over I called out,—"Jump up, Bill, we can lick him!"

We were both strong boys and quick as any in the country, and not at all averse to fighting. Presently up got the burly farmer, and putting himself into an attitude stood upon the defensive, his wind a little damaged by the fall. As my brother was now sixteen years old, I fancied he was quite man enough for the clodpole before us; so I advised a rush with a straight arm in his wind. Away went Bill like an arrow; and down went the mountain of guts and garbage, rolling over like a porpoise and retching like a sick hippopotamus. There we left him to his own conclusions, while we, after about an hour's hard labour, succeeded in getting the drove together and proceeded on our way; not without some misgivings lest we should be brought before the magistrates, and made to pay for the damage done to the standing corn. However, we never heard any more about it. I have thought since that our assailant was ashamed to tell how he had been boy-beaten; a joke which, if known, would have stuck to him for life.

It cannot be wondered that we both began to get disgusted with this servile and monotonous occupation, and therefore agreed on requesting our mother to endeavour to make some more suitable arrangement for us; our present being at best but a degraded position, without the slightest hope of advancement. Within a few weeks from this time we gave up the drove; my brother being put to one of the first butchers in Cambridge to be finished in the business, at which he had previously worked during some three years at home.

CHAPTER II.

MY APPRENTICESHIP—SPARROWS AND SPECTRES—I BECOME A 'JUVENILE OFFENDER' AND AM SENT TO PRISON—THE INDENTURES CANCELLED.

I WENT to live with my grandmother, who kept a dairy. My duties were various; such as fetching up the cows to be milked, going to the brewhouse for grains, carrying out milk, cleaning out the cowlodge; in fact, anything and everything that I was thought capable of doing. However, this kind of life did not exactly agree with my tastes and inclinations; so that I was frequently in trouble. My grandmother too was hasty and passionate; and never having had any other children than my mother, she could hardly be expected to put up with an obstinate and self-willed boy, who was constantly in some mischief or other: indeed I was a source of great trouble to her, and to myself also. She was not in possession of the great secret, the magic rod that would have unlocked my heart, and brought gushing forth the milk of human kindness in as pure and ample a stream as ever flowed. It was not her fault; for I appeared the very opposite to what I really was.

The old lady soon got tired of me; and I cared but little about myself, whom I regarded as an outcast.

Thoughts of the future forced themselves upon me; what was I to do when arrived at manhood? how was I to get the daily bread I had been taught to pray for night and morning? I felt alone in the world; but at once made up my mind to fight my way through life, keeping truth and justice in view. I had often expressed a wish to learn a trade, as that seemed to offer the most certain means of independence, the thing of all others that I desired. It appeared to me that a mechanic could live in any country without being dependent on any one: I therefore, when asked what trade I should like, chose that of a shoemaker. The next step was to find a respectable master, and of course a religious one, as the old lady herself was very constant in her attendance at church; hail, rain, wind or snow, it mattered not—nothing to her could be a justifiable excuse for staying away. In a few months a master was found just to my grandmother's mind, and I was sent for a month on liking, as it was termed. My first attempts, I was informed, gave great promise of future excellence; and I fancied there was nothing so difficult in the art and mystery, but I should be able to accomplish it.

Thus far all went smoothly: I was treated with great civility, lived exceedingly well, and felt perfectly satisfied. Under such favourable auspices, it was soon agreed on both sides that I should be bound to my employer. The morning having arrived for this eventful business, all parties, according to previous arrangement, repaired to the lawyer's office for the purpose of witnessing the Indenture, and paying down the £25 premium. This important act of the drama concluded, I returned to my work with a suitable admonition from my aged relative, and threepence from the purse of my generous master; which was the first and the last money he ever gave me as a gratuity. He had at this time been married only a week, and I had not yet seen the face of his wife my new mistress.

My master was one of the leanest men I had ever seen; his head seemed much too large for his body, and he possessed an elongated visage, staring grey eyes, a mouth with projecting teeth, and a nose of such immense proportions, as I have never seen before or since. His legs were like two dropsical tobacco-pipes; and he walked leaning backwards, as if he was afraid the weight of his nasal projection would pull him to the ground. Such was my master's figure: as yet, I had known but little of his disposition; but by degrees it developed itself, and to my sorrow. Instead of a mess of milk for breakfast, the diet I had been accustomed to from childhood, I was put on sour broth, so thin it might be best described as good water spoiled; I never could prevail on dog or cat to touch it. Then for dinner, the bits and scrapings of the plates were served up to me in the kitchen; and there was the pump of course, if I felt thirsty.

Such treatment inspired me with the feelings of a young savage, and I began to look on my employer with the most unqualified hatred as well as contempt. My indignation was roused at his villainous hypocrisy, as I measured the sanctified scoundrel's bearing before the canting crew with whom he associated. Never did any thing in human form appear to me so truly ugly and despicable. It soon fell to my lot to be ushered into the presence of Mrs. B., as 'the new boy,' for her approval or disapproval, as the case might be. After a patronising but contemptuous survey, I was dismissed with a sort of yawning,—"Oh, that will do!"—which led me to conclude that I had not made a very favourable impression upon her mind. Be that as it may, it was quite certain she had not impressed me with a very lofty opinion of herself; for I perceived during this short interview that she was intolerably affected. This for me was quite enough, had she been beautiful as Hebe; but she was the very opposite to all that I had ever imagined of female loveliness. Her tall and lath-like figure was surmounted by a little white face, short and flat, with eyes so small that they looked like two sloes stuck in a dumpling. During my short visit, I saw she desired me to understand that she thought herself quite a lady; but in this opinion we did not exactly coincide. I was in my way a small philosopher. I made it my business to study human nature, and could distinguish between the bearing of true nobility and its 'brummagem' counterfeit.

In truth, I could not conceal my unqualified contempt for such a precious pair: it was plain to me that they existed only in sham. Their 'my dear' and 'my love,' in the absence of any genuine affection on either side, were but miserable attempts to deceive each other and the canting maw-worms their pious friends; amongst whom was the saintly minister, who came frequently to tea, and prayed with 'Susan' in private. He was a nice soft-spoken gentleman, with straight hair combed flat to his forehead, and his face drawn out to its full length in that most approved form supposed to be expressive of ultra sanctity. Nevertheless, I strongly suspect he yearned after flesh-pots; I certainly caught him once with the lid of one in his hand inspecting its contents, while his pocket seemed to stick out, as if it contained something a great deal more like a piece of pork than a handkerchief. If I had seen him take the pork I dared not have said so, because I should not have been believed; besides which I must have borne the infliction of a long yarn of methodistic cant, and have been shewn up as a lying monster for venturing to impugn the character of such a holy man. Moreover the pork was not mine; so I locked up my suspicions in my breast, and let them pray, deceive, and cheat each other as they pleased.

My living, as already stated, was of the worst description; but that was nothing as compared with other degradations I experienced. My bedroom was a dark garret, the window of which had been plastered over, no doubt to save the window-tax. To this pigeon-hole I had to ascend an old-fashioned staircase in the dark, groping and feeling my way on the large landings, where at first I frequently lost myself. However, after a time I got used to the road, and could reach my nest without much difficulty. I was greatly indebted to the sparrows for letting a little light into my sleeping kennel. The house had been shut up for years in consequence of a report that it was haunted, and the birds had pecked holes through the mortar, and domiciled within so long, that I suppose they considered it their own freehold. At all events, they made noise enough the first night I disturbed them in their snug warm roost, and fairly screaming with fright, flew about the room in such hurried confusion, that if at all superstitious, I might have thought these were the spirits of the departed who had been murdered in this lonely den. I have since known some poor boys (aye, and men too) who would have been rendered idiots for life by such a scene, or rather uproar. There must have been a large family of them, for the birds were at least twenty minutes before they all got clear of the place; in fact, the holes that they had made were only large enough to admit one at a time; and the poor things, in their hurry and flight, whilst scrambling to get to the apertures, flew against each other and fell down stunned.

After all the birds had got away that were able, I searched about by the glimmering light that came through the holes in the mortar, and picked up thirteen that appeared nearly dead with fright and were panting for their lives. I placed the poor creatures on the bed, where they remained without attempting to escape; whilst I soliloquised upon my own helpless condition, and felt for them as companions in my misery. At length, in no very happy mood, I laid myself down and slept soundly, till St. Mary's bell awoke me from my slumbers. My first thought, on getting out of bed, was for the prisoners I had captured overnight. I had secured them by fastening the door and blocking up the holes with my stockings; so when I let in the light, there sat huddled together my little captives. Having ascertained that they were all young ones, I shook up my bed and went to open the shop windows; resolving after breakfast to take them up some soaked bread, which, as I knew, would serve for both victuals and drink.

For I had taken many a bird's nest with young ones, in brighter days; when I had a happy home with brothers and sisters, and large bedrooms comfortably carpeted, and four-post bedsteads with curtains, and a good-natured servant-girl to light us to bed and tuck us in after saying our prayers. Here, indeed, was a change: it seemed the work of a lifetime! In thought and feeling I had become a man; I was all alone in the world; I saw with sorrow the craft and treachery around me, and no way left but to oppose cunning to cunning, though I despised the spider-like system.

But to return: breakfast time arrived, and sopping some bread, I took it up to my young family; but holy nature would not have her rights usurped by me. The parents had been before me and fed their young, and were perched against the holes when I entered, whither they had most likely fled on my approach to their dark and solid breeding-cage. Some time passed: the sparrows became quite used to my appearance, and took no notice of me; they always passed through the holes at peep of day, and I saw no more of them, as they were always gone to roost long before my bedtime.

Meanwhile I had suffered wrong upon wrong: I had undergone every species of insult and humiliation; I had been beaten with the buckle-end of a strap, for breaking by accident an earthern vessel worth a groat. But what finally exhausted my patience was the being sent on a degrading errand especially devised to make me figure in a ridiculous light before all the urchins of the neighbourhood. For this public insult I forthwith vowed to be revenged. That day passed heavily indeed; I felt no pleasure in life; it appeared to me all a vapour, a mere blank. I retired to bed overwhelmed with grief; and being far from the hearing of any one, gave vent to my pent-up sorrows; it seemed as if the little birds understood the tones of grief, for they joined with me in plaintive notes. I began to think how I should get away from this dark prison: and it occurred to me that the report of the house being haunted might be made useful, with the aid of a little invention.

Next morning, on meeting the servant-girl, a vulgar addle-headed creature, I told her that I had seen, on the landing of the first floor, a little old woman,—but could not touch her, for when I tried, my hand went right through her—yet there she stood. I thus worked upon the girl's ignorance and credulity, till she fancied she saw the ghost in the cellar as she was going down for coals,—and came back screaming as if the fiend had seized her. To keep up the delusion, I offered to go with her, if she would get a light; and so we fetched the coals, but not without great trepidation. My plan began to operate: all day this imaginary spirit followed the fool up and down stairs, and when it grew dusk she was fairly demented. I went into the kitchen just as the bell rung for a candle, and answered it myself as if in a terrible fright. My hair, which was very wiry, I had stuck bolt upright; and my face was rubbed slightly over with chalk from the palms of my hands. In this guise I suddenly opened the parlour door, met the mistress face to face, and in a terrified tone cried out, "The ghost, the ghost!" The girl, like a good second, bawled out lustily, "The ghost, the ghost!" The mistress, poor silly creature, soon joined in chorus, and even fancied she saw the spectre vanish up my old-fashioned staircase.

Just at this precious moment, in came Daddy Spindle-shanks, and at his heels about twenty young ladies from a boarding-school next door. They too had often heard noises in the attics, and had seen a figure (just such as I described) gliding about in the kitchen by moonlight; nay, when I told how she was dressed, they had all seen her often, and thought she was one of the family, either Mr. or Mrs. B.'s mother! I think this goblin tale was a sort of god-send for Mr. B.; since the 'haunted house,' as it was called, had been taken and fitted up at some expense to receive his new wife, who no doubt thought it derogatory to her breeding to reside at a shoemaker's shop. Be that as it may, my plan succeeded; we all left the haunted house, and the poor sparrows held quiet possession of the solitary attic. The boarding-school too was removed immediately, but whither I never heard. The two houses had originally been one mansion, tenanted by persons of considerable property and local consideration; for there were still attached to it extensive stables, outhouses, and a beautiful garden; all denoting the rank of its occupants in former days.

Our household now became more closely associated; for we henceforth lived within a very small compass, and were severally accommodated in the least possible space. The place where I was stowed at night was a lean-to sort of loft, over a kitchen in the yard. It was approached by a ladder, at the top of which was a square landing about a yard each way; and at the further end of this dormitory, my bed (if that be really the name it deserved) was placed on some boards. In turning into this bunk, if I happened to forget its peculiar conformation, my head came in contact with the rafters; and when I lay at full length, my toes touched the tiles.

This convenient apartment served also as a workshop for myself and a journeyman, who was my tutor in the art and mystery of the gentle craft. This poor fellow had himself been apprenticed there, and knew he was a doomed man; since there he must remain,—for this reason, that no one else would employ him. As soon as I began to understand the nature of work, and could distinguish betwixt good and bad, I resolved to be free by some means or other. Here was a fair sample of what I must become, if I served seven years in this botching den; here sat beside me every day a living monument of human misery.

The contemplation of my forlorn position drove me to desperation; I became reckless of consequences; I hurled open defiance in their teeth; I had been starved and degraded, I had been beaten like a slave,—but my determined and indomitable will could not be broken; they could not manacle my soul, they could not make shackles to bind my spirit; and I felt that both would triumph over hatred and malice. I was remarkably strong and active; I could do more work, and do it better, than my poor instructor; I began to feel that I could earn my bread, if set at liberty; I yearned for the opportunity, and it soon occurred. I had been making paste, and was in the yard filling the horns which we used at our work, when I heard the squeaking affected voice of my beautiful mistress calling out "Mr. B., Mr. B.!" I could not resist the temptation to mimic her, which I did loud enough to reach her ear in the bedroom above. She opened the window and asked who it was that called. I replied, scorning to tell a lie, "Oh, that was me!" The grand climax had arrived; I went up to my stinking den, and sat down to my work, which I had no sooner resumed, than I saw the shadow of my cold-blooded tormentor through the window. I suspected his errand and prepared for the conflict. He opened the door, and drew forth the well-known strap and buckle; but before he had time to strike, I ran into him, and seizing him by the loins, threw him down the ladder into the yard below. It was fortunate for him that he slid down the hand-rail, or his worthless neck might have been broken by the fall.

This scene had scarcely passed, when in walked the parish constable with his long staff of office. I was given into his custody, and taken through the street to the magistrate's house. This functionary was sitting in a parlour with his daughters, before whom I cut a pretty figure, with my black basil apron, dirty hands and face, my hair uncombed, and without a hat. Here my heart swelled in spite of me; I could not forget the respectability of my childhood; and fairly overwhelmed with grief, burst into tears. Presently my persecutor arrived, and laid a heinous charge against me, involving the most barefaced and wicked lies; telling the magistrate he had taken me from motives of charity, whereas he had received with me a premium of £25, and my grandmother was to find me in clothes.

However, upon the statements of this religious monster, I was committed to prison for a month. On my arrival there I was locked in a cell where a man, whom I had known, had hanged himself only a fortnight before.

Here was another splendid lodging of my persecutor's providing—but it mattered not; I slept till morning, and was then let out into the yard, where I washed myself, combed out my hair, and thanked God I was released, for a season, from the most hypocritical tyrant that ever crossed my path in life. After I had walked about the yard some time, the governor made his appearance. He was a fine specimen of an Englishman, standing over six feet, with a countenance expressive of all the good qualities of our nature. He very kindly questioned me about my present misfortunes, and being himself a shoemaker by trade, examined me concerning my capabilities and the progress I had made: as to which, I am happy to say, my answers gave entire satisfaction.

On the conclusion of our discourse, the governor went into the house or lodge where he resided, and shortly after I was called into his keeping-room, where I had the pleasure of seeing his wife, a most benevolent old lady, who gave me tea and bread-and-butter, offered with such kindness that the act has made an indelible impression on my memory. Indeed the treatment I received at the hands of these worthy people can never be effaced from my mind. To speak of a prison as a place of comfort, and even happiness, is rather novel; but, gentle reader, just consider what I had suffered both mentally and bodily, and you will arrive at something like a just conclusion as regards my feelings in this otherwise unhappy place. Being requested by the governor to state the exact and positive truth, I did so, omitting nothing. When my tale was ended he asked who my father was, and on being informed exclaimed: "He was an honourable man, I knew him well,"—at the same time consigning my devil of a master to the custody of a certain old gentleman, with a character that would ensure him every attention his peculiar case deserved.

Had I been idle or stupid, and so proved a burden to my employer, he would have had some excuse; but as it was he had none: for I could do things that no one so young in the trade had been known to accomplish. On the day of the installation of the Duke of Gloucester as Chancellor of the University, I made two pairs of shoes for a gentleman of Queens' College; I saw Sadler's balloon ascend over the houses as I was sitting at work, not being allowed a holiday, like other apprentices in the town, on that memorable occasion. But that did not grieve me, as I took great delight in doing something to be spoken of; besides, I knew that by my own exertions I must work my way through life. To an active tradesman I should have been a prize of the highest value; but to such a psalm-singing drone, such a drawling idler, I was really hateful because he knew I despised his laziness and ignorance. Through his own neglect he lost his business, and had not half enough work for me to do. Thus being on the verge of bankruptcy, he desired nothing better than to get rid of me, and could see no more creditable mode of doing so than that of branding me with disgrace. Yet with all his hypocrisy he did not succeed; for I passed through the fire unscathed.

To return to my prison discipline: after reading to the old lady at her request, she very courteously asked me to read a chapter in the Bible to the prisoners. This duty I thenceforth performed every day during my confinement; and being a better reader than most boys, I was treated with great respect in consequence. I became indeed a favourite with the old people, who watched with parental care over the unfortunate beings under their charge. Thus the time passed on for three weeks, without anything particular occurring; except the appearance of the great comet, which I had the pleasure of looking at through the bars of my cell.

My grandmother all this time had been ill, and was confined to her bed, so that I did not expect to see her: however, some person informed her of my disgrace; and although very unwell, she came to inquire what monstrous crime I had committed. I detailed all the circumstances as truly as if I had been before the last tribunal; when, after remaining for some time in thought, my relative asked the gaoler how I had behaved in prison. He gave me an excellent character, said that I had been shamefully treated, and spoke of my master's conduct in terms of honest indignation. His good wife too advocated my cause with nature's kindliest eloquence. After some further conversation, —as I was resolved on not returning to my master's abode,—the governor politely offered to accompany my grandmother at once to the magistrate's, and endeavour to effect some arrangement.

Things now began to assume a more favourable appearance; the old gentleman returned in about an hour, released me from the prison walls, and himself acted as my conductor. I shall never forget the peculiar sensation I experienced on emerging into the open air; a sort of dizziness came over me, and I reeled like a drunken man: but it soon passed away. Having reached the place where all parties concerned had met to decide upon this momentous business, we found two magistrates and their clerk, who appeared to be recording the last sentence spoken before we entered. It ran thus: " besides the premium, I lent him £25." The magistrate who had committed me now began to question me in mild and considerate language, both as to my capabilities, and regarding the treatment I had received at my master's hands. I answered in respectful terms, and carefully avoided the slightest exaggeration. At the conclusion of my examination, we all, except the magistrates, left the room; but were soon recalled to hear the important decision, for which I stood listening in breathless anxiety.

The senior magistrate then addressed my chap-fallen tyrant in the following terms: " Mr. B., we have given this case our most serious consideration: and have arrived at the conclusion that you have not only violated your agreement, but have exercised the most wanton cruelty towards this poor boy. It appears in our judgment very unacccuntable that you should be so eager to get rid of him, after the statement you have made; for you say he can earn fifteen shillings a-week, though only eighteen months at the trade. This is indeed strange: however, as the youth says he would rather serve the remainder of his time in prison, and his grandmother consents to the indenture being cancelled, we advise you to pay over the £25 which you borrowed of her, before we destroy this document; and you had better fetch the money at once, for your own credit's sake." At the conclusion of this well-timed advice, its humiliated recipient sneaked off to get the money, which I was sorely afraid he would not be able to raise. He did however obtain the amount—by what means I know not; it was sufficient for me that the cash was paid, and the indentures cancelled.

CHAPTER III.

I THROW MYSELF ON THE WORLD—LONDON—THE 'TRADE' QUARTER—MY LODGING, AND NEW ASSOCIATE—I MAKE A VERY POOR BEGINNING.

The next thing was to see my poor old grandmother, to assure her that I could earn my living, and to state my intentions. Our meeting was of a sorrowful character; but in the end she came to the conclusion that I must pursue my own course. London was to me the great centre of attraction, whereof I had heard much and read more; for whatever books fell in my way I always read if possible. Thus buoyed up with hope, I won my aged relative's consent that I should try my fortune in the world.

The next morning at a very early hour I took my leave of her, after receiving some good counsel and an affectionate farewell. Then with bundle on shoulder, and a little money in my pocket, I started for the great Metropolis, intending to go as far as I could the first day: and being a good walker measured eighteen miles without stopping. I first pulled up at a roadside public-house in the village of Barley; here I asked the landlady to let me have some bread and cheese and half-a-pint of ale,—which the woman very civilly brought, together with a knife and a little salt. Just before I had finished my frugal meal, a tall rough-looking fellow entered, who after saying 'good morning' to the mistress of the house, turned to me: and asked how far I had come? I answered, from Cambridge; and told him that I was going to London. Hereupon he became inquisitive, and seeing my apron twisted around me, inquired what trade I was, and if I was not an apprentice. Having nothing to fear, I answered all his questions promptly; until at last he said I was a runaway apprentice, and that it was his duty as parish constable to take me back. To convince him of his mistake, I had to go through the history of my apprenticeship, my incarceration in gaol, the cancelling of the indenture, and the parting with my grandmother.

When I had concluded, the woman of the house, who had been listening all the time, remarked that it was impossible I could make up such a tale if it were not true; and the burly constable allowed me to pursue my journey without further molestation. I had not anticipated anything like this occurring when I started; but now the possibility of its being repeated, haunted me during the remainder of the journey. I felt annoyed, and dreaded being interrupted in my progress—but nevertheless continued to march along at my usual rate, until I had accomplished forty miles. Then, beginning to feel tired, I again stopped at a public-house, and was supplied with some cold meat and a cup of tea. After paying for what I had taken, and ascertaining that I could have a bed, I amused myself for an hour with a newspaper that was lying on the table, drank a pint of ale, and retired to rest early.

Having slept soundly until the servant girl was stirring in the morning, I rose about seven o'clock, had a good wash at the pump, and again took the road. But my pace was now slower, for my feet were rather tender from not having been used to walking so far, and my limbs too were stiff. This however gradually wore off by exercise, and at about a quarter to eleven I entered the modern Babylon. The din and bustle, and the never-ceasing stream of vehicles of every description rattling backwards and forwards, here completely bewildered me; whilst the crowded streets, and the shops displaying an inconceivable variety of articles, struck me dumb with wonder and astonishment.

On recovering from my confusion, I bethought me of inquiring for a place I had heard much talk about, as the quarter where a great number of the trade resided. It was formerly called Grub-street, but is now named after our great poet Milton. Here in many different windows I saw 'Lodgings' advertised in a great variety of character; but the shops and houses all bore the appearance of squalid misery; the inhabitants too seemed of the lowest description: and drunkenness and disorder appeared to revel uncontrolled. Squalid sallow-faced beings reeled about with short pipes in their mouths, cursing and swearing in the most horrible manner; whilst their ragged vestments fluttered in the wind, exposing their naked persons at every gust. But this was nothing to the disgusting conduct and wretched appearance of the women, who kept tumbling in and out of dirty gin-shops, screaming and blaspheming, with infants in their arms half naked and in the most filthy condition. Some were so helplessly drunk, that they dropped their babies in the noisome gutter and rolled over them: being incapable of getting up until set on their legs by some of their acquaintance, and assisted to their foul dens in the most bestial state imaginable. The children were the most pitiable objects my eyes had ever beheld. Almost in a state of nudity, begrimed with filth and dirt, it was impossible to tell whether they were blacks or whites; for their hair resembled a dirty thrum mop. But I must give up attempting to describe this scene, and leave the shocking picture to be completed by imagination. I turned from the spot with loathing, and wandering up a side street, almost wished I had consented to bear the ills I had been so eager to fly from.

Whilst thus ruminating, my eye fell upon a card in the window of a small shop, whereon was written in an excellent schoolboy's hand, 'Lodgings for single men.' I made a scrutinizing survey of the shop and its contents; everything appeared arranged in the most exact order, the scales were bright, the counter perfectly clean, and the floor bestrewed with white sand: moreover, nothwithstanding the variety of articles, I observed a place for everything, and everything in its place. There was a nest of drawers all neatly labelled with the names of the articles they contained; there was soap and candles; gums, pitch, and resin; starch and stone-blue; sugar, mustard, pepper, and salt; with every variety of article for domestic purposes. These, as I learned afterwards, were retailed to the poor of the neighbourhood in the smallest possible quantities. They dealt also in sand, brick-dust, small beer, glass, crockery, birch-brooms, bread, butter, cheese, bacon, and other items more than I can enumerate.

After a little hesitation I entered the shop, and was received by a woman of about the middle age, wearing a widow's cap white as snow; her mourning dress too appeared of excellent quality, and her countenance expressed sorrow blended with resignation. In the little room behind I could see a boy about twelve playing with a young child; they also were in mourning. Upon being asked my business, I said I had just arrived from the country, and wanted a lodging. The mistress judged at once from my bnndle and apron that I was one of the craft, and asked: "Are you a shoemaker?" I answered in the affirmative, not without a blush, for the orgies I had witnessed a few minutes before made me feel ashamed of my calling. She then said that many of the trade had gone away in her debt, not only for their lodging but for shop goods also. I hereupon offered at once to pay every week in advance, and give ready money for what I might have out of the shop. Nothing, she admitted, could be more fair: so I was shewn upstairs to a room where a man about forty sat at work on a pair of jockey boots, the closing of which appeared to me most beautiful. We agreed about the lodging, and I paid half-a-crown in advance for the week ensuing, which was to be my weekly rent.

I next addressed myself civilly to the person who was now joint tenant with me. In answer to a few inquiries as to where I came from, and how I came to be on my own hands so young, I gave him a brief history of my trials and travels. We then got into conversation about our fellow-craftsman Bloomfield, whom my new acquaintance had worked with in the garret in which he wrote his 'Farmer's Boy.' This talk resulted from my noticing a volume lettered 'Bloomfield's Poems'; but there was besides a long shelf containing the works of our best poets, though the books were old and the binding here and there dilapidated. First in order stood the sublime Milton; next him the immortal bard of Avon: with Goldsmith, Cowper, Gay, and Gray, Pomfret, and Kirke White,—to whose memory a tablet has been erected in one of the churches of my native place. Here were also translations of Homer, Virgil, Ovid, Juvenal, and many others both ancient and modern. Of all these works I had read or heard more or less; for to me reading was the greatest luxury of which I had any conception.

We sat talking like old friends; for there was something in the expression of this man's face that made me feel quite at home. An old Dutch clock that hung in one corner of the room struck four, when my companion laid down his work, and began to set his things for tea. He used no tray, but arranged on the table a little black teapot, two cups and saucers, a little brown jar with moist sugar, a plate with a small quantity of butter, and a japanned tea-canister. Whilst he was thus engaged I ran down to the shop, and having procured four nice rashers of bacon, through the kindness of the landlady got them cooked, and sent up by the little girl I had seen below. Just as my fellow-lodger was about to pour out the tea, "Why," said he, "did you not say you were going to have meat, and I would have got you a clean knife and fork?" However he soon surmounted that difficulty by the use of his rubstone, a thing used by shoemakers to sharpen their knives.

We set to and had a most excellent meal. I was rather sharp-set, not having had much food since the day before; my companion ate but little. After we had finished and were chatting together as if we had been friends for years, he proposed a stroll, and to take what he called 'a picture-shop fuddle,' that is, looking at the shop windows, or anything you happen to meet with that may attract your attention.

He led the way through Smithfield, where pointing out St. Bartholomew's hospital, "That," said he, "is one of the noblest institutions in the world; none, my friend, but the poor can appreciate its value: I only regret that I am poor, because I cannot assist my fellow man." Thus conversing we walked on to Holborn, the best part of the town I had yet seen. The goods in the shop windows were nicely arranged and set out in the most tempting order; the company generally in the shops were well dressed ladies, and the passengers in the streets of the same description. Walking leisurely, and contemplating the multiplicity of objects that demanded our notice, we turned down Drury-lane and looked at the Theatre, as also that of Covent-garden; thence we went by the Strand as far as Charing-cross, and returned by Somerset House through Temple-bar into Fleet-street. The shops and buildings of this great thoroughfare struck me with admiration; St. Paul's, that stupendous and magnificent masterpiece of architecture, riveted my attention, and drew from me an exclamation of wonder, to the amusement of the passers-by, who could easily see that I was green from the country. Proceeding along Cheapside, I took a long stare at the Mansion House, Bank of England, and Royal Exchange; my companion all the time explaining things as we continued our walk to Leadenhall-street, and came out by the East India House. Hence, after striking down St. Mary Axe into the Jews' quarter, crossing Bishopsgate-street, passing over Moorfields, and threading some narrow courts and alleys, we regained our humble dwelling; by which time I felt pretty well tired.

Just as we arrived, a pot-boy came to the door with a tray of porter in pint and quart pewters. So I took up a quart in my hand, by the aid of which, together with bread and cheese, we made our supper; and afterwards each selected a book, and read for about an hour. This was the first time I ever had an opportunity of reading Shakspeare; the book opened at that beautiful speech on Mercy, put into the mouth of 'Portia' in the *Merchant of Venice*. Never before had my senses been so completely captivated. I could have read all night; but observing that my friend had closed his book and looked as if inclined for rest, I put up mine also, and we both retired to bed. Yet even here, what I had been reading haunted me in my sleep. The whole *dramatis personæ* were before me palpable as life; I watched the proceedings with intense anxiety, till the Jew approached to cut the pound of flesh from the Merchant's breast,—when struggling to arrest the knife, I awoke,—and thanked God it was a dream! However, I soon fell asleep again, and being tired did not stir until called in the morning.

The breakfast things were set, the kettle boiled, and all was ready by the time I had washed and performed my toilette, which was not long. During breakfast

I sat thinking what I should do; for the time had arrived for action, and this was a new start in life. But my shopmate (as I must now style him) soon began to point out the course I must pursue. When we had finished our meal, "We must now," said he, "go and seek for work." So off we started through Chiswell-street, Barbican, and Long Lane, 'occasioning'[1] the shops as we went along, but without success. Having crossed Smithfield, we entered Cow Cross; where, at a shoemaker's on the right-hand side, seeing a man at the cutting board, I asked if he had any occasion for a 'man's man.'[2] To which he answered, "Thee means a man's *boy*, don't thee, friend?" I can never forget the feeling of shame and helplessness that came over me; the quiet satire of the quaker completely overwhelmed me, and I bowed my head in sorrow.

There must have been something in my appearance that excited the pity and kindly feeling of the facetious quaker; for in the next moment he asked me if I could make a good strong shoe? To which I modestly replied, that "I thought I could." "Well, friend," he said, "I will try thee," and so gave me a pair of boys' ancle boots to prove my skill upon. Oh! how delighted I felt as the stuff was tied together and delivered to my care. Having now all that I desired on earth, I went over to my shopmate, who seemed pleased that I had succeeded in obtaining work. We returned to our lodgings, and prepared for what appeared to me the

---

[1] Simply 'asking for work,'—or inquiring whether there is any 'occasion' for a hand.

[2] This is a term used by the trade to denote what sort of work you have been used to.

great trial of my fate. I finished my task that night, and took my work to the shop next morning with indescribable fear and doubt. When I entered, the master was at his board, and stretching out his hand he took the boots from me. With intense anxiety I watched his countenance as he examined the work, and read my destiny in the expression of his features. After looking at me, and then at the things I had (as he said) spoiled, he gave me eighteen-pence and told me that he was sorry he could give me no more work. Heavy at heart I returned to my truly compassionate shop-mate, and in sorrowful accents told my pitiful tale. He seemed to feel for me, and tried to alleviate my sufferings by kind and gentle words. But he could not lose time and neglect his work, however inclined to serve me; neither could I expect him to do so. Thus situated, I determined to stroll round the City by myself, and try my fortune again; hoping the next time to be more successful. Having screwed up my courage, I started forth on my second expedition; taking care to avoid all the shops where the work appeared evidently above the reach of my ability. I traversed the meanest streets that I could find: and, after many unsuccessful attempts, applied at a shabby-looking shop on Saffron Hill. Here I saw an old woman who had all the appearance of an Egyptian mummy. I asked her if she could inform me whether they wanted a 'shoe-man;'[1] at which request she opened a pair of such eyes as I never beheld before or since. I shrunk back in terror at her satanic stare, and stood on the step of

---

[1] A term applied to persons in the trade who make nothing but men's shoes.

the door ready for a bolt; fearing I might be pulled in and chopped into sausage-meat, or made into penny pies, for I had heard tales of the kind since my arrival in this bewildering town.

Just at this moment, a man entered about half dressed, and, in conformity, about half drunk, who staggering past me asked with a hiccup what I wanted? I replied that I was desirous of getting work. I soon discovered that this was the old woman's son who managed the business; and from the conversation that passed betwixt them it seemed he had been at a public-house in Field-lane all day playing at skittles, to the great annoyance of his amiable mother. The language that passed is rather too refined to be here set down; however, the male specimen of humanity gave me some work, though merely, I believe, in sheer opposition to his crabbed mother, who seemed to have but little of the milk of human kindness in her dried-up composition.

Having received the materials and instructions from my new master, I hastened back to my kind-hearted friend, who said all he could to cheer me under these trying circumstances. When I looked around, and considered my lonely position in the world, my spirits sunk; I felt incompetent to struggle with the difficulties that surrounded me. The world seemed all dark, and I appeared to myself as if not belonging to the common brotherhood of mankind; there was no one on whom I had a right to call for help, and my deficiencies stared me in the face at every step I took. It is difficult for persons more happily circumstanced to imagine the feelings of youth in a state of helpless inability. I knew that I must do the work I had taken out; yet knew as well that I was not master of that which I had undertaken. What would be said by that fiery old woman when I took in the shoes? This was my first theme of dread; next I pictured a vulgar quarrel betwixt the ogress and her son, about giving me work; and thus my affrighted fancy conjured up accumulated scenes of horror until I started from my seat in despair. After remaining some time in a state of mental abstraction, I resolved to try and muster courage to accomplish what I had undertaken.

So having wetted[1] my stuff, and tucked up my shirt sleeves, I sat me down to work, with a determination to succeed if possible. Alas! what misery I suffered from beginning to end of this my second undertaking. The stuff was wretched and insufficient in quantity; the soles were foreign[2] and hard as stone, breaking my awls and turning the edge of my knife. By the time I had finished, my hands were crippled and the skin flayed off my fingers. All this could have been endured; but I could not bear to look on the sorry botching piece of work that I had perpetrated. Thus, overwhelmed with shame and sorrow, I proceeded to face that fiendish old woman. I would almost as soon have faced a legion of evil spirits in the lower regions; but compelled by necessity, I submitted to the will of fate, and entering the shop placed the—the *things* (I dare not call them shoes) on the cutting board. The 'old

---

[1] The materials composing the sole, and connected therewith, require thorough soaking before they can be operated upon.

[2] This is the great difference between English and imported 'butts,' as they are called, that the latter are intensely tough. The 'butt' is the portion of the hide used for the outer soles.

one,' for I believe she was an incarnation of the devil, came forth from a little back room, and casting an evil glance at me took up the 'things,' which after a glance she threw in a burst of hellish passion at my head. The blow sent me staggering against a glass case, which was thereby smashed: and seldom was such a storm raised in so short a time.

A dog (in waiting?) now seized my coat tail, and ragged urchins chased and hooted me from Saffron Hill down Peter Street, where I outran them and made my escape. Never was a poor wretch so hunted; when I had got clear of my pursuers I stood still, panting for breath, whilst a crowd gathered round and inquired what I had been doing. With tears running down my cheeks I told my pitiful tale; some laughed and others pitied me. A well-dressed man who stood by expressed his sorrow for my forlorn position, and secretly put into my hand a half-crown, telling me at the same time to walk away from the deriding rabble by whom I was surrounded.

CHAPTER IV.

I GROW DESPERATE—BUT 'ALL'S WELL THAT ENDS WELL'—MY CIRCUMSTANCES IMPROVE—THE 'STRIKE'—THE RECRUITING SERGEANT.

ON entering my obscure abode, I felt humbled to the dust, and sitting down cried like a child over the miseries I had encountered, and the utter hopelessness of the prospect before me. My older shopmate tried all he could to soothe my afflicted mind, and foretold that I should one day surmount all obstacles, and stand proudly on the pinnacle of fame. Alas! how was this bright prophecy to be realized, when I was now in the lowest depths of despair, and feeling the full force of the text which says, "man is born to trouble, as the sparks fly upward."

After a little further conversation, I reached from the shelf the "Economy of Human Life," and at my companion's request read it aloud. I felt great relief in reading that beautiful little work, and drew sweet consolation from its refreshing springs. After having read the book entirely through, I fell into a gentle sleep, and under its influence was transferred back to the days of my childhood and my early home, surrounded by all those endearing objects that are associated with that happy period of our lives, when the whole face of nature seems to wear one glowing blush of brightness; when every sound that floats upon the airy tide falls sweetly upon the ear, charming the sense to gladness; and all around bears the impress of universal benevolence.

How disappointed I felt, when I awoke to that cold and cheerless world where thousands are running the mad race of ambition, passing by unheeded or trampling down their wretched competitors who fall in the struggle But I began to feel more resigned to my fate, and prayed to God to direct me; calling to mind at the same time the hardships and trials of many great and good men, of whom I had heard. Thus in reading and contemplation, I passed this day in the room which served for shop, parlour, and sleeping apartment: the bedstead being turned up in the day to give us room to move about and do our work.

When we had finished supper, my friend filled his pipe, and requested me to read a portion of *Hamlet*. I complied at once, and derived unspeakable delight from that marvellous creation of the immortal bard. Had my young soul been at ease, how I could have revelled in his honied expressions, so refined, so truthful, so grand! I read over and over again, the soliloquy, "To be or not to be," &c., until I had committed it to memory. I felt at that moment truly thankful for the little education that I had received; and the more so, because at that time few of the middle and lower classes were educated at all. My good friend to indulge me sat up later than usual, and by his sage counsels soothed my afflicted spirit. Oh! how welcome is sympathy in our misfortunes: ' 'tis balm of Gilead to the heart'!

The old dutch clock struck eleven, warning us that it was an hour beyond our usual time; so I closed my book, and we retired to bed. But again I could not sleep; my spirit was ill at ease, and vague apprehensions haunted my disturbed brain; but the one engrossing idea was a dread of the dark future that lay before me, that mysterious book whose pages are beyond mortal ken; for

> "Ne'er hath been to human eye lent
> Sight, the Future's gloom to break;
> God hath charged it to be silent,
> Till the day all things shall speak."

Wearied nature at last asserted her prerogative, and like a kind mother lulled me to sleep. I awoke as the clock struck six, and donning my clothes felt one stage removed from the miseries of the previous day; my heart, at all events, was lighter. I made a fire, swept up the shreds, and prepared for breakfast: and the meal quickly despatched, was off on a fresh voyage of discovery. For truly, in the midst of a vast city, I felt myself a sort of Robinson Crusoe; I knew no one, nor did any person know me, save my kind old shopmate, who was indeed a sensible and good man.

But to proceed: I started again to try my fortune, and walking down Snow Hill saw in a shop window —'boysmen[1] wanted.' I entered, and on asking for

---

[1] This seems a strange term, though well understood by the trade; it means hands to make boys' shoes, the wages given for which are inferior to what is allowed for men's work.

work, was told by the 'clicker'[1] that I could be set on. After taking down my address, the 'trotter'[2] was despatched with me and the 'stuff'[3] for a half-dozen pairs, together with a form to be signed by my landlady,—a sort of security for the materials. These preliminaries being completed, I set cheerily to work; never having felt more buoyant and happy in any portion of my existence.

I had by this time, from my own observation and the explanations of my shopmate, acquired a better knowledge of the principles of work. This gave me greater confidence, so that by the time I had finished the sixth pair, I not only felt quite pleased with my own performance, but had the unspeakable pleasure of my friend's unqualified approval. My prospects now began to brighten, and with a light heart I took in my work, which being deemed satisfactory, I received nine shillings and a fresh supply of materials, with orders to make all possible haste; as this was part of a shipping order, and must be completed within a given time.

I now kept working steadily, made rapid progress, and began to feel myself quite a man; when one day, passing with my bag of work over my shoulder, I saw in a shop window—'Shoemen[4] wanted.' This was one of the first-rate shops in the city; and it is usual, in asking for

---

[1] The foreman and cutter-out; usually manager of the entire business.

[2] Shop messenger and errand boy in general.

[3] The 'stuff' includes everything necessary to make a pair of shoes or boots; but in 'the trade,' the term more particularly designates the raw material for soles (inner and outer) and heels.

[4] For *men's* shoes only: the best workmen being implied.

work at such places, to shew a sample of your skill. The thought struck me that I would go home and take great pains in making a shoe to "occasion" with. Having therefore completed a piece of work to my mind, I repaired in perfect confidence to the shop in question, and in the usual way, exhibited the evidence of my abilities. The master, a wiry-haired Scotchman, exclaimed on examining it—" This is a vara weel wrought shoe; did ye mak it yoursel?" I affirmed the fact; whereupon, though apparently rather sceptical, he said he would give me a trial. So fitting up the stuff, he tied it together with the welts, and then in the most workmanlike manner inserted the lasts like a pair of reversed wedges; making the whole as compact and secure as possible. I could not but admire the business-like style in which all was done. He next shewed me a shoe of the substance he required, having examined which, I took up my work and left the shop, calculating as I went along (like the girl with her basket of eggs) upon my future prospects. Arrived at my dwelling, I threw down the stuff with a feeling of exultation; my old friend too seemed delighted at my success. Here was a grand change. When I untied the stuff and looked at it bit by bit, I felt pleased in observing how everything was suited to its purpose; the lasts too were in beautiful form, nor had I before seen anything so perfect and so mechanical. I proceeded with my work in the most careful manner, bestowing the greatest pains on the minutest portions of it, until all was completed.

When I had finished, I handed the shoes over to my shopmate to 'crown', or inspect; who, after having thoroughly examined the work, told me I might take them in without the slightest fear of 'getting the sack.' Thus assured I marched off to my little Scotchman, who was standing at the board in a clean white apron, with his shirt sleeves tucked up, having all the appearance of a man of business. On entering I placed the shoes on the cutting-board, and retired a few paces to give him an opportunity, as is usual in such cases, of examining and pronouncing his opinion upon the work: and happy indeed was I, when he expressed himself satisfied with my performance. He then handed me over two other pairs of stuff, with instructions how they were to be made, which I took home with feelings of no small satisfaction.

Thus matters continued for some time; I could earn a guinea a-week, and began to be spoken of by the trade as a lad of singular promise. My old shopmate was quite proud of his protegé, and on Saturday nights, I used to accompany him to take a pint or two of porter and smoke a pipe. About this time I thought myself as good a man as at any period of my life; I was getting on swimmingly, buying clothes, books, tools, in fact any thing that I desired; and everything looked bright around me. I took much delight in my work, and felt happy.

I used to go sometimes to the theatres, and felt great delight in hearing the language of my favorite Shakspeare delivered by Kemble, Young, and other great actors of the day. This, indeed, appeared to me to be the perfection of human enjoyment. I revelled in their masterly impersonations of the wondrous *creatures* of the immortal poet's brain. Frequently was I up till after midnight reading Shakspeare,—when all around was hushed in silence, save the distant rattle of some vehicle over the stones. Milton's lofty emanations also cost me many hours of luxurious labour; in very truth, I feasted on these sublime works. But I read every book that came within my reach, and also committed a great amount of matter to memory, which I would recite for the amusement of my shopmate, who pronounced me a tolerable declaimer. It appeared quite natural to me to aid the language with action and expression; and this I sometimes essayed in company, not without éclat. I was in consequence regarded as superior to the persons by whom I was surrounded; but as these were for the most part wholly uneducated, the fact need be no matter of wonder.

Thus I passed twelve happy months, with nothing to interrupt my dreams of future prosperity. So soon as I was settled in a regular seat of work, it became necessary that I should join the trade or shops-meeting, which is a combination for the support of wages. With this end in view, each member pays a certain amount monthly, in order to raise a fund for the support of families when a strike takes place, whether in one shop or more as the case may be: the men being at the same time furnished with 'tramping money',[1] to enable them to go into the country until the dispute betwixt employer and employed is for the time adjusted. All persons subscribing to this fund are called 'flints', whilst those who do not join are honoured with the dignified title

---

[1] An allowance of twelve or fourteen shillings from the general Fund, to start them on a journey in quest of work.

of 'scabs'. During these struggles, fights and consequent imprisonments are very common.

The long war in which the country had been engaged had raised all articles of consumption up to famine price, so that men having large families could not earn sufficient to buy them food. Hence a feeling of discontent arose in most trades, and a general 'strike' was the result in our own. I attended meetings at the different public-houses where they were held, and heard the great orators of the craft, men in ragged habiliments and of squalid looks, pour forth in touching and eloquent language their appeals to the unmarried men, to support them in the death struggle. It was agreed that the strike should be general, and as none could in consequence subscribe towards the relieving fund, some hundreds of pounds were borrowed from the farriers, carpenters, and other trades in support of this lamentable cause. Nearly all the single men packed up their kits and went on tramp, as they were not allowed any relief; but I remained in town, and determined to pledge my clothes, books, and such valuables as I possessed, in hopes of redeeming them when I got to work again.

Thus week after week passed on: the pawnbroker's store-rooms were crowded; families were reduced to the greatest misery, having parted with their beds, furniture, clothes, in fact anything and everything that would fetch money; the men were reduced to mere shadows, with countenances expressive of despair; and mothers were crying over their starving children, whilst the little ones clamoured for food. Such scenes of indescribable misery I hope never to witness again!

The tenth week of this siege had terminated, and we appeared no nearer our end; the wretchedness by which I was surrounded became intolerable; I resolved to pack up my all and go elsewhere. I felt reckless; all my little store was exhausted but a couple of shirts; so putting my tools together and wrapping them in my apron, I took leave of my old friend with a sorrowful heart. I walked moodily along, without thinking or caring which way I went. The amount of my worldly riches was tenpence-halfpenny. In a state of almost stupor, I wandered as far as Oxford-street, and there stood gazing at the shops and carriages, and the well-dressed people as they passed by. Then again, without any definite purpose, I strolled along till I had got clear of London, and found myself on the open road. As it mattered not whither I bent my steps, I now walked on as far as Brentford. Here I put down my bundle on a seat outside a public-house, called for a pint of porter, and, with a twopenny twist from the nearest baker's shop, made a modest dinner. When I had finished, I requested the landlady to allow me to leave my bundle while I went round the town to seek work. After trying such few shops as there were to no purpose, I returned for my bundle and retraced my steps to London.

I was by this time tired, so went into the park, stretched myself under some trees, and fell asleep. When I awoke the sun was fast declining; my senses reeled as I again commenced creeping along pressed by hunger, and with only sixpence in my pocket. I found myself at last in Saint Giles's, where entering a low looking tavern, I asked for three-pennyworth of bread and cheese and a pint of porter: with which I was served, receiving one *halfpenny* in change. My last sixpence was now gone, and I felt bankrupt both in purse and mind.

Whilst I sat thinking over my forlorn and destitute position, a smart looking sergeant entered, who soon began to talk about the war; and, amongst other fine things, said—'what a chance there was just then in the army for young men with a little education, as they were sure of promotion.' He talked on in this strain until my weak imagination was wrought up to the proper pitch; when, perceiving the effect of his rhetoric upon my inexperienced mind, he questioned me respecting my prospects. I did not attempt to conceal their real nature, whereupon he offered to enlist me 'as a sergeant.' However, I told him I knew better than that: since, as sergeants were the schoolmasters of the army, they must needs be well disciplined soldiers, and able to teach others. He then shifted his ground, and said I should be sure of arriving at that honour in ten or twelve months, as there were few men in the army who could write. Then producing pen, ink and paper, he asked me to give him a specimen of my abilities, and on my compliance with his request praised the style, and politely begging I would stand up, measured my height by his own, saying that I was just the height for a light company. Thus by degrees I was prevailed upon to take the shilling, and pronounced myself free, able, and willing to serve the King.

I had now given myself up to the service of my

country, but I could not bear the thought that any one should know I had become a soldier; so I made up my mind thenceforth never to write to my friends, for I felt ashamed of the course I had taken.

HULKS ON THE MEDWAY.

PART II.

THE VAGABOND ASHORE AND AFLOAT.

CHAPTER I.

MY MILITARY CAREER; RATHER BRIEF THAN GLORIOUS.

WHETHER the man who enlisted me was really a soldier or not, I have often since doubted; but however that may be, he possessed an oily and persuasive tongue, which in every way qualified him for the part he enacted, and I felt much pleased with his conversation. After some time spent in talk, he proposed a beefsteak and onions—an offer which I readily accepted, having fared but poorly of late. The repast was soon prepared, and after a hearty meal, we amused ourselves at draughts till bed-time. I had no great devotion to my new profession; I did not embrace it with very ardent feelings; I acquiesced in it as a necessity, and went like a lamb to the slaughter-house.

About ten we retired to bed, where I lay absorbed in thought until I fell asleep. We rose about eight, took breakfast, and then visited the Doctor who ordered me to strip, and examined me something after the fashion of a dealer when about buying a horse,—the walk, trot, cough, and leap not excepted: for desiring me to get on a table and jump off, he after that performance pronounced me perfectly sound. The next thing was to go before a magistrate, to be sworn in and take the usual oaths. This done, and having received twelve pounds bounty, I spent another week in town, walking about in the day time, and going to the theatre at night; but when the sergeant had got about a dozen of us, we were marched off to the Depôt at Chatham. Here we were put under the standard, and our heights, ages, and complexions were set down in a book. After this, we were marched to the Infirmary, and passed the regimental Doctor. This ceremony over, we were taken by a corporal and put into different barrack-rooms with old soldiers. I now received my clothing, which fitted like a sack on a pitchfork, and my hair was cut short to my head. I felt fit to cry with vexation when I looked at myself in the glass: what a transformation!

The next morning I joined the awkward squad, and was marched about in the sun till almost ready to faint, having had nothing but 'skilly' for breakfast. Thus we went on day after day—drill, drill, drill, eternal drill. How I pitied myself, and the miserable machines around me, all doomed men: but in truth they did not feel as I did,—for the most part were poor ignorant fellows picked up from the plough-tail. However, by degrees I became more reconciled to my fate, and tried to make the best of it. I was eventually attached to a company, and becoming tolerably expert in the performance of my duties, was noticed by the sergeant-major as being clean and smart in appearance. My clothes had been altered to fit me tight as my skin, and I began to acquire the style and bearing of an old soldier; it became known too amongst the non-commissioned officers that I was a good penman.

I was consequently often requested to write out the company returns which had to be shewn to the sergeant-major, who was a strict disciplinarian and one of the smartest soldiers in the world. There was no violation of the rules of the service in getting those things written out by another person; but one foolish fellow, for whom I had executed such a trifling job, desired me to write his return in a disguised hand, to the end that he might claim the credit of it for himself. And so indeed he did; but the crafty old sergeant-major was not to be deceived. The poor fellow was upon detection deprived of his stripes, and reduced to the ranks; whilst I, on being questioned, told some lame tale designed to screen the corporal, and received for my pains a slap on the cheek. This was a degradation I could not brook; so I watched for an opportunity to desert.

The officers used to get up plays, which were acted

in the large room of the barracks, and at such times my services were made available in copying out parts, prompting, and looking after the wardrobe. This latter duty favoured my secreting an old wig, a countryman's smock-frock, and a pair of canvass trousers; which, together with an old cap, formed a tolerable disguise. The next time I had to stand sentry at night, I managed to place all these things in readiness, where I could shift my clothes unobserved, putting my great-coat on over all, and my cross-belts again over that. Thus equipped, when my turn for duty came, I marched out with the relieving party, and was posted at the corner of a lane near the dock-yard. I soon left my regimentals behind, swam the Medway, and then went straight across country, avoiding turnpike roads and every thing that looked like a town; for I knew that there were 'look-outs' stationed in every direction.

CHAPTER II.

THE STROLLERS—I BECOME AN ACTOR—OUR WAY OF LIFE.

ABOUT break of day, hearing a number of voices, I very cautiously made my way to the spot from whence the sounds issued; and after listening for some time, gathered from their talk that they were a travelling company of players going to a fair. No sooner had I made myself quite certain of their quality, than I ventured into the road and shortly overtook the party. It soon appeared that two of their companions had quarrelled with the manager, and joined another set of strollers. The manager thus driven to shifts presently addressed me—'You don't,' said he, 'talk much like a countryman.' I replied, that I had been living a long time in London, but was now out of work, and should be glad to do anything. On this he asked if I could read; and my answer was—'Yes, tolerably well.' It was now daylight; so taking a book from his breast pocket, he asked me to read a speech of 'Henry,' in *Speed the Plough*. When I had finished, he said—'That will do excellently well; so you study that part by to-morrow night. We are going to do the regular drama in a barn where we always get good houses; and it strikes me that you will take amazingly.'

This matter arranged, on we trudged: they talking, and I studying, as we went along. About eight o'clock we pulled up at a roadside public-house, where we had ale and bread-and-cheese. I ate very heartily, having a good appetite; and we took about an hour's rest, which I also needed. The manager then called for the bill, and having paid it, proceeded to look after the waggon and prepare for a fresh start. He was a sharp rough-looking little man, who had, as he said, run away from school, and whilst yet a boy joined a travelling company like his own. After a while, he married a widow in a country town who possessed some property, and during her lifetime always lived like a prince. But in about three years she died, and the property went to her nephews and nieces; upon which event the bereaved husband, after selling what moveables remained on the premises, left the place and joined another strolling company. The proprietor of this concern had made a good sum of money, and possessed an only daughter; whom, after being nine months in the establishment, our friend, without the old man's consent, married: at which the 'governor' was very wrath. But this state of things could not last; so they became reconciled, and were tolerably happy together. However, it was not long after their marriage, that the old man was taken ill and died, leaving all his property to the son-in-law, who, being persuaded into a speculation, lost the whole, and was forced to take up again with his old way of life.

Our manager nevertheless seemed a light-hearted merry fellow, and whistled and sung scraps of comic songs as we walked along. Nothing particular occurred until, having reached our destination, we stopped at an old-fashioned inn, and drove into the yard. Here we refreshed ourselves by a good wash at the pump; and then entering the house, the little manager desired the landlady to get ready some chops,—pending the appearance of which we discussed four or five quarts of beer, being somewhat thirsty after our journey. By this time the chops were served in the next room, and on the landlady announcing that all was ready, we took our seats and fell to without ceremony. After a hearty meal, the cloth being removed, pipes and tobacco were introduced. And now my companions began to get merry; and a jovial set of fellows they were. They narrated many strange adventures they had met with in their professional career: each man was on excellent terms with himself, and fancied he was good enough for the Theatres Royal.

But my own want of rest, and the anxiety that I laboured under, began to tell upon me. So requesting to be excused, I withdrew, and was shown up to bed. I was taken to an old-fashioned room, very large, containing four beds without hangings, and having much the appearance of a barrack-room. On the ceiling was traced in rude letters with the smoke of a candle, ' Good quarters for the 37th Foot,'—and other regiments. Indeed the whole ceiling was covered with hieroglyphics that would have puzzled Dr. Adam Clarke or the great Dr. Carey to decipher.

After recalling all the circumstances of my perilous adventure the night before, and thinking over the marvellous escape I had achieved, I thanked God with sincerity of heart, and prayed to be forgiven for what I had done. I considered again and again how to disguise my appearance; for I knew well enough that I should be accurately described in the 'Hue-and-cry,' and at this time there were recruiting parties in every town in the kingdom. My distracted imagination conjured up the most frightful scenes: I was perfectly aware that, according to the articles of war, if taken, I should be shot; no person in the land had the power to reverse the sentence. This terrible picture was constantly before me: and although tired almost beyond nature's endurance, I could not sleep. I took a retrospective view of my short life, and fancied I must have been born under the influence of some malignant planet, thus to become the shuttlecock of capricious fortune. In this state of mind, I passed one of the most wretched nights that mortal ever endured.

Next morning, however, I was up and dressed as soon as I heard any one stirring: and walked into the fields, taking with me the part I had undertaken to study. After about two hours' reading, I found myself tolerably perfect, the language being simple and natural; and as the part was not very long, I soon made myself entirely master of it. About eight o'clock I returned, and found the whole company ready for breakfast. The little manager complimented me upon my industrious habits, not doubting that I had been preparing for rehearsal. Breakfast over, I walked into the yard, and seeing in a stable some clean straw, threw myself upon it and slept soundly for two hours. By this time they had collected together for rehearsal: the ladies had arrived, and all were waiting to begin. 'Henry!' was now called, but no 'Henry' could be found; the house was searched upstairs and down, and the most private places were looked into, but without success. The clamour was at its height, when the manager came running out in a tearing rage, looking as if he had been possessed by ten thousand furies, and turning a corner ran against the ostler, of whom he asked if he had seen me—giving a brief description of my person. The man replied—'Aye sure, he be asleep in stable, and I shut door to keep 'un from catching cold.' The little man now somewhat calmed, came in, and told me they were all waiting to begin; so I walked with him to the barn, and was formally introduced to 'Miss Blandford,' 'Dame Ashfield,' and 'Lady Handy'; to all of whom I made my most polite obeisance.

This little ceremony over, we began the rehearsal: when, as I was a novice at stage business, they all took great pains in teaching me, and expressed themselves pleased at my readiness to profit by their instructions. I was indeed so utterly inexperienced, that the manager suggested going through the piece a second time; to which all acceded. For myself,—despite my unhappiness,—I was anxious to come off with credit, both for my own sake and that of the company. When we had finished and returned to the house, tea was ready; cold meat was standing on a side table, together with plenty of boiled eggs, and, as is the custom in some parts of the country, a jug of ale with glasses on a tray. Had my mind been at ease I could have been well contented; for the men seemed full of spirits and fun, and the women were pleasing and ladylike, without any ridiculous affectation.

Having finished my dinner-tea (for it was two meals in one) I retired to read over my part, prior to my first appearance on any stage. Whilst thus engaged, the individual who united the offices of wardrobe-keeper and property-man brought me in, as he styled it, 'Henry's suit,' which was just like what I have seen gamekeepers wear. I now dressed, and making my appearance behind the scenes, was highly complimented by the manager on my fitness to represent the part; he also hoped I might not be seized with stage fright.

Before the time for ringing up the curtain, the barn was crowded; posters had been stuck about the town a week before our arrival, which accounted for so large an audience. With gun on my arm, shotbelt over my shoulder, my hat a little on one side, and my shirt collar turned down *à la Byron* (as the fashion has since been styled), I presently made my *entré*, and was received by the audience with evident favour. On my quitting the stage, the manager, who was acting as prompter, congratulated me on my success. The piece worked on very smoothly, the actors all coming in for their share of applause; but in the course of my great scene with 'Sir Philip Blandford,' the bursts of approbation swelled into a perfect hurricane. I felt frightened at the noise I had occasioned, which perhaps made the scene appear more natural than it otherwise would have done. I had no sooner made my exit, than the whole *Dramatis Personæ* gathered round me, and declared they had never seen better acting. I really believe that, under the circumstances, the play went off exceedingly well; and the audience retired to spread a favourable report.

When we were snugly seated and smoking our pipes,

all well satisfied with the business of the evening, the manager announced that the same pieces would be repeated the next night, by particular desire of some of the principal persons in the place. A number of young men of the town soon came in, who appeared to be familiar with the 'governor' and most of the company. After having shaken hands, and offered their congratulations on the evening's performance, they also sat down to their pipes, and gave their orders to the waiter, every one according to his liking.

Some one now proposed a 'free and easy' sitting; and it was voted that our little manager should assume the chair. This, like a man of the world, he did without ceremony; and in a neat and appropriate speech opened the session; after which, as there was not much time to lose, one of the company forthwith called upon the chairman for a song. The 'governor' responded to the call by favoring us with the 'Wedding of Ballyporeen', which he sung with a rich Irish brogue. I certainly never heard an Irish song sung better, and I have heard a great many. He then gave a toast which to me was quite new, as I believe it was also to the rest of the party:—'Poverty in a bush, and the devil throwing stones at it!' After a few minutes' light talk, in which all joined, our chairman called upon one of the young men of the place, who sung 'Within a mile of sweet Edinborough town' most beautifully, giving the Scottish accent; at which I was not so much surprised when I was informed that he had been some years in Glasgow with an uncle, who had brought him up and taught him the trade of a working jeweller. The time flew fast, as the poet sings, while toasts and songs went round, and all were joyous and happy. In this scene of hilarity, I too partially forgot the dangers by which I was surrounded.

As the night wore away the company grew small by degrees; the clock struck two as we retired to the old barrack-room, and having taken more drink than I had been accustomed to, I was soon in a sound sleep. On getting up in the morning, I rambled over a neighbouring common, again carefully studying my part, which I well knew was necessary to impress it clearly on the mind. On my return, I found the breakfast things set, and the ladies also looking over their parts. I returned their cheerful greetings with as happy a face as I could assume; for my expressions were in no way akin to my feelings. In about half-an-hour the manager made his appearance, and, after shaking me by the hand, gave me a fresh study for the next evening. It was the part of a sailor lad in a then popular farce, which I looked through, and found very agreeable. On the rest of the men making their appearance, we all sat down to breakfast; but our appetites were indifferent and our heads a little disordered from last night's excess. The manager, perceiving our state, prescribed a 'hair off the old dog'; so we each took a small glass of brandy, which seemed to resuscitate the dying spirits within us, for we all felt better after taking it. I then went straight to the pump, and sluiced my head well with water; it was cold as ice, and wonderfully refreshing.

The before-mentioned common was not far distant, and here I occupied myself until the clock struck twelve, when it was time for repairing to the barn, as a rehearsal was called for that hour. The company were assembling as I arrived: as however we were all perfect, the business was soon over; indeed, we galloped through it in double-quick time. This being a banyan day, we had bread and cheese for dinner washed down with beer. Being determined to acquit myself as well as possible, I again resorted to my favourite haunt, where I could read aloud, un-noted, save by the cows, on whose information I did not dread being taken up as an escaped lunatic. Here, like Demosthenes on the sea-beach, I could declaim without fear of interruption, and found it of great service to get accustomed to the sound of my own voice; besides, I soon discovered that the tongue will mechanically repeat familiar lessons, even when the memory is shaken by fear, or when a tremulous feeling comes over one before an audience. When *my* audience, the cows, commenced drawing towards the common gate, I gathered that it was near milking time, and consequently almost four o'clock. I therefore pocketed my book, and walked to our hotel tolerably well up in the part I had been studying.

We took tea as usual, and then repaired to the theatre, which, by-the-bye, really deserved the name; for although it was in a barn, we had a raised stage, orchestra, wings, drop-scenes, and everything complete; the boxes, pit, and gallery were also managed very well, and the whole made a very respectable appearance. As it took me but a short time to dress, I was soon ready, and amused myself by peeping through a hole at the audience as they came in. Amongst them were many persons of unmistakeable respectability; and before we began the house was crowded in every part. On the curtain's rising, the people evinced their friendly disposition by a hearty round of applause. Thus auspiciously the play commenced, and its interest kept increasing as we advanced. At the conclusion, 'God save the King' was sung by the company, and responded to by the house rising and giving three hearty cheers. These little things are dear to both manager and actors.

The business of the theatre over, we retired to our quarters. On entering the house, it struck me that the sitting-room we had occupied the night before was much larger; and on looking up I saw that they had removed a partition which ran across the centre. When I entered there could not have been less than a hundred persons present, and in less than half-an-hour the room was crowded to suffocation. They were all smokers to a man; and the ceiling being rather low, it was impossible to distinguish persons at the opposite end of the room through the dense cloud of smoke. This night was spent like the first, in revelry and song. The party did not break up until daylight peeped in at the windows upon the Glasgow jeweller singing—'If we fa', we get up again, we always did sae yet.'

CHAPTER III.

I AM COMPELLED TO REFUSE A MOST NOBLE OFFER—CHANGE OF QUARTERS AND CHANGE OF BUSINESS—THE CLOWN—THE INUNDATION—CLOSE OF THE SEASON, AND BREAK-UP OF THE COMPANY.

THE smoke, drink, and noise had given me an intolerable headache, so that I got but little sleep, and in the morning I found myself quite unfit for 'mine own purposes'; my head was ready to split, and I also felt oppressed by a combination of conflicting feelings. The dreadful uncertainty in which I lived preyed upon my spirits, and bowed me to the earth. Oh, how the morning of my life was overshadowed by the consequences of one false step! Whilst indulging in this train of thought, I was informed that a gentleman wished to speak with me in the parlour. Thither accordingly I repaired, and found myself in the presence of an elderly man of benevolent aspect and gentlemanly bearing. I bowed respectfully to the stranger, who bade me be seated, and then began referring to my last night's performance. He gave me great credit for what he was pleased to term my noble feelings. 'My young friend,' he continued, 'your's was not acting—it was the working of your own soul that flashed upon the audience, and brought down those sudden bursts of applause. I have seen too much of acting to be mistaken.

But I did not come here to speak on that subject; I have determined to make you an offer. I am a merchant and banker in this town; and, if you think proper to accept it, I will give you a situation in my counting-house at a salary of a hundred guineas a-year, upon the bare condition that you render me a just account of yourself without reserve. I will ask for no reference whatever, but take you on your simple word of honour.' He paused for a reply; whilst I in bitter anguish turned my eyes from him, to hide my overflowing emotions. Thus for some seconds I stood silent, with my head drooping to my bosom. On somewhat recovering, I turned round and thanked him from the bottom of my soul; but plainly told him I was so circumstanced, that it was impossible for me to accept his offer, kind and generous as it was beyond compare. 'Well,' said he, 'I am sorry for it.' In taking leave, he put a £5. note into my hand and bade me good morning.

As soon as I had regained my self-composure, I had a good wash, and calling for a glass of soda-water and brandy, drank it off at once. Feeling no appetite for breakfast, I desired the servant to say as much to the manager when he came down; and then, crossing the common at a good pace to get my blood into circulation, sat down to study my part. My companions the cows were grazing peaceably around, the lark was singing high overhead, and linnets warbled in the hedgerow that grew by the brook where I was seated. How bright, beautiful, and calm did every thing appear! I paused to admire the scene, and to indulge in a luxury of feeling beyond the painter's or the poet's skill to pourtray; until roused from this dream of elysium by a sense of duty, I started up to wend my way to business. The clock struck twelve as I passed the church, which was not far from our place of assembly, and they were just preparing for rehearsal when I arrived; by which time my headache had just left me. We soon commenced work, the little manager taking his stand in the centre of the pit.

In the character I was to personate, I had made up my mind to imitate a young sailor, who spoke to me one day as he was passing the barrack-gate leading into Chatham. He told me he had just come ashore, after being about four years and a-half at sea on the coast of Africa among the darkies; and he pressed me to go with him and take a glass of grog. Being off duty, I accepted his invitation, and accompanied him to the 'Globe,' which I pointed out as a respectable house; and advised him to avoid those taverns, which at that time were common brothels, frequented mostly by soldiers and prostitutes of the lowest description, who made it their business to plunder sailors whenever the latter were foolish enough to get into such company. As my young tar had never been at Chatham before, I shewed him over Rochester and Stroud, and pointed out what there was of interest to be seen. Having spent about three hours very pleasantly, we retraced our steps, for he had to be on board by sunset. On reaching Chatham lines, we shook hands and parted, he going towards the 'hard' or landing-place, and I returning to barracks, where I arrived about twenty minutes before evening gunfire.

There was something about this youth so truthful and buoyant, such a jolly laugh, such an absence of care, such a restless sort of happiness, as became contagious; his perfect innocence and good-nature have left an impression on my mind that will never be effaced. Taking this youth for my model, I went through the first scene, which being short, elicited little notice. However, as we advanced, the little manager was quite in ecstacies, and coming behind the scenes shook me by the hand, saying, "Your 'Henry' was good, but nothing to this; I have never seen such a conception of the part before." He asked me whom I had seen play it? And I told him truly—no one; I had taken it from nature.

Rehearsal over, we went in to dinner, and being now hungry, I played an excellent part here. The bill of fare was simple but substantial, being ribs of beef baked over a pudding—than which, in my estimation, there is nothing better. After taking a glass of ale, I walked to my out-of-doors study and played my sailor in earnest to a mute audience. For on this occasion the beasts left off eating, and walking my way stood with their eyes fixed upon me, as if in wonderment at the antics I played, while going through my nautical attitudes accompanied by the full power of my voice. They paid great attention to the performance, till I began my hornpipe; when, as if by some pre-arrangement, they cocked their tails out, each straight as a gun-barrel, and started off galloping like a herd of deer. It was most absurd to behold them flying away to the other side of the common, and the sight upset my business. I could not proceed with the hornpipe for laughing; I was however quite perfect in the part, so the little interruption I had met with was not of much consequence. On reaching our quarters, I made direct for the stable where I had been discovered when they missed me at rehearsal. The place was empty, and the straw quite fresh and clean; so I again lay down in one of the stalls, and slept soundly for about an hour. It is my firm conviction, that nothing can be more comfortable for an afternoon sleep than a bundle of clean straw; at all events, I awoke much refreshed.

The time was now approaching when I was to make my appearance in a new character. I found, on looking over the wardrobe, a white jacket trimmed with blue, a pair of duck trowsers, and a straw hat tied round with a blue ribbon, together with striped socks and pumps. The only thing wanting was a black tie for my neck: but it struck me that the landlord's son usually wore such things; so sending the property-man with my compliments he obtained one, which I adjusted in a sailor's knot, and then taking a survey of myself in the glass, almost fancied that I saw before me the young friend whom I had chosen as a model. The company now began to arrive; and, as on the previous night, the house was crowded some time before the hour at which the play was advertised to commence. The audience indulged in a round of applause as the curtain drew up, the little manager appeared in high spirits, and the actors were bustling about behind the scenes. The house was well prepared for my *entré* by the preceding action of the piece; and as soon as I made my appearance the applause was deafening. For a moment I forgot myself; but turning quickly round, took the word from the prompter and went on. To give here a description of each scene as we proceeded, would appear tedious and egotistic. But the sum total is, that even Garrick's unappeasable appetite for praise might have been sated with the amount I received.

Thus passed away a week: after which the fair commenced. Our theatre was now removed to a field; and whilst it continued here, the business was entirely changed. We enacted such 'raw-head-and-bloody-bones' work as I had never witnessed; nothing went down with the poor ignorant country people, but some tale of blood and murder, involving always a ghost in blue flames. This was followed by a bit of pantomime; but upon 'John Audley' being called (which means that a sufficient number is waiting on the stage outside to commence again), the curtain would suddenly drop, and the audience be played out by the band amid the shouts of the paraders, who keep bawling out, 'Enquire the character!' As the people descend the steps, those waiting on the stage outside take their places, and the same piece of mummery is repeated as fast as the people can be got together to succeed each other. Thus business is carried on frequently till twelve o'clock at night; and the amount of cash taken in this way is immense,—indeed to persons unacquainted with such things, quite incredible.

As outside show was every thing at this game, I asked to be allowed to play the clown; feeling satisfied that that would be the best disguise I could assume. There being no particular rule for that line of business, I amused myself with cutting extraordinary capers, and always kept my features more or less distorted to avoid being recognized. We were at this brutalizing work for a week: and as the weather was fine, the little man made a tolerable harvest.

It was one Monday morning that, our time for starting having arrived, we took the road at an early hour, leaving the waggon laden with scenery, and our other luggage, to follow at leisure. I had purchased of a Jew a second-hand suit of clothes, with the money given to me by my never-to-be-forgotten patron the merchant; and I think I may say, without vanity, that I was really a smart looking young fellow. My whiskers were growing fast, and black as a sloe, although I was not yet seventeen; my face too was bronzed by the sun; so that I think my friend the sergeant would hardly have known me: for when he last saw me, I was lean and pale, as is always the case with persons of sedentary employments working in a confined atmosphere. In fact, I was so much altered that I could scarcely recognize my former self.

After a journey of sixteen miles we arrived at a market town. It happened to be horse-fair day, and the country people were pouring into the town from every quarter; all seemed bustle and confusion, every description of vehicle was in motion, the public-houses were crowded, and the inhabitants appeared unusually busy. As our little manager was an annual visitor, his arrival was anticipated: and mine host, after giving us a brief welcome, soon produced some refreshment in the substantial form of a round-of-beef and excellent bread and cheese; to which we did ample justice. In about an hour and a-half up came the waggon, which we accompanied to the place where the fair was held, proceeding at once to a piece of ground which was reserved purposely for our use. The carpenter in the town, who always had the job of assisting to put up the theatre, had got holes dug ready to receive the posts, and half-a-dozen men to assist; so that by two o'clock we were all ready to begin. The musicians then struck up, and we commenced a country dance; the people soon gathered round, and in about ten minutes the theatre was nearly full; when the little man, with his usual tact, called out at the top of his voice,—'All in to begin.' This had the desired effect; for the people flocked up and soon crammed the house. In a few minutes we began with performance number one; and, to use a shoemaker's phrase, soon 'balled it off.'[1]

This being the first performance, we gave them as much as we could afford for the money: until, the parade getting crowded, 'John Audley' was called, and in less than ten minutes we began again. Thus we kept it up till eleven o'clock, when the people gradually retired; yet even at that hour we managed to raise spectators enough for one more performance; after which, having got rid of the audience, we pigged in upon some straw under the parade where we had been playing the fool for nine hours to amuse the gaping crowd. Never were poor devils more completely used up; my joints ached with the fatigue I had undergone: but nature would be obeyed, and I slept like a millstone after a hard day's grinding. We did not creep from our rest till twelve o'clock next day; and I believe I slept the clock round.

On going outside and looking upwards, I perceived white fleecy clouds skimming along from the horizon due south; and it soon appeared that the wind blew from that point of the compass. The afternoon was tolerably fine,

---

[1] Finishing off; in which glass-paper and hot irons are employed.

although occasionally overshadowed by clouds which sailed along the firmament; but towards evening these grew gradually together into a dense mass, and the rain fell gently for a while,—just giving the people time to reach their homes. In about an hour, it appeared as if the flood-gates of heaven had been opened; the rain fell as if in one unbroken sheet, and so continued all that night, and the next day without any appearance of intermission. We lay down upon our straw, which by this time was considerably damp; and I had fallen into a dozy state between sleeping and waking,—when suddenly I heard a confused noise, as if a number of voices were crying for help.

On rising to ascertain what was the matter, I found myself ancle-deep in water. I now whipped up my clothes, and running to the highest ground to dress myself, became aware that the river had overflowed its banks and was inundating the country. The water came rushing in like mad; booths were washed down; chests, stalls, and beds floated about; women were crying in despair with naked infants in their arms; and men were scrambling after their property, that was swimming about in all directions. Such a pitiful scene I had never witnessed! Towards night, most of the things, with the aid of boats, were recovered, but a great quantity of goods was completely spoiled. The respectable neighbours contributed bundles of clothes for the women and children, which were given out according to their necessities; they sent also ready-made tea and coffee in large cans, with pots and jugs for them to drink out of; not forgetting more substantial refreshments.

We remained here a fortnight, before the waters had

subsided, so that we could get our theatre down and remove it; and even then, the earth was so soft that we had to lay planks on the ground for the wheels to run on, or we should not have got off at all. During our stay, the inhabitants raised a subscription and divided it amongst the sufferers according to their losses and necessities, which went a great way towards alleviating the general misery. Whilst this was going on, we went about to the public-houses of an evening, and recited, or sung songs; by that means securing more than five times the amount of our salaries. The 'governor' too was allowed to perform three nights in the town-hall; so that, upon the whole, I think we all had occasion to be thankful.

The business being now over in that town, we quitted it, and took the different fairs as we went along, until the end of September: when our chief drove into London, where he resided in the 'Borough' on the Surrey side. After unloading the waggon, and stowing away the scenery, lamps, stage-properties, and other things, we all adjourned to the manager's private abode, which was well furnished and had a very snug appearance. Here we had supper served up in first-rate style, with sherry and champagne, and every thing in fact good enough for a prince. Our host had taken the precaution to secure us lodgings at a house close by: and when we broke up, accompanied us to our domicile for the night, with an invitation to breakfast in the morning—of which we thankfully promised to avail ourselves.

On the following day, accordingly, we repaired to the little man's dwelling, where all was in readiness for our reception; made a good breakfast, and chatted over our late adventures. After some time spent in social talk, the 'governor' rose from table, and drawing out his keys unlocked an escritoire that stood in the room. Then taking out a canvas bag, he presented each of us with a £1. note, saying at the same time, that he should be glad to engage us next season, if we were not otherwise situated to our minds. Upon which understanding, we shook hands, and bade him good-bye.

CHAPTER IV.

A RESOLUTION—THE 'TENDER'—SCENE ON BOARD—AT CHATHAM AGAIN—FRENCH PRISONERS—I SAIL IN THE 'TIGRIS'—THE IRISH STATION—'OVER-LAND' WAGHORN—LIFE ON BOARD-SHIP.

MOST of our late company had some sort of a home to go to; but as for myself, I had sundered every tie that bound me to my family, which, though poor, was honourable. I had been strictly trained up in principles which, by one rash act, were grievously violated. What could I do to retrieve that which I had lost? If I surrendered myself, it was to certain death; and my country would not be benefited. I thought the only way left to be of any service to the country, was to enter the navy; so turning to the only one of the theatrical corps that remained with me, I told him my determination; which, instead of opposing, he approved, and proposed that we should share our wayward fates together. This individual had always evinced a particular friendship towards me from my first joining the company; and as I could not dissuade him from his purpose, I took him by the hand, resolving to stand by him even to the death. For I clearly saw that he would have gone with me anywhere; and such natures are not found under every bush.

Being both agreed, we started for the '*Tender*,' where on going alongside we were hailed from the deck: the waterman told our business, and we were requested to come on board, which we did with the agility of old topmen. The officer on deck gave us a hearty greeting, for volunteers at that time were very rare; and the press-gangs had become so obnoxious to the poor people about Bermondsey, Thames Street, Tower Hill, Whitechapel, Shoreditch, and all the low neighbourhoods, that they were afraid to send out parties! Indeed, one of their men had lately been killed by the Billingsgate fish-women, who rose *en masse* to rescue a lad seized by the gang in that quarter. The war was at its height; and men of all countries were to be found both in our army and navy, from the pot-bellied Hollander to the coast of Guinea 'nigger.'

As we stood looking over the side of the vessel, an eight-oared cutter pulled alongside; out of which, with some difficulty, the boat's crew hauled up a young man whose head was bound up with a handkerchief saturated with blood, the crimson fluid still trickling down his cheek on to the bosom of his shirt. A surgeon was soon in attendance, who dressed the sufferer's wounds and administered restoratives which brought him to his senses. Oh, what an agonizing scene followed! The poor fellow raved like a maniac; they could scarcely keep him from jumping overboard; he called in vain for his brothers to aid him in this hopeless state of misery; he bewailed his mother and sisters, and his beloved 'Mary,' to whom he was to have been married on the morrow.

Never did I see a poor fellow in such a state of distraction; he kept on raving and crying until exhausted, and then lay sobbing like a child in its nurse's arms, and moaned so piteously it would have melted a heart of stone. In this prostrate state the sailors took him down the hatchway; and we also, being ordered below, were served by a black boy with some three-water grog and hard biscuits, along with some rank stuff called butter, which, if put to its proper use, ought to have served for cartgrease. We drank the grog and ate the biscuits, but the butter we did not meddle with, as the smell alone was poison. After sitting here for three or four hours, we heard the bell on deck strike eight. Of this I did not then know the meaning; but soon learned that in the navy the bell is struck every half-hour, and at noon and midnight always strikes eight. We were now again called on deck, and ordered into a boat alongside, which conveyed us to a vessel getting ready to drop down the river.

Having a favourable breeze, we soon reached Gravesend, and were thence marched to Chatham by the petty officer who was sent in charge of us. I had become so much altered in appearance, that I did not fear being recognized; besides I knew that the regiment to which I belonged had been sent to the seat of war to join the Duke of Wellington's army. In fact, there was hardly an able-bodied man left in the country; the war had continued so long, that every available source had been drained; and mere boys were enlisted, who were not able to shoulder a musket. Having reached the dockyard, we were taken into the Commissioners' office, and our names entered on the books of the *Tigris* frigate, a fir-built vessel not quite finished. We were consequently sent on board the old *Brunswick* 74 (then dismasted and used as a prison-ship) until the *Tigris* was ready; and here we remained three months.

On board our hulk were about 700 French prisoners, the most lively and animated beings I had ever seen. It would be impossible for me to describe their various occupations and amusements: there were tailors, shoemakers, snuff manufacturers, fancy box makers, domino and card makers, and other artists in great profusion. They even exercised their ingenuity so far as to make £5 notes; for which a poor fellow was hanged on the little island opposite Chatham lines, who had given one to a marine to pass when going ashore on leave. Their amusements were various; such as small-sword, broad-sword, single-stick, quarter-staff, cards, dominoes, fiddling, dancing, gymnastics,—in truth every kind of game that their inventive genius could suggest. Some of these poor fellows had been in prison nine or ten years, and could speak English like natives. It was truly wonderful to witness men bearing captivity with such buoyancy of spirits. Their food was not of first-rate quality; the brown bread was very coarse and by no means sweet to the taste; the beef generally was miserably lean, such as an Englishman would consider unwholesome; the salt fish I believe was generally pretty good. However, as they were nearly all versed in the art of cookery, they made dishes of which few Englishmen would have any conception.

A great many of these captives were officers, who had been at Stilton and other inland prisons, but having forfeited their parole, were now confined on board these prison-ships, and strictly guarded night and day. It was not very uncommon for them to cut a hole through the ship's side just above the water-line, and swim for their liberty; in attempting which, however, they were generally drowned, or shot, or stuck fast in the mud, and, being captured, were punished as the commander directed. The prisoners were always driven below before sunset, and the hatchways secured by strong iron bars; so that there was no chance of their getting a breath of fresh air till they were let on deck in the morning. The hatches were then unlocked, and such a horrible sickly stench issued from below, as no person could conceive who had not felt its effects. Just fancy 700 human beings crowded together between decks, with no ventilation but small cross-bar holes, and some even of these blocked up to keep out the cold! I can only say they bore their sufferings with amazing fortitude; they were indeed laughing philosophers, yet seemed to a man attached to Napoleon and their country.

As soon as our frigate was ready to receive us, we went on board and commenced scraping the pitch off the seams of the decks, and getting in guns, stores, and provisions together, with all things necessary for sea. We then dropped down to Sheerness, where the ship was got into proper trim for sailing: and here we lay all that hard weather which marked the commencement of the year 1814. As soon as the frost broke up, we weighed anchor and sailed for the cove of Cork, where we moored in one of the most spacious and secure harbours in the world. We had not remained long at anchor, ere we received sailing orders. These were promptly obeyed; the *Tigris* being manned with as smart a crew as ever went aloft. Our business was to cruize round the Irish coast, to keep a good look out, and to protect merchant vessels going to the Mediterranean. This was what is called a 'full-belly' station; and we got plenty of potatoes, which we either purchased or took in exchange for biscuits. Moreover, as we frequently put into harbour for water and provisions, the girls from the town came on board to see the ship, and the consequence was, that a great many of them got *bona fide* married to our men. And beautiful creatures some of them were; fresh, graceful, and I believe, generally good.

Our ship's company was what might be considered a tolerably happy one. The captain was a strict disciplinarian, but in the main might be called (as things went at that time) a good man; the first lieutenant was one of the noblest specimens of humanity that ever walked a quarter-deck, and the officers generally were a fair sample of their class. One youthful midshipman was an especial favourite of mine; his name was WAGHORN; he was the son of a butcher at Chatham. The little that I knew I imparted to him, and he repaid my services with gratitude. This youngster became in after days the celebrated Lieutenant Waghorn, the originator of the Overland *route* to India. Many hours has he remained on deck talking with me, when he might have been in his hammock. There is no accounting for the friendships that spring up between persons so situated: man must love something, and I felt for him as if he had been my younger brother. He belonged to the larboard and I to the starboard watch: many, many times has he saved his rum, and brought me up a 'tot' in the middle watch, when the night has been unusually cold; and would even then stay talking, until I have forced him below.

We had on board an excellent band composed of about twenty instruments, which was a source of infinite delight. Often of an evening when the weather permitted, 'all hands' was piped to dance; and it was fine fun indeed to see how some of the merry devils would hammer away on the deck in nature's stockings. This was good exercise, and contributed greatly towards keeping the ship's company in a healthy condition; which in our case was evinced by the fact, that no vessel, in any port we put into, could furl sails and strike top-gallants so quick as we could. This was the pride of our first lieutenant, for whom the men would fly aloft like lightning; his words on such occasions were,—' Now, my lads, let 'em know you're here'; which had more effect than all the swearing and bullying that ever disgraced humanity. It has always appeared clear to me that men will do their utmost when kindly treated; whereas the reverse process renders them savage and morose.

I never knew an instance of any one being made better by flogging; human nature revolts at treatment which is calculated only to make man an ungovernable monster. I have seen some of the most brutal natures subdued by kind words and civil treatment, when severe punishment has had an opposite effect upon the very best. The use of the 'cat' is the greatest disgrace recorded in the annals of our country: I have seen eight or ten men tied up of a morning, and the skin flayed off their backs, while the blood ran down into their shoes; and this too for the most trifling faults.

I once witnessed the flogging through the fleet, of a man who had stolen a pint of rum; for which crime he received 300 lashes, taking a proportionate share of his punishment alongside of each ship in harbour. When brought on board again he died immediately; and what was this but cold-blooded murder? 'Starting' too was a common practice at this time; it was frequently inflicted on the man who was last on going aloft, or the last up with his hammock. Now, where all are struggling to be first, surely some one *must* be last; and the penalty thus generally fell to the lot of some poor weak fellow; for the strong man, to save himself, would shove the weaker aside, and thus the man least able to bear it came in for a severe beating with a ropes-end, suited to cut him in pieces. Often have I seen poor creatures writhe in agony under this brutal treatment, praying in vain for mercy: let us hope such scenes will never again be enacted. This degrading and demoralizing punishment was the cause of many of the best seamen in the navy running away, whenever they could find an opportunity. It was no uncommon thing for an entire boat's crew to desert, and leave the boat upon the beach; although they knew it was at the hazard of their lives they did so: this is all that such a species of discipline ever effected for the service.

Our style of living was, of course, rough and ready, as there is but little time allowed for ceremony: we generally had burgoo or cocoa for breakfast, which was fetched from the coppers by the cook of the mess, whose duty it was to wash up the breakfast and dinner utensils. For this service he received the *plus* of grog,—which is managed in this way: if there are twelve men in a mess, they have as many pints of grog (full-measure) served out by the purser's steward; and this again the cook of the mess serves out to his mess-mates with a short measure 'tot' holding about two-thirds of a half-pint,— giving each man two of them, and mostly taking care to insert his thumb as far as he can into the measure, so as to make his *plus* the greater. The liquor thus saved he takes care to bottle off for the evening, when he generally invites a friend to grog with him, one most likely from another mess; thus keeping up a sort of visiting acquaintance. Upon these occasions they smoke a pipe, sing a song, and are very jolly. Good singers are sure to be invited out. But further, as regarding this grog business,—whatever number of men there is in a mess, all act as cook in succession, beginning with number 'one' who serves for that day only; then number 'two' takes his turn, next day number 'three', and so on, until number 'one' begins again; so that in the end, no one gets more than his regular allowance.

If skilly or burgoo be served out for breakfast, it is generally taken with pepper and salt, and a piece of butter; some I have seen use sugar, but very seldom. Each man has about a pint, which he takes from a tin pannikin; and when breakfast is finished the cook gets hot water from the coppers and washes up the things, scours down the table, cleans out the berth, and arranges every thing in order; which if he neglects to do, he is subjected to a punishment called 'cobbing'. It is effected by four men seizing the culprit's arms and legs, and bending him with his face downwards on to the end of the table: where he is held fast, whilst a fifth slaps him on the breech with the tailor's sleeve-board borrowed for the purpose. This is considered a most degrading punishment. On certain days, flour, fruit, and suet are served out, which the mess-cook has to convert into a pudding, and deliver (tied up with the number of the mess attached) to the ship's cook. It is the latter's business to get all ready by 'eight bells', which means twelve o'clock; for as there are no ordinary clocks on board ship, the large bell, which is struck every half-hour, does the duty of a time-piece. There was but little variety in our dishes, the food being alternately pork and beef. The latter is called salt junk, in consequence of its resemblance to a piece of old cable. I have often pulled it to pieces in long strings, something like rope-yarn. It is usual on pea-soup days to make what is called 'dog's-body'. This is done by pouring off the soup, and turning the peas that remain into a piece of canvas, which two of the mess twist at opposite ends until all the liquor is squeezed away; it is then turned out upon a dish, and appears in the form of an excellent pease-pudding; but I beg that you gentlemen cooks at Trinity kitchen will not be too severe on my rough sketch of a rough style of living.

Exactly at four o'clock (eight bells again) the boatswain pipes to grog, which is a very grateful announcement, as there is generally but a limited supply of drinking-water. In half-an-hour the watch on deck is piped up; this is called a 'dog-watch', and ends at six o'clock; when the second dog-watch begins, and concludes at eight. The reason of these two-hour watches being fixed, is to give the ship's company an equal chance of getting the same amount of rest. Thus the larboard watch gets the middle watch one night, and the

G

starboard the next; and so on alternately. From twelve till four A.M. is called the middle watch; then commences the morning watch, when the men prepare for washing decks. A few buckets of water are thrown down just enough to wet the deck, which is then bestrewed with sand, and rubbed with bits of a substance something like what is used for hearth-stones. This process is called 'holy stoning', and makes the planks when dry look beautifully white. In performing this duty, the men kneel down without shoes or stockings, having their trowsers tucked up above the knee. When the deck has been sufficiently rubbed, the sand is sluiced off into the scuppers, and dry swabs are used, which answer the same purpose as the common mop. The decks being dry and every thing set square by seven bells (half-past 7, A.M.) the boatswain or one of his mates pipes up hammocks. Then comes a grand scramble, each man lashing-up and conveying his bed on deck as quick as possible; so that before eight bells, they are all stowed snug in the nettings, and covered over with tarpaulings, which, besides giving the vessel a snug and neat appearance, serve to protect the bedding from rain, the dampness of the atmosphere, or from the spray of the sea. This being completed, as the bell strikes eight breakfast is piped; and the cook of each mess hastens to the coppers for the burgoo or cocoa, whichever is served out. Should the ship be rolling heavily, they have some difficulty in getting down the hatchway ladder in safety; whence it frequently happens that a portion of the precious cargo is spilt, and the unlucky bearer comes in for a hearty 'damn!'

I once saw a young marine coming down with a kid

of burgoo, who for safety had set it on the shot-locker on the main-deck, while he got three or four steps down the ladder; but in the act of reclaiming it, the ship suddenly lurched or rolled, when down came the scalding contents upon the poor fellow's head. In endeavouring to claw the vessel from his head, he next frightfully scalded his fingers,—all the time dancing about, and screaming in the most frantic manner. As soon as possible assistance was rendered, but not in time to save the young fellow from being frightfully burned; insomuch, that the skin came off along with the tenacious substance that clung to it.

At one bell, that is half-past eight o'clock, the watch is piped, and those whose duty it is go on deck; whilst the watch below clean the lower deck, and put every thing in order. This when done is reported by the master-at-arms (an active petty officer) to the officer of the watch, who orders the mate on duty to inspect, and further report whether every thing is arranged for the day. The men off duty now prepare to mend their clothes: and the lower deck has the appearance of a house of industry, being bestrewed with jackets, trowsers, shirts, stockings, and every article composing a sailor's wardrobe. The majority thus find employment; but those who have no work, either pick out a soft plank, and 'caulk' it for an hour (which means taking a nap), or read, play draughts, prepare tobacco, or do any thing they please till eight bells (twelve o'clock); unless 'all hands' is piped, when every man in the ship must jump on deck, whether it be night or day. This sometimes happens when the watch below have not been five minutes in their hammocks, and occasionally three or four times during a watch; a very, very wearying process, as the men must take the next watch even if they can't go to their hammocks at all; so that those having the first turn, if wanted on deck throughout the middle watch, must take the morning watch in due course, and thus be on duty for twelve consecutive hours; which is very distressing, and particularly so in a cold climate. However, if nothing more is needed to be done on deck, at the sound of eight bells, the boatswain and mates pipe all hands to dinner. This meal is soon despatched, and the grog drunk; the watch below then go on deck: whilst those off duty do whatever they please, until summoned to take their turn at eight bells, or four o'clock.

About this time the captain's dinner is served up, to the tune of 'the roast beef of old England'; after which the band continues playing until the captain and his guests retire from table. The men composing the band are called 'idlers' (a term I shall explain in my next chapter), and as such are excused from ship's duty,—except when the boatswain pipes all hands; for then every mother's son is expected to pull his pound, and must remain on deck till the watch is called.

CHAPTER V.

SHIP'S 'IDLERS'—FLOATING THEATRE—BANTRY BAY, AND KINSALE—DEALINGS WITH THE NATIVES—A SAILOR'S ACCOMPLISHMENTS — STATE OF DISCIPLINE DURING THE WAR—FRIGHTFUL USE OF THE 'CAT', AND OTHER ARBITRARY INFLICTIONS—AN UNJUST PUNISHMENT, AND ITS MELANCHOLY RESULTS.

THERE is always a good number of 'idlers' in a man-of-war, such as the officers' servants, the barber, tailor, and the shoemaker; for though the fore-mast men can go without shoes and stockings, it would not be decorous to see the officers walking the quarter-deck with naked feet. Besides those I have mentioned, there are others also excused from duty, who are required to do various things for the captain or officers: such as cabinet-makers, painters, writers, &c. &c. We had one hand on board who never did anything but decorative painting. These men are generally found among the marines; they are mostly such as, through some act of indiscretion, leave their homes and enlist as soldiers, hardly knowing what they are about at the time. From all I could learn of them, it appeared that drunkenness was the chief cause of their embracing a kind of life so comfortless for them.

They were generally poor miserable creatures, who from having been tenderly brought up, were quite unfit for their present mode of existence.

The 'captain's painter,' as he was called, had been apprenticed to the scene-painter at Drury-lane theatre; and an excellent artist he was. His handicraft was displayed from stem to stern; the cabin was beautifully ornamented, and every part of the ship decorated like a ball-room. This man was employed to paint the scenery for a portable theatre, the framework of which was made by the ship's carpenters. This was set up when we went into port, and a performance was given by the officers, to which the principal inhabitants of the place were invited. Both the acting and all the accessories were most respectable; the band formed an excellent orchestra, and the whole wore the appearance of a regular theatre. After the performance, the company repaired to the quarter-deck, which was fitted up like a ball-room with an awning overhead, and decorated with flags in the best taste. When tired of dancing they withdrew to the cabin, and took refreshments; after which, at an early hour, the boats were manned and the visitors conveyed on shore. Thus ended what appeared to me a most pleasing entertainment; and in the morning all was stowed away as if nothing of the kind had taken place.

As our only business in harbour was to get in water and provisions, our labours commenced as soon as breakfast was over. The men, I may observe, feel the beneficial influence of an entire night's rest, which is a luxury they can never hope for at sea. But a short time only was allowed us; the stores were shipped as quickly as possible; and all being complete, the captain held himself in readiness for sea. On the signal being given, we at once weighed anchor and put to sea; cruising according to the orders or instructions from the admiral of the port or from head-quarters. This naval guard-mounting is very dull and monotonous work; there are no fresh scenes, and it was also very cold and often stormy. The only places we put into, during two years, were Bantry Bay, and Kinsale—or Barehaven. This latter is, or was, a (truly) bare and barren-looking place, where two sterile promontories exhibited equally naked and hungry features. The people we saw here were of the most filthy description; their hands and faces had all the appearance of smoke-dried bacon; the rags (I dare not call them clothes) that hung about their mummy-looking bodies, were scraps of various material, and of more colours than I have ever noticed even in a rag-mop. Two or three families of these precious beings came alongside in something betwixt a wash-trough and a canoe, each bringing articles for sale or barter; such as butter, eggs, chickens, young pigs, potatoes, or anything they had to dispose of. They did not care so much about money, as biscuit and tobacco; the latter being their idol, which, on concluding a bargain, they clutched with inconceivable greed. One man exchanged a bag of bread for a hog of immense frame, but without flesh; it was the most racer-like animal of its kind that I ever beheld, of great length, and nearly as high as the mess-table. This living skeleton was butchered in the hope of getting some fresh pork,—but alas, not an ounce of meat could be scraped off his bones; so, after consulting what was best to be done, the purchasers concluded by throwing the carcase overboard. This circumstance gave rise to a standing joke among the crew, which was an eternal source of annoyance to the party thus taken in.

Among the articles brought for sale were some fowls, which turned out to be game to a feather. These were a source of great amusement to the tars; who, though no great adepts in cock-fighting, trimmed up the birds, and turned the lower deck into a cock-pit. Their usual method was to fight single battles, as it may be supposed they knew but little about mains; the stake was generally a gallon of ship's grog, which went to the mess of the winner: there usually being a joint interest in the combatants. When the fighting was over, the fowls were killed, and together with ship's pork made into a sea-pie. This is done by cutting up the meat into small pieces, and placing it at the bottom of a round boiler; enough water is then poured in to cover the meat, over which is laid a crust of dough; then over that, another layer of meat with additional water, and over that again, another crust. A third tier of meat is now put in, and the crowning crust being laid on the top, the sea-pie (called a three-decker) is complete. The boiler is then taken up to the galley, hung before a large fire, and turned round as in roasting a joint of meat. After hanging thus for an hour, it is placed on the top of the fire, and so finished off. This is considered the most luxurious dish that a seaman can prepare with the means supplied to him.

But besides being his own cook, a sailor is also his own laundress; he washes and gets up his linen himself, and excellently well I have seen it done. You would hardly suppose that some of them take in washing and ironing, which is paid for either in money or grog. This business is generally done in the first or middle watch, when the copper fire is lighted and the water boiled ready by the time the watch is piped to wash clothes and scrub hammocks. For each man has a spare hammock, which he keeps under his bedding, and exchanges for the dirty one whenever the order is given. Fresh water being a precious article at sea, the quantity allowed for individual use is but small, and is husbanded with great care. Therefore, after having washed out the dirt, they rince in salt water, wring out, and then hang up the different articles in the rigging to dry. The majority of the sailors wear their linen rough-dried; though some, who are more particular, iron it out in regular laundress fashion. This washing scene would appear rather novel to our mothers and sisters, whom indeed I have found almost sceptical as to facts;—especially when, dissatisfied with my linen, I have told them—'I could get it up better myself.'

I have now given a tolerable account of our domestic arrangements; and thus for twelve months we cruised about, ever, whilst at sea, on the look out for an enemy, but ocasionally going into harbour for provisions and water; and also (as I suppose) for a change, and to allow of some rest to both officers and men. The officers had permission to go on shore for a little recreation, but not so the men; for the navy was, on the whole, far from efficiently manned, and desertions were common whenever an opportunity offered. In consequence of this, the greatest severity was practised towards the men; so much so, that they were, in many cases, liable to be cut up like pork into sausage-meat.

The officers had been trained to this horrible work through a long and protracted war; and some in course of time became perfectly dead to all feelings of humanity, looking upon those committed to their care as savages to be ruled only through savagery. I do not however attach so much blame to the officers, as to the system, which is altogether wrong on principle. I certainly often wondered that these gentlemen could not discover how degrading such a system was both to themselves and to the men, and how calculated to destroy the innate dignity of their common nature. If the tender feelings of the heart be crushed, and self-respect destroyed, man's true courage is annihilated; and he either sinks under the disgrace, or becomes by degrees a perfect demon.

I once witnessed an instance of this in a young man of excellent disposition. He was a romantic boy when he entered the navy; who had run from home upon some slight family misunderstanding; he was well educated, having been brought up at the grammar school of his native place; a pleasant lively companion was he, and as smart a sailor as ever went aloft. This youth was my particular friend and messmate; we shared our grog together, and were constant companions: we were friends in more than mere words, for, in all truth and honesty, I loved him as a brother. It one day so happened that we had got the *plus* of grog; and, having the second dog-watch below, had invited one or two shipmates to a free-and-easy at the mess-table. Here we enjoyed ourselves till eight bells; when, ours being the first watch, as soon as it was called we jumped on deck. However, as the ship was gliding along under easy sail, and there was nothing to do, we walked the deck till tired, and then lay down to take a nap—a thing always allowed if there is no work going on. I had not slept more than an hour, when I heard the boatswain's mate's shrill pipe, and his hoarse voice sing out —'Watch a-hoy!' Yet so faintly fell the sound, that it scarcely reached me. The order was to reef topsails, as a smart breeze had sprung up. Having gone aloft and performed the duty required, we were about to descend to the main deck; when the mate of the watch called every man aft to answer his name. On the list being called over, eight of the watch were missing; and amongst them my poor friend. The consequence was that they were all put in irons, sitting in a row with shackles round their ancles fastened to a long bar of iron, which is locked at the end to prevent their leg-cuffs from slipping off. The men all declared that they did not hear the watch piped: and I was not surprised, for (as already stated) the sound was so faint, that I scarcely heard it myself. If any one was in fault, it was the boatswain's mate for not blowing his call or whistle louder. As for his voice, it was destroyed by constant bawling, and could not rise above a hoarse whisper; this is generally the case with men holding the office and performing the duties of a boatswain.

I was not allowed even to approach my unhappy friend; but walked the deck, and watched him sitting with his head betwixt his hands resting on his knees, whilst I could hear the stifled sobs that burst from his manly breast. The scene roused feelings of sorrow and anger within me. Those only who have experienced the feeling of disinterested friendship, can understand or appreciate the harassing and conflicting thoughts that distracted me, and made my heart sick.

Thus for two hours I paced the deck in a state of bewilderment, until, the watch being relieved, I retired to my hammock,—but not to sleep. Throughout the middle watch I lay in a state of restless anxiety; but before the last sound of the bell had died away that announced the morning watch, I was again on deck,—when going directly to the officer in command, I requested permission to give my messmate a drink of water. Leave was obtained as soon as demanded: I must needs however here observe, that this was the only lieutenant in the ship of whom I would have asked such a favour. It happened, in fact, to be our noble and gallant first lieutenant's watch; I therefore did not dread a refusal. On going below for a pannikin to fetch the water, young Waghorn beckoned me to the midshipmen's berth and gave me a tot of rum, well knowing the use that would be made of it. Having drawn some water at the tank, I accordingly mixed the grog, and handed the welcome draught to my unfortunate friend; who with a sorrowful face thanked me, drank the contents, squeezed my hand, and in the saddest accents that ever fell upon my ear, said—'God bless you: I am done for!' He well knew the degradation that awaited him; mercy was a thing unknown. You might as well appeal to a block of granite, as to the stolid form of our human commander; if once reported, there was no chance of forgiveness.

The business of the watch, such as washing decks, coiling up ropes, and putting things in order, having been completed, 'up hammocks' was piped. I went below with a heavy heart, lashed up my messmate's bedding and my own, and took them on deck to be stowed in the nettings. Having thus a double task to perform, I was nearly the last man up; and was on that account spoken to in the most offensive terms, by the same boatswain's-mate who had been the cause of my friend's degradation. The tarpaulings being put over the nettings and eight bells having struck, the word was passed for breakfast; and the men went below to eat with such appetite as they could. A feeling of gloomy sorrow pervaded the entire ship's company; for every one anticipated the bloody scene that would shortly be enacted; and the victims were well-conducted men whom all respected. Our own berth was in as much grief as if the favourite son of a family was about to be sacrificed.

When the cook of the mess came down with the burgoo, I took our captive friend his allowance with some biscuit and butter; but alas, he touched it not. I spoke to him; he heeded me not, but stared as if looking on vacancy; his eye was fixed, the muscles of his face were rigid, and a deadly pallor pervaded his countenance. The bright jewel of his soul had fled; his reason was dethroned! This conviction shot through my brain like an electric shock; and in a moment of despair, I uttered a bitter curse on those who imposed more upon man than God ever intended him to suffer. I rushed below, and conveyed the dreadful tidings to the crew. Every man left off eating, and sprung to his feet: had I brought word that the ship was sinking, it could not have produced a greater feeling of consternation. All appeared as if struck dumb at the horrid news; and then again the entire crew sat down in silent sorrow to await the issue. The duties of the vessel were carried on in the usual way until four bells (ten o'clock), when all hands were piped 'for punishment'.

The gratings being fixed and strong lashings attached to seize up the unhappy victims by the wrists and ancles, the boatswain's-mates advanced, with their shirt-sleeves tucked up, all in readiness to perform their bloody business. The captain and officers took post on the quarter-deck, and thence gazed on the area below, where stood the ship's company compulsory spectators of the cold-blooded murder that ensued. The captain with studied complacency addressed the heart-broken victims, the men who were then, as ever, the safeguard and bulwark of our native land; and in calm accents told them that, 'his country expected him to do his duty!' Victim number one was then called and ordered to strip, which being done without a sigh or a murmur, he was next seized up as high as his hands would reach, when stretched out across the grating, so as to bring his breast flat against it, and prevent the possibility of his flinching. His feet were similarly disposed and made fast; and the whole process constitutes what sailors derisively call, making a 'spread-eagle' of a man. The boatswain's-mates now produced that disgusting and abominable instrument of torture, a cat-o'-nine-tails; the mere sight of which is enough to cause the flesh creep, and the heart's blood freeze. This fiendish contrivance is made with a thick handle about a foot and a-half in length, and about the substance of an ordinary broomstick; there are nine cords attached about three feet long, and about as thick as a tobacco-pipe; the cord is about the consistency of whipcord, and there are three over-hand knots tied on each cord, making altogether a bunch of twenty-seven. This elaborate tormentor when drawn across the shoulders tears away the flesh in the most shocking manner, leaving the bladebones and backbone bare.

All being in readiness, the order to proceed is given. A man of powerful frame steps forth, who holds up the cat by the handle in his right hand and combs out the tails of it with the fingers of his left: he then grasps the ends altogether in his left hand, and swinging the whole round over his head, brings it down with concentrated force upon the back of his helpless victim. As the blow falls upon the body, it produces a sound from the inside something like the noise made by a man when using a pavior's rammer. After every stroke the cords are deliberately cleared by the operator's fingers, and the cat swung overhead to give the next blow additional force. At about the fourth lash blood begins to flow, and trickles down upon the deck; the flesh next begins to get rotten with beating, having the appearance of scarified bullock's liver; whilst the knots of the infernal scourge tear away pieces, which bespatter the deck at every cut,—as the butcher's bloody fingers are drawn through the cords saturated with the life-blood of his fellow-man. When the judgment or caprice of the captain is satisfied, he orders the sufferer to be cast loose; who goes below an altered man, and feels himself a degraded wretch. Thus many of the finest men in the service have been rendered worthless: and this was called discipline! Some men bear this horid punishment in sullen silence, being determined that those who have caused the inhuman exhibition shall not enjoy the luxury of hearing a single cry escape their victim's lips.

I have known instances of men putting a leaden bullet in their mouths, to bite in their agony; which, when produced at the conclusion of the punishment, has been as flat as a sixpence. Others again scream out, and beg for mercy in the most heart-rending tones; calling upon their God in the most frantic manner,—praying to be put to instant death, rather than suffer such uubearable torture. But no attention is paid to their cries; all is apathetic silence and perfect indifference, save perhaps a stern order from the captain to the boatswain's-mate to—'do his duty.' This disgraceful punishment has been the cause of both mutiny and murder; petty tyrants have been seized and thrown overboard in the dark, and no one the wiser; for the men grew secret and sullen, under such savage treatment.

I once heard of a horrible revenge taken upon a petty officer, who was constantly in the habit of reporting men and getting them flogged. The vessel to which he belonged was chasing a privateer, a fast sailer which had captured several English merchantmen; and on this occasion, in order to get the ship into good sailing trim, gratings loaded with eighteen-pound shot had been slung in different parts. One of these was over the main hatchway; and as the man in question was descending in the dead of night, this heavy weight of metal was let down upon his head, crushing him like a spider.

There was another tale too, current in my time, of a man who had become desperate in consequence of being flogged at the instigation of some boy-midshipman. He vowed to be revenged—and a dreadful revenge he took; for one day, when the wind was blowing great guns, and the sea rolling mountains high, he seized the lad in his arms, and (being close to the gangway) jumped overboard with him, ere a soul could interfere to prevent the accomplishment of the horrid deed. Human aid was not further available, as no boat could live in such a sea.

There were other modes of punishment, which under some circumstances were very severe. There is a man now living in my neighbourhood, who was on board a brig in the French war: and being an able seaman was once set to look out on the bowsprit;—it was on the coast of Norway. There came on a furious storm of sleet and hail, which so battered his face and eyes that he could not see (as he has told me) half-a-mile ahead, and then only at intervals. The commander by-and-bye hailed my friend and told him to come in, 'as there was land on the starboard bow.' Now the officer had the aid of a powerful glass, which also protected his eye, whilst the man was nearly blinded by the driving wind and sleet: still, for not performing an impossibility, the latter was ordered aloft to sit on the cross-trees for four hours in the most inclement season of that frozen climate. The result was that when the time had expired, he was fixed there a sitting statue, with every joint rigid, his flesh numbed, and without a particle of feeling left. When hailed by the officer to come down, he could neither speak nor move; upon the discovery of which his messmates went aloft, and lowered him down apparently frozen to death. They succeeded however in pouring a little spirits down his throat, then wrapped him in warm blankets, and as soon as he was restored to some degree of animation administered a full pint of rum,

H

which the patient drank off without being able to tell whether it was rum or water that he had taken: so completely deadened was every sense by long exposure to the cold, with no better clothing than a common jacket and canvas trowsers. Hundreds of men would have died under such circumstances; however my old friend is still living, and although approaching seventy, walks as upright and with as firm a step as any man on earth. There was another mode of punishment, to which no one could object if men neglected their duties; that was, to stop their grog and put them on the black list. But to hack the flesh off men's bones, or perch them aloft to be frozen to death, is a disgrace to the British flag and a foul blot on the escutcheon of our country.

My poor friend received his three dozen in an apparent state of unconsciousness, and when taken below sat down and with a bitter smile muttered something about his mother. He seemed to fancy that he was again a little boy at home, and that he had been beaten for something he had done wrong; and then he cried to be forgiven, and promised not to do the like again. Here was a scene to witness! Here was the most grievous change that ever wrung the heart of man! A gallant youth, just springing into manhood, with the fresh bloom of nature upon his glowing cheek, the bright flash of intelligence in his eye, and naturally gifted with faculties of the highest order, was thus in a few short hours reduced to simple idiocy; and the shadow on the dial of his existence had retrograded to childhood. But it was useless to complain: it was impossible to redress. When we arrived in port the poor prostrate youth was sent to hospital, and there in a short time so far recovered as to give the address of his family; which, as I learned from the bumboat woman, was at Taunton in Somersetshire. A letter, it appears, had been sent to his father, who came to him as quickly as possible. The latter was described to me as a fine old gentleman with powdered hair, wearing a white neckcloth, blue coat, nankin small-clothes, and white stockings with silver buckles in his shoes. On his arrival, the resident surgeon cautiously informed him that there was no hope of his son's recovery; an inflammation of the brain having supervened, which defied human agency. The old man took the good doctor by the hand, and wept over his long lost son in speechless sorrow; but the boy was already too far gone to recognise the parental voice.

He lay in a state of unconsciousness bordering upon death, which continued for nearly a fortnight. In the meantime his mother also arrived, and remained in close attendance on her unhappy child during several days of agonizing suspense, whilst the tide of life was ebbing fast. At length the fatal malady subsided, and the afflicted sufferer was restored to reason: but not till nature was completely exhausted. He had only time to receive his parents' blessing and forgiveness, when falling back into his mother's arms he yielded up his afflicted spirit to the eternal Source from whence it sprung: and so ended the career of one who well deserved a better fate!

"Peace to his gentle spirit now, where'er it flies:
Whether moored in heaven, or sailing in the skies!"

His funeral obsequies were performed in an humble and quiet but solemn manner; no pompous hearse, nor well-trained steeds with nodding plumes were there; no mimic mourners followed; for this was no mere mockery of woe. None but his aged parents paced behind the coffin with aching hearts, as their lost one was borne to his resting-place,—save indeed the good nurse, who, clad in decent black, attended the sorrowing pair. A simple head-stone was set up, whereon was inscribed in plain letters these words:

Sacred to the Memory
OF
FREDERICK WILLIAM JOHN HAWTHORN.

CHAPTER VI.

CHASE OF THE 'PEACOCK'—CHRISTMAS EVE IN HARBOUR—A QUARREL—I COME TO GRIEF AND TO THE GRATINGS—MY SUBSEQUENT FEELINGS, AND RESOLVE—A SULLEN CREW—AN ATTEMPT AT ESCAPE—IT IS FRUSTRATED, BUT NOT DISCOVERED.

HAVING filled up our provisions, we received orders to put to sea with all speed, in search of an American privateer called the *Peacock*. She was a remarkably fast sailer, and was committing sad havoc among our merchantmen; having captured several and taken them into French ports, where it was easy to dispose of both vessels and cargoes. There was no English man-of-war on the station that could come up with her; and so our frigate, being considered one of the fastest in the navy, our captain was now instructed to repair to the scene of the privateer's depredations, and capture her, if possible.

We soon weighed anchor, shook out our canvas, and, once clear of the land, packed on all the sail we could carry: and having a good quarterly wind, ploughed the sea in gallant style at the rate of thirteen knots an hour. Thus we kept on all day and night; until, at about 3 A.M., just as day was breaking, the man at the mast-head cried out—'A sail to windward!' The officer of the watch, on going aloft with his glass, knew her from description to be the identical craft we were in search of. Orders were instantly given to haul close to the wind; and with the frigate put into the best sailing trim for the chase, we kept gaining gradually until about six bells, when we came within gun-shot of the privateer. A long eighteen-pounder was then brought to bear upon her through one of the bow-ports in the forecastle; but as the sea was rough and a considerable swell on, it was difficult to get a correct aim.

We still however kept gaining ground, and could see the men on deck throwing things overboard in order to lighten the vessel; but just at the moment when she appeared to be our own, the frigate's tiller-rope broke; which threw us all aback until we could ship a new one. This took some time, and gave the *Peacock* an immense advantage; however, as soon as the fresh rope was adjusted, we again started in pursuit. A very stiff wind was blowing, and as it kept increasing in strength the spars bent before the blast: until, with a sudden crash, away went the fore-top-gallant-mast, once more throwing us aback and causing additional delay. Ere this damage could be repaired, the chase was far ahead; but having made a fresh start, we again gradually diminished our distance, and just as the sun was disappearing below the horizon came within reach of her. The frigate now kept up a running fire, whilst the crew of the flying craft could be seen working for their lives; throwing overboard their guns, chests, and everything of a heavy nature,—including live-stock, such as pigs and sheep, casks of provision, bags of bread; even their gun-carriages came floating along as we pressed upon her stern. It was now towards midnight, and the prize within our grasp; when suddenly there came on a fog so dense, that we could not see the bowsprit's length ahead. The enemy most likely took advantage of a circumstance for him so fortunate, and squaring his yards went off before the wind; and as we kept our former course, the ships were soon far apart.

At all events, when the fog cleared off, and the beautiful rays of the morning sun glittered and sparkled on the water, nothing was in sight. The vessel we had been chasing had disappeared like a phantom; the wind was hushed, the sea was calm, and we appeared to be in an immense field of fountains produced by whales and grampuses spouting to a considerable height. The water in its descent had the appearance of crystallized weeping willows, as the sun's rays danced and played in the falling stream of liquid glass; and altogether it was one of the most beautiful scenes that the eye of man ever looked upon. As there was no immediate hope of again falling in with the American privateer, we retraced our course: and on arrival in port heard that the *Peacock* had gone into one of the French harbours to refit and prepare for new adventures. Our next business was to convoy eighty sail of merchantmen to the Mediterranean,—which we accomplished in company with a seventy-four and a gun-brig. This service at an end, we returned to our cruising station off the Irish coast, and there remained all the winter. On Christmas-eve it began to blow hard, and the captain anchored the ship in Bantry-bay; when, being in harbour at this particular season, the ship's company were served with a double allowance of grog.

The captain and his lieutenants had gone on shore to spend Christmas-day; and while the men on board were smoking and drinking in their berths, the mates were enjoying themselves in their cabin, which was partitioned off from the steerage: one of the mates and a midshipman however remained on deck to keep the watch. About a quarter before eight P.M. the second lieutenant came on board to take charge of the ship for the night. The men were now getting elated after taking an extra tot of grog, and all 'went merry as a marriage-feast'; some of Dibdin's songs were sung in true nautical style; and comic recitations were given in much better taste than any one would expect. For it must be remembered that our crews in that day were composed of strangely assorted materials; numbers were sent to man our ships, who in times of peace would have been transported. Some of these men had seen a great deal of London life, who, first acquiring idle habits, eventually progressed as far as robbing their employers, picking pockets, or anything else that fell in their way. Thus, after a short career of crime, they sooner or later fell under the strong arm of the law, and were handed over to the naval service; where some of them, under strict dicipline, became tolerably useful.

During this scene of revelry, it fell to my lot to be called on for a favourite recitation called 'The three drunken sailors': and as this was a sort of standing dish, all the men were very attentive; until, at the conclusion, one of the worthies I have just been describing made use of a filthy and most insulting expression towards me. This brought on angry words, and destroyed the harmony of the evening: whilst I, feeling indignant at an attack for which I had given no cause, demanded an apology; but instead thereof received the most unqualified abuse, and at length a blow. And now, thrown off my guard by liquor and excitement, I struck the miscreant in return, and paid him back his coin with compound interest; but, on attempting to close with my antagonist and throw him, we fell together against the thin partition that separated the midshipmen's berth from the steerage: and the feeble barrier giving way, both of us rolled through the opening. This was all done in a breath; the noise occasioned by the shivering planks was heard by the lieutenant on the quarter-deck just overhead; and he at once called to the master-at-arms, to know what was the cause of all that noise below?

The functionary addressed knew well enough, having witnessed the whole proceeding from beginning to end: nor would he willingly have reported us,—as he was very fond of a fight, being himself a good boxer. I once saw him cut up a fellow in fine style who had been very insolent, rather than report him; and this was considered by the men a good trait in his character. But now, being called upon, he was compelled to do his duty; and the end of it was, that we were both ordered aft on the main-deck, and put in irons till the captain came on board. This did not happen until the morning after Christmas-day; so that, on the day of festivity and thanksgiving, we took our dinners in the bilboes, where we were kept confined all that day and the next night. But as soon as the captain came on board the following morning, we were ordered to be released for punishment, and did not remain long in suspense.

All hands being piped 'for punishment', the entire ship's company was assembled as usual; the grating was rigged out to receive our doomed carcases, and the butcherly boatswain's mates stood ready for their infernal work. Just as the captain was about to address us, a deputation from the crew at large ascended to the quarter-deck, and presented a petition in my favour; detailing the provocation and ill-treatment I had received from the other party, and pleading all else that could be alleged in extenuation; but it was of no avail—they might as well have supplicated a rock. I myself then begged rather to suffer death than be subjected to this horrible degradation. In the best language at my command, I set forth the enormity of the hellish practice and its demoralizing effects; I spoke of the sufferings and melancholy death of my friend, and pointed out other instances of men once cheerful and happy, who had been tortured into misery. I endeavoured to shew that our common manhood was outraged at every lash; that human nature revolted; and that the law of God was violated by such cruel and unsuitable inflictions: I referred to my character and past conduct, my services, and the ready hand with which they were ever performed. But, alas! all was useless; the man's humanity was effaced by the horrible system under which he had been trained; the eye had dwelt unmoved upon these brutal scenes, until the heart was petrified. The individual I addressed had no feeling left for his kind; and had possibly even arrived at the conclusion, that he was himself made of different material from other men.

Having in vain urged every plea that my poor brain suggested, I was peremptorily ordered to strip.

My spirit now sank within me; a tear stole from my eye; and I cast an imploring look up to that Power, of whom we are told, that His holiest attribute is mercy: and that man is most like God, when he is merciful towards his fellow. I then drew my shirt over my head, and as the keen air fell upon my bare skin, a shudder of horror came over my whole frame. With sorrow in their countenances, my shipmates seized me up by the wrists; and even the boatswain and his mates approached their bestial task reluctantly. For I was a general favourite with the ship's company; I wrote letters, and read the answers from their friends, for nearly all of them; and for such services I would never receive anything in the shape of remuneration, not even a tot of grog; and I was as much in love with honour, truth, and justice, as the best educated in the land.

The captain was now uttering the fatal words,—'Boatswain, do your duty!' when a man of athletic frame stepped forward, and offered to take the punishment in my stead; saying, that it was a pity to cut to pieces so young and delicate a boy. For I had not then seen nineteen years; and consequently my muscles were not fully developed. The proffered sacrifice was rejected, my friend told to stand back, and the executioner directed to proceed. This last order was given with all imaginable complacency; the soft utterance of the words being a masterpiece of mockery. Such tones I had heard before from the tongue of canting hypocrisy; but they never sounded so unnaturally, as when associated with the never-to-be-forgotten formula—'My country expects me to do my duty: boatswain's-mate, do yours!' The operator boggled at the first lash, and the cat fell lightly on my back; he was severely reprimanded for not striking harder, and promised, if he did not do his duty, to be tied up in my place. Again the man essayed to strike; but his arm appeared paralysed, he trembled from head to foot, his face assumed a deathlike hue; and he staggered back fainting into the arms of the men who caught him. The boatswain himself, the chief butcher, was then called forth; he was a quick muscular man, and could hit with the sharpness of lightning. The first stroke from his master-hand made me writhe in agony not to be expressed by words; cut after cut succeeded, the blood trickled down my back, and every blow appeared to strike inwardly. The feeling was as of molten lead being poured upon the parts where the scourge fell; but this acute sensation gradually subsided into a dull and aching pain, which seemed to pervade the entire nervous system, and communicated itself to the heart: this is all I remember, for vitality was suspended; and had they flogged on till doomsday, I should have felt no more.

But how shall I describe the feelings, whether mental or bodily, which I experienced on again coming to my senses! All that imagination ever painted of the eternal torments of the damned, could not compare with the sufferings I endured. I was possessed as with a demon, and vowed to be revenged; I made up my mind to murder the man who had thus disgraced me. I secreted a pistol, taken from the armourer's chest for the purpose, and kept it loaded nearly a week, watching an occasion to execute my design; but no favourable opportunity presenting itself, my passion gradually subsided; and I resolved on going into port, to swim ashore and desert.

It is impossible to depict the crushing influence that weighed me down. Where now was my free Briton's boasted birthright,—where the title of 'man,' that I inherited from my Maker,—where all the ties of brotherhood which should bind the human family together? All that I most loved and valued had been trampled under foot, the scoff and scorn of a petty tyrant. More than forty years have passed away since then,—and I am fast approaching the goal of life; but I still feel the scorching degradation as palpably as when I was branded with it in my country's name. * * * But, enough of this!

I resumed my duties in sullen silence, and soon perceived that a feeling of depression akin to my own had possessed every man in the ship; it was plain too that the officers equally understood this, and began to look upon the change with sorrow. The men moved like automatons—all life and spirit had fled; nothing was heard beyond low murmurs and whispered sounds; the light of contentment had been put out, and all was darkness. The dreadful silence that now reigned, appeared to affect our tyrant more than the tears and groans of his agonized victims; he seemed to grow thoughtful and serious, indeed a great change came over him; the detested cat was laid aside, and milder punishment was substituted in its stead. But it was too late, the mischief was done: nothing now could have restored the men to that light and buoyant state of mind they once enjoyed. 'Tis true, that they became in some degree reconciled, but never again joyous and happy. How little did our ancestors know of that true government which consists in the greatest amount of happiness to the greatest number; they seem to have arrived at wrong conclusions from false reasoning, and to have believed that their own happiness was enhanced by the misery they inflicted on others!

We continued to observe the usual dull routine of duty until our return to harbour, when I began to meditate an escape from this unbearable position: and also communicated my determination to a young man about my own age, whom I knew to be dissatisfied and wretched as myself. After consulting together as to the best means to be adopted, we concluded to cut down the jolly-boat which hung suspended at the stern of the ship about a yard from the water. The greatest difficulty was how to evade the sentry stationed betwixt the mizenmast and the signal-chest, over which latter we must needs get, so as to slide down the tackle into the boat. I proposed waiting until we could ascertain who would be put on sentry from twelve till two in the middle watch, at which time it is very common for all to creep below, either to smoke or sleep, except the sentries; and even they sometimes take advantage when in port, where all is supposed to be safe.

After waiting several days, and having all things in readiness for the accomplishment of our plan, I learned who would be on sentry during the first two hours in the middle watch; and as I had always been on good terms with this man, I asked him if he would have a tot of rum, it being a cold night. To this he readily assented, and I took care to let him have nearly half-a-pint from a bottle that had been given to me by one of the officers for doing some writing. By degrees the men retired to their hammocks and were all soon fast asleep, except myself and my partner in this dangerous enterprise. We waited anxiously for the bell to announce the hour of midnight; the hour arrived, we heard the sentries relieved, and in a short time the men off duty and the sergeant of marines turned in. When all was still, and a death-like silence seemed to favour our design, we crept from our hammocks with the stealthiness of cats; and creeping up the fore-hatchway, went directly to the ship's-head, as an excuse for being on deck in case we should be seen by any one. But all continued still, and the night was dark as pitch: the next thing to be done: was to manage the sentry. I approached him accordingly, and found he was pacing to and fro across the deck, half-asleep; so that he did not notice me until I was close to him, and (thinking it was the officer of the watch) still kept stepping out the tedious time.

On making myself known, I said I could not sleep in consequence of a pain in my inside: and presently added 'that I should go below and take a drop of rum'; and that if he thought proper, as there was no one about, I would give him a dram also. This was not the man to refuse: so taking him about a quarter-of-a-pint in a basin, he quickly drank it off. I staid talking and watching the effect of the sleeping draught I had administered, until observing that he was asleep on his walk, I bade him good night; saying, that I should go below and turn in. Instead however of doing so, I continued to watch my man from behind a gun, and soon saw him drop down on the signal-chest quite overpowered; then, after having ascertained that his sleep was sound, I crept softly below, and communicated my success to my companion in this hazardous undertaking.

We ascended the hatchway-ladder with our bundles, which contained a change of clothing; so that when safe on shore, we might not be known by any description of our attire. Thus provided, we stole along the deck, and passed the sentry asleep on the signal-locker; then softly climbing over the stern, we slid gently down the tackle by which the boat was suspended. The next thing to be done was to cut the tackle at each end of the boat simultaneously; our knives had been well ground for this purpose, and were both equally sharp; indeed, we had been very particular in comparing them, as the least mistake in cutting through the tackle would destroy our plan. The tide being at the flood, we agreed to lie down in the boat and let her drift ashore; and as it was perfectly dark and few vessels in the harbour, there was little fear of our being observed. The word 'now!' was the signal agreed upon for cutting through the tackle. It was given in a whisper; but, by some unaccountable mishap, my end only was severed, and I was consequently pitched head-foremost into the water, together with our bundles containing our disguises. My companion climbed up by the tackle of the boat which now hung stern uppermost with her bow in the water; we luckily did not wake the sentry. My friend having reached the main-deck, let down a rope through one of the portholes under the forecastle, by the use of which and his assistance I scrambled on board.

The next thing was to find my bag, and get dry clothing; and this done, we went softly to our hammocks, which we had the precaution to let down, so that they hung considerably lower than the rest. This is frequently done for the benefit of the air, and likewise to make more room for those sleeping above. Secresy was now the main object; a single look might draw suspicion upon us, and lead to our destruction. When the hammocks were piped up in the morning, we went about our duties in the regular way as if nothing had happened. Meanwhile, the jolly-boat boys, being the first to discover that the tackle had been cut, set to work and spliced it at once; so that the entire affair passed off as an ordinary accident.

CHAPTER VII.

A GALE IN THE BAY OF BISCAY—GIBRALTAR—OUR SHIP PLAGUE-STRICKEN — AWFUL MORTALITY — QUARANTINE — THE IRISH WIDOWS—PLYMOUTH SOUND—NAPOLEON I. ON BOARD THE BELLEROPHON—PAYING OFF—A LARK WITH THE ISRAELITES—A PLUCKED PIGEON.

A FEW days afterwards we weighed anchor, and again convoyed a large fleet of merchant vessels to the Mediterranean. This duty had fallen to our lot, in consequence of the frequent capture of merchantmen by privateers. Having seen our charge safely on their way according to instructions, we were to return to our proper station; the weather was remarkably fine, and the atmosphere seemed to sparkle with light; the sea was like a mirror, the sky clear and beautiful on every side as far as the horizon; the ship rolled lazily on the sleeping waters; and the sun about mid-day was overpowering, as there was not a breath of air stirring. Thus becalmed we lay for several hours; at length a favourable breeze sprung up, and we glided smoothly through the glassy element under every stitch of sail that the ship would carry. She, with her canvas wings expanded, moved majestically along, and looked like a thing of life. No sight could be more pleasing: and it was the first time I had witnessed such a scene in full perfection. The wind however gradually increased, and we shortened sail by degrees, until reduced to close-reefed topsails; the clouds gathered dark and thick around; rain fell in torrents, and the storm came on apace. The men were now ordered aloft to furl topsails; and this had not been many minutes done, when it became necessary to furl the foresail and close-reef the mainsail.

It was by this time blowing a gale, which in a few hours became a hurricane of the most fearful nature; the mainsail was blown into tatters, and the pieces were cracking and fluttering in the wind; a stay-sail was then hoisted, but shared the same fate, flying into ribbons as soon as it was set, with a sound resembling the discharge of artillery. The vessel rolled and pitched like a cork on the mountain billows; the wind and waves seemed to contend with the dark and threatening clouds that lowered overhead; and the rain poured down as if the flood-gates of heaven had been opened. In this helpless state we were the sport of the raging elements; the wind whistled and howled through the rigging, as if the universe were in its death-struggle, and all nature seemed convulsed. Our bowsprit and masts shook like reeds, boats and spars were swept from the booms: and the men were clinging like cats to anything they could grapple, in order to avoid being hurled with desperate force into the lee scuppers. For two nights and days we drove before the howling storm, sometimes on the pinnacle of a mountain wave, and then suddenly dropped into the valley of waters below: the sudden transition producing a sensation such as can only be compared to that of falling from a stupendous height into a fathomless abyss. I have sometimes experienced this extraordinary feeling in a dream. Every moment we expected to go down; and sometimes lying on her beam-ends, the vessel appeared as if she would never right again. There was no interval of respite or repose; and this wretched state of affairs had continued so long, that the strongest men were nearly exhausted; whilst the weaker rolled about the deck in the most pitiable condition.

In this hapless plight, we were driven into that dangerous sea the Bay of Biscay; and it appeared certain now, that nothing but the interposing hand of Providence could save us from a watery grave. Many who had been at sea all their lives, had never witnessed such a storm; the vessel creaked and groaned like some living monster of the deep; all hope had fled, and each man had resigned himself calmly to his fate. During this state of suspense betwixt life and death, the fury of the elements fortunately subsided, and by degrees settled down into a dead calm. But the swell continued to be very heavy; and the ship staggered under its ponderous assault, as wave after wave burst in angry foam against her sides. Thus we continued pitching and tossing; until by slow degrees, the heaving ocean sank into repose, and the vexed sea became gradually passive, as if its mighty powers were exhausted.

On going below to examine the ship's state, it was discovered that she had sprung a leak, and had taken in a considerable quantity of water; whereupon, the pumps were instantly manned, and all hands took a spell in turn. Under these trying circumstances, the order was given to 'splice the main-brace': which had the effect of raising the drooping spirits of the crew. We kept on pumping incessantly, until our arrival in port; when the carpenter and his crew set to work to stop the leak, fish the masts, and make all 'taut,'—as the phrase is. Using great diligence, we soon put to sea again, taking under convoy another fleet of merchant vessels proceeding to the same destination as before. The weather was fine; so that, with a favourable breeze, we soon reached the Mediterranean, and there meeting with other men-of-war, made over our charge to them.

On our return we sailed down the Gut, and entering the bay of Gibraltar, noticed two French frigates lying at anchor; a spectacle, the meaning of which we could not understand. However, our sailing-master steered in betwixt the two; which was close shaving, as our yard-arms touched theirs in passing. They received us with a cheerful salute, and we returned the compliment with three cheers, whilst the band struck up 'Rule Britannia.' Upon the captain hailing one of the Frenchmen to know the cause of their presence, somebody on board answered in unmistakeable English, that a great battle (Waterloo) had been fought, and that Napoleon had surrendered. This was glorious news indeed! Liberty once more dawned upon me; my hopes by day and my dreams by night were on the eve of being realized; all that I had suffered seemed as nothing, and I felt as if nought was wanting to consummate my earthly happiness.

Whilst we lay here at anchor, the Spanish peasants came alongside in boats laden with grapes and oranges.

The former were the finest specimens I had seen, yet we bought them at only three-halfpence per pound; we did not however enjoy this luxury beyond a few days. All on a sudden, it transpired that a raging epidemic had broken out among the population on the Rock: and our captain, fearing the contagion, came on board immediately, and gave orders to weigh anchor and put to sea at once, in the hope of preventing the frightful malady from being communicated to the ship's company. But, alas, it was fruitless; the fatal scourge was brought on board by his own boat's crew, who shewed immediate symptoms, and were all dead within twenty-four hours.

One after another the hands sickened, and died like sheep with the rot; more than half the men were affected; the dead were quickly sewn up in their hammocks and committed to the deep. It was a solemn scene to witness at midnight the corpse lying on a grating ready to be launched into the deep. An officer read the funeral service by the dim light of a lantern, which cast a sickening ray upon the pallid faces of the men who stood mournfully round, no one knowing whose turn would come next: for several of the most robust were seized and carried off by the insidious enemy in a few hours. As I lay in my hammock sick with the horrible sensations produced by this destroying plague, I cast my eyes on either side, and beheld many of my comrades expire in a last convulsive struggle with death; the skin changing the while from scarlet to purple, and then to a deadly paleness, when all was soon over. But I will not dwell upon this scene of horror; the weather happily grew colder as we made northing; the sharpness of the breeze revived the drooping spirits of the sick; and this devouring pestilence gradually abated: but all who recovered were sadly emaciated, and looked more like shadows than living men.

However, the virulence of the disease had expended itself ere we arrived in port. No sooner had we dropped anchor and furled sails, than a boat came off making direct for the ship: which being perceived by the captain and officers on deck, the jolly-boat was instantly despatched with orders that no one would be admitted on board for four days. The shore-boat contained the wives of several victims to the devastating scourge under which we had suffered. On being told that they must return without seeing their husbands, the women set up a cry of lamentation, as if they foreboded some dreadful calamity. It was therefore with great reluctance they returned to land, crying and wringing their hands, and exhibiting the most intense grief at their disappointment. For hours they lingered on the beach indulging their sorrow, and at length they moved away with their heads bowed down as at a funeral procession. It was a sorry sight to us, who knew that most of their husbands were dead, some of whom had only been married when we were last in harbour.

Being safely moored and every thing made taut, all hands were now set to cleanse and purify the ship fore and aft; every article of clothing was washed and scrubbed; the bedding was exposed to the air on deck; the ship was fumigated in every part, and the decks besprinkled with some purifying liquid prepared by the doctor. This short quarantine having been observed, on the fifth morning the women were allowed to come on board; then, as each learned the sad fate of her husband, they tore the caps from their heads, and let their hair hang dishevelled over their shoulders. In this state they ran about the deck raving like maniacs, calling upon the departed, and crying—'Och hone! och hone! why did ye die and lave me to the wide world?' Their cries and lamentations were truly pitiable: and what made the scene more heart-rending was their youth; for not one of them, I believe, had seen twenty years, and several were much younger. Their grief was respected by both officers and men, and every thing was done that could be thought of to alleviate their distress; but it was of no avail, as they refused to be comforted, and seemed to indulge in a luxury of woe.

This sorrowful scene continued from nine A.M. until sunset on a long summer's day; they were then kindly informed that they must go on shore. On receiving the order, they set up a concert of the most hideous howls that ever assailed the sense of hearing; and then, adjusting their hair and clothing, proceeded to obey. They were gently handed over the ship's side; and, in a state of mental and bodily prostration, took their seats in the boat which waited alongside to convey the poor miserable creatures ashore. The ship's company gazed after them, until on landing they raised their hands imploringly to heaven, as if asking its protection; and then, looking back towards the ship, waved us a last and sorrowful adieu. Thus ended this strange and singular exhibition of grief.

Two days after we weighed anchor, and bade farewell to old Ireland; the weather was fine and the wind favourable; so we soon saw the English coast, and made direct for Plymouth Sound: the band playing merrily as we passed the different vessels lying at anchor, until we came in line with the *Bellerophon*, or, as the sailors called her, the old 'ball-of-rope-yarn.' Almost within cable's length of the floating prison that contained the mighty Napoleon,—the man who made continental Europe his play-ground, and crowned heads his puppets,— we dropped anchor amid the shouts of thousands who had congregated from all parts of the kingdom to get a sight of this wonderful man. The Sound was covered with every available craft that could be set afloat, all crowded with anxious spectators waiting the ex-emperor's appearance on the poop; and on shore also the people had gathered together in a dense mass, which appeared so compact that you might have walked upon their heads for miles. At length the fallen conqueror came on deck, accompanied by a guard of marines; and having taken his stand upon the poop, cast an eagle glance upon the surrounding multitude, and taking off his hat saluted his innumerable visitors. A settled gloom hung upon his brow as he viewed the stern realities before him; the muscles of his face were rigid, his lips compressed, and his penetrating eye fixed steadfastly upon the imposing scene.

Here then had ended his dream of universal conquest; here he lay prostrate at the foot of the altar, on which he had sacrificed not hecatombs, but pyramids of human victims. As his ambition was boundless, posterity will not weep his fall. But that he had insinuated himself into the hearts of a generous people is too true; they worshipped him as a demigod, until their zeal became a species of infatuation, and took such firm root in the breast of the devotees, that they would go through fire and water at his bidding. For a time his adopted country was enriched by the spoils and plunder of other lands; he formed the bulk of the population into an organized banditti, and led them forth in martial pomp to do the unholy work of bloodshed and robbery; the palaces of kings, the dwellings of princes and nobles were ransacked, and the most sacred places plundered to satisfy his insatiable cravings; the finest works of art were stolen from museums, and splendid altar-pieces torn down to adorn the national gallery of France;—until all the remaining independent states of Europe leagued together to put down this infamous system of national plunder. And here stood before me, as a prisoner, the greatest destroyer of industry and domestic happiness, that ever waged war upon his species in modern times. Had he been desirous of establishing just principles on earth, and of crushing despotism, the sympathies of the entire human race would have been enlisted on his side. But instead of doing this, he merely put down one despot to set up another.

After a few days passed at anchor, notice was given that the ship would be paid off. On the morning fixed for this important business, several boats came alongside laden with goods of various descriptions; such as jackets, trousers, shoes, hats, hosiery, jewellery, watches,—in fact all sorts of things calculated to coax the cash out of poor 'Jack.' The vendors of these articles were mostly Jews; however, be that as it may, they were all equally unscrupulous in their dealings with the simple tars, who knew as much about the value of things on land as the fishes in the sea. The dealers set up their wares and exposed them for sale betwixt the guns on the main deck, with a sort of counter extending from gun to gun; behind which they took their stand and exhibited their goods to the inexperienced customer, whom they fleeced of his hard-earned pelf in a manner incredible to persons experienced in the traffic of the world. The prices charged according to the quality of the articles were enormous, the sellers taking every possible advantage of the ignorance and simplicity of the buyers. From the break of the quarter-deck to the forecastle, the main deck had all the appearance of a fair; each stall-keeper having his goods laid out in the most tempting order. During the day some funny things occurred. The sailors having discovered that they had been cheated in their purchases, resorted to a novel mode of retaliating on the 'land-sharks,' as they designated the Jews. One of these specious gentlemen, who had reaped a good harvest from the credulity of his customers, had a box standing close to one of the gun-carriages full of all sorts of trinkets; round which was buckled a leathern strap; through this strap and the box a strong cord was inserted and made fast to the breeching of the gun.

Now, it so happening that a whip-tackle had been left suspended from the main-stay, directly over the hatchway, one of the men secretly attached the ready hook to the strap of the box, while another cut the cord that secured the latter to the gun. Thus, upon a signal concerted by the parties who had planned the trick, up flew the box into the air,—whilst Moses, not being in the secret, on seeing this apparent miracle raised his spectacles in astonishment, and cried out most lustily—'Mine got! mine got! there goes the tevil vith mine pox and all mine coots!' Then perceiving the tackle, from which the box hung suspended, he scrambled up the ladder on to the upper deck thinking to secure it; and nothing could be more ludicrous than the bewildered appearance of the Jew when he discovered that his property had vanished. For while he was ascending, the box was lowered into the hold, and the tackle being whipped up hung dangling in the wind as if nothing of the kind had occurred. The disappointed Israelite stood staring in amazement at the conclusion of this magic trick, and then with woeful countenance approached the quarter-deck to make his complaint to the captain. The latter could not refrain from laughing outright, as he heard how the sailors had out-witted the Jew:—and telling the victim that he should not interfere, advised him to keep a better look-out in future. The miserable creature returned to his stall in a state bordering on distraction, and began to pack up his goods, uttering the most lamentable cries and venting the direst imprecations upon the 'plooty tieves vat schtole his pox.'

Whilst this sport was going on, a scene of the most ingenious description was being enacted by one of the 'Old Bailey gentlemen,' as they were termed, who had been sent on board-ship for committing petty thefts. One of the Jews had placed a sack full of shoes standing upright against a gun at the end of his stall, which happened to be the last on the larboard side next the cabins. This being situated under the quarter-deck was rather dark, which gave the cunning thief a more favourable opportunity of accomplishing his purpose. Several of the fraternity engaged in the plot congregated together in conversation, so as to screen the operator from notice: and while others occupied the Jew's entire attention by asking various questions under pretence of becoming purchasers, the principal actor crept behind on his hands and knees, and cutting a slit in the bottom of the sack drew forth the shoes pair after pair. These he handed to a confederate stationed close by the hatchway, who dropped them down to another on the lower deck. As these shoes were drawn out, the sack gradually sank down; so that the Jew did not perceive any change, until it disappeared below the gun and two-thirds of the contents had vanished. Then first discovering his loss he lifted up the sack in order to ascertain how the shoes had been abstracted: which seemed to puzzle him exceedingly, as the mouth was securely tied with a strong cord.

However, on turning up the bottom, the truth flashed upon him like an electric shock, and he fell back against the gun pale as death, exclaiming: "My got! I am a ruined man: dare vas tventy pounds' vort of shoes in dat shack, and dish is all dare ish left! Oh, my got! my got! vat shall I do?" He cried and bewailed over his loss in every tone that could express human sorrow and despair. It brought to my mind the agonizing grief of Shylock at the loss of his jewels and his daughter: with this difference, that no actor could so truthfully have pourtrayed the workings of nature. Being still very weak from the illness I had undergone, this scene affected me considerably: and feeling tired of the noise and bustle of the day, I went below and laid down in an empty berth, where I had not remained long, when an order was given for all the sick to be sent to Haslar Hospital the next morning.

By this time, all the men had been paid: and having received their discharge, some of them went on shore that night, while others stopped on board till morning. When the hammocks were piped down, I turned in; but could not sleep. I felt all over in a burning fever, and the same excruciating sensations affected me as when I was first attacked by that dreadful Gibraltar pestilence. The dreary night at length wore away, and with the little strength I had left I managed to get on my clothes; but as I feebly descended the ship's side, it seemed as if it were my last move in life.

As I sat in the boat wrapped up in an old jacket, and half insensible, my young friend Waghorn descended to take charge of us. I happened to be nearest to him, and we entered into conversation for the last time.[1] He spoke in kind and soothing terms, and tried to inspire me with hope: but while fully appreciating his goodness, I felt as if I should never master this dreadful malady; my frame grew gradually weaker, and a sort of dizziness seized my brain. Arrived at the landing-place, we saw one of our men standing on the beach without a hat, and not a sixpence left of the hard earnings which he had received the day before—amounting to upwards of £70. His face was so contused and disfigured that we hardly knew him: and what made it worse, he could

[1] We met no more. My young friend subsequently entered the Bengal Pilot service; and his successful exertions on behalf of the Red Sea *route* to India, China, &c. are now matter of history. Waghorn seems to have retained a considerable affection for the Royal Navy; and his great ambition was to become a commissioned officer therein. It was thus upon his own earnest petition, that the rank of lieutenant was somewhat grudgingly conceded to his distinguished merits. I have also heard that his services were, in other respects, not very munificently requited.

render no account of how or by whom he had been thus ill-used. We left the poor fellow there, as we moved slowly towards the Hospital, and could hear him entreating the officer to take him back on board; but that of course was out of the question. I heard afterwards that the crew raised a subscription to pay his coach fare, and sent him to the place whence he came from. This was quite as much as he could expect, and more than he deserved; for all sailors well know what sort of entertainment awaits them in a seaport town, at the hands of prostitutes and bullies, if once inveigled into their filthy dens.

CHAPTER VIII.

HASLAR HOSPITAL—A RELAPSE AND CONVALESCENCE—SINGULAR MEETING WITH AN OLD ACQUAINTANCE—I AM DISCHARGED, AND OBTAIN A FREE PASSAGE ROUND TO CHATHAM.

On arriving at the Hospital, I was ushered into a ward by the porter: and was forthwith consigned to the care of an elderly woman the nurse of the ward; to whose kindness I believe I am indebted for being now in existence. She requested me to go to bed immediately: as indeed I was very glad to do, having hardly strength to stand; and in a few minutes she brought me a cup of warm gruel, which was very grateful, for I had taken nothing that morning but a drink of water. In about half-an-hour the doctor, an elderly white-headed man, entered attended by six or seven young ones: who surrounded the bed, apparently eager to ascertain the nature of my complaint, and the treatment to which I was to be subjected. The senior addressed me very kindly, and seemed to know perfectly well how I felt, and what I suffered. By the questions he put to me, I was convinced that he was a man of great experience and sound judgment. Having felt my pulse and looked at my tongue he ordered two of the young men whom I judged to be students to bleed me in either arm; which operation they performed with great care. Leeches were next applied by the nurse to my temples; and as the blood drained gradually from my veins, I felt a fainting sickness at my heart, which ended in total unconsciousness. In this state I lay for a short time, and on my recovery the nurse administered a gentle stimulant which had a beneficial effect. Feeling now somewhat easier I fell into a heavy slumber, which lasted about three hours. On awakening my mouth was dry, and my tongue felt like a piece of burnt leather: I asked for drink, and was supplied with barley-water which the burning fever dried up in an instant; it seemed like pouring liquid upon heated iron.

I had not lain long in this state when the doctor came into the ward, and on looking at me and feeling my pulse said I must be blistered on each side, and have my head shaved. To these operations I resigned myself with patience, feeling perfectly indifferent to life; nay, I rather desired to die, and begged forgiveness for the errors of my past existence. I would now gladly have written to my mother and my brothers and sisters; but, alas, I had not strength to lift a hand; my mind too had become weak, so that I have no recollection of what passed around me. At times only I could just distinguish the nurse, and felt her bathing my face and temples. In this prostrate state I lay for eight days; when the malignant fever took a turn, and consciousness was restored. But, oh, what a living skeleton I found myself, with limbs all shapeless, and shrivelled to the bone! However, through the kind attentions of the nurse, who watched me night and day with the solicitude of a mother, I gradually recovered so far that in a few days I could sit up in bed and read. This was a source of great comfort to me, and the good old nurse buoyed me up with encouraging words; so that I soon felt strong hopes of being myself again.

During all this time, I had taken nothing but liquids; and when at the expiration of a fortnight the doctor asked me if I could eat the leg of a chicken,—I eagerly answered, 'Yes!' adding that, 'I began to feel hungry;' at which he smiled and told me that I was now out of danger. The extra diet thus authorised proved truly grateful: though, even when the kind old woman raised me up in bed and placed the food before me already cut into small pieces, I had barely strength to raise my hand to my mouth to feed myself. Upon such fare, together with rice boiled in milk, and an occasional glass of wine-and-water, I after a few days gained strength enough to dress myself and walk across the ward; and gradually attained so far as taking gentle exercise up and down the apartment. I was now permitted to indulge in a little talk with my sick companions: telling them occasionally a tale or anecdote, which destroyed the monotony of the scene and helped to pass the tedious hours away. It struck me at the time that a cheerful companion was of great service to the sick, and contributed greatly to their recovery.

Thus days passed away; and I still kept getting stronger. I had been about a month in Hospital, when on rising from my bed one morning, the sun shone beautifully bright, and the sky was so serene, that I was tempted out into the square to enjoy the benefit of the balmy breeze. Those who have never been confined to a sick-bed, can have but a faint idea of the pleasurable sensation of going forth under the vivifying power of a genial sun; it seemed to put new life into my dilapidated system, and supplied me with a vigour such as I had not felt for a long time. I strolled leisurely about the court, occasionally leaning against the wall of the building to rest and enjoy the warmth of the sun which appeared to renovate my yet delicate frame. Whilst thus whiling away the time, I fell into conversation with a man about thirty years of age, who began telling me a doleful tale of the sufferings he had undergone.

His story was that one fine evening, as he returned from his work in the city and had just cleared London Bridge, he was seized by a press-gang with whom he struggled hard for his liberty; but in vain, as they knocked him about the head till he became senseless, and then threw him down. He remembered no more till he found himself on board the '*Tender*,' and the doctor was dressing a wound which he had received on the forehead, just over the left eye. The speaker removed his hat, and in the region indicated, I perceived a scar about an inch and a-half long. 'This,' said he, 'I shall carry to the grave; but it is nothing to the wound they inflicted on my heart. For on the news reaching my beloved and patient Mary, as she sat at needlework, she clasped her hands together, the work fell at her feet, and, as if chilled into marble, she never spoke more: but retired to her bedroom, and died without a groan or one relieving tear. Her poor mother survived her but a few months, and the old man her father is bowed down with sorrow, under the weight of his sad bereavement. Should I recover, what have I to care for in this world? True! I may be the means of consoling the stricken old man in his misery; and this, if I am spared, shall be the business of my life: for he loved me as if I had been his son.'

I at once informed my new acquaintance that I had myself witnessed on board the '*Tender*' just such a scene as he described; and on calling to mind the expressions then made use of, he declared that no other person than himself could have used the words. Poor fellow! his was indeed a sorrowful fate; we now met every day during our continuance in the Hospital, and held conversations which seemed a great relief to his mind: for I always acted a friendly part towards him, and expressed my genuine sympathy with his misfortunes. There was a quietness and mournful sincerity in his manner that enlisted my feelings in his behalf; but he frequently said with a sigh that he should never be happy again. One morning, as we conversed in our usual way, the porter gave my companion a letter sealed with black; and in accordance with my sense of delicacy I walked onwards while he made himself master of the contents. On rejoining me, he exclaimed in a sorrowful tone—'The poor old man is gone to his long home, and I am not sorry that it has happened so!' Then again, glancing over the letter, he observed that it was dated July 31st, and that the present day was the fourth of August.

This at once reminded me that the same fourth of August was my own natal day; and that I had arrived at nineteen years of age, during which short period of time I had seen more changes than some men have witnessed through a long life. Without stopping for a second thought, I asked my sombre friend to walk outside the gates and drink a glass on the strength of my birth-day. He assented, for we were now getting well apace, and needed only time to gather strength. Entering the street that leads from the hospital, we turned into a grog shop where I ordered two glasses of rum-and-water, paying for them with a shilling taken from a piece of canvas containing all my worldly riches, which amounted to about thirty shillings. Having received the customary compliments from my companion we returned to our quarters. This was the first and last birth-day I ever observed, since I was a little boy at home.

Day after day passed on, and each succeeding one found me stronger. I had always practised running and jumping from my childhood, and now fancied that I would try the strength of my muscles by jumping over a leaping-bar which I set up for the purpose. Feeling satisfied with the experiment, and being desirous of resuming an active life, I now told the doctor that I was quite well: and expressed a wish to be discharged. "Very good," he replied, "I will report your case, and you may rest satisfied that it will be attended to." A week passed in anxious expectation, at the end of which came the order for my removal, together with the discharge and the pay due to me; for the sick, I should observe, did not receive their money on the day the ship's company was paid off. Eight weeks had passed since I entered the hospital a living skeleton; I was now quite well and daily gaining in condition. After packing up the few things I possessed, which consisted of three checked shirts, my best jacket and trowsers, and a German flute which I had been taught to play by the master of the band, I went directly to the doctor to express my gratitude for his kindness and attention to me. He seemed pleased, and asked me to take a glass of wine which I most respectfully accepted; he then enquired where I was going. I answered, to London. "Well," said he, "then I can render you a little service. There is a gun-brig about to sail for Chatham; and if you think proper, I will secure you a passage in her. You will then be within forty miles of your destination, which you can reach in a few hours by coach; besides it will be a great saving to you." I thanked him for his kindness, and told him that I should be only too happy to avail myself of his generous offer. The good doctor then wrote a note addressed to the commander of the brig, which he handed me to deliver. Again I thanked him; and was taking my leave, when he rose from his seat, and shaking me cordially by the hand wished me a pleasant voyage; whereupon I made my obeisance, and retired after a most agreeable interview.

Well pleased with the treatment I had met with, I returned to bid farewell to my kind nurse, and the inmates of the ward. Having shaken hands with the men, some sitting by the fire and others lying in their beds, I went to thank the nurse and bid her good-bye. She was sitting in a small private room apparently asleep in her arm-chair: and although I felt anxious to get away, I deemed it sacrilege to rob her of nature's holy influence so beneficial to a careworn frame. I therefore quietly withdrew, and took a seat on the form by the fire, where I sat talking quietly for an hour; by which time I could hear the old dame moving about the place. I then again approached the door of her private room, and said: "Nurse, I have come for the purpose of offering to you my poor thanks for your kindness, and the great care you took of me in my helpless condition." The poor old woman held out her hand and with tears in her eyes leaned forward to kiss me. Although it was more than I had ever allowed my mother to do, I yielded to the good creature from feelings of gratitude. After giving me her blessing, and still holding me by both hands, she went on to prophesy that I should one day make, as she was pleased to term it, a bright man. Thanking the old lady in all sincerity of heart, I shook her aged hand, and having implored the blessing of heaven upon her declining years, bade her an affectionate adieu. I now took up my bag, and left the place; tears starting from my eyes in gratitude for the kindness that I had experienced at the hands of strangers.

Having arrived at the landing-place, I engaged a boat to take me to the brig which was lying in the harbour. Getting alongside, I went on deck, and paying my respects to the officer of the watch, presented my letter of introduction. This he sent immediately to the commander, who was in his cabin, but in a few minutes appeared, and asked if I was the person named in the note from the Hospital surgeon. I answered of course in the affirmative, and was told to bring my things on board. In an instant I descended the side, paid the man who brought me off, hauled up my bag, and proceeded below. As soon as I had got betwixt decks, one of the men presented me with a tot of grog, and taking my bag stowed it under the forecastle with the rest, at the same time pointing out where he had put it. How different the Sound looked since I saw it last! all the bustle and tumult had subsided; the mighty concourse of people had retired to their homes; the great Napoleon had departed in the '*Northumberland*' for St. Helena, and the only activity displayed was by those engaged in making the breakwater across the entrance of the Sound for the security of ships riding at anchor.

The time and place combined to seduce me into a reflective mood; and I indulged in a varied train of thought until the lights were put out, when, turning into my hammock, I still lay musing until ever welcome sleep sealed my eyelids; yet as soon as the hammocks were piped up, I went on deck. The sun shone brightly, the song of birds was audible from land-ward, and the sky-lark had ascended so far into the etherial space that he looked no larger than a bee, whilst his thrilling notes were far beyond the hearing of man. I stood gazing aloft, till I could see nothing but dark specks floating before my aching vision; but soon recovering my sight, I cast a rapid glance along the shore and beheld the ripe golden harvest, upon which the reapers were already busily employed. I involuntarily recognised the beauties of the scene, and said to myself: 'Why cannot man renounce war and bloodshed, and vow eternal fidelity to the arts of peace?' But after puzzling my brains almost to bewilderment, I (as might have been expected) left this all-important question still unsolved. A fresh breeze now springing up, the hands were piped on deck to weigh anchor: which being accomplished, we proceeded on our course for Chatham, and arrived in the Medway after a fair run.

HASLAR HOSPITAL.

PART III.

I RECOMMENCE LIFE AT HOME: AND MEET WITH VARIOUS 'UPS' AND 'DOWNS.'

CHAPTER I.

I REFIT AT CHATHAM—A DISPUTED IDENTITY—AN AGREEABLE FELLOW-TRAVELLER—ARRIVAL IN LONDON—MY 'BOTTLE-GREEN-BLACK' COAT—A DAY IN TOWN—MISS O'NEILL—I BID ADIEU TO MY TRAVELLING COMPANION.

WHEN the brig had reached her destined port, there remained nothing for me to do but thank her commander for my passage; after which, having bid adieu to the men, I hurried on shore happy as a bird let loose from its cage. I bounded across Chatham Lines, passed the barracks, and entered the town making direct for the Globe tavern; where I booked myself for London by the earliest conveyance. As however the coach would not start till four o'clock, I had two hours to spare: and thus it happened that, seeing a clothes store nearly opposite, I went in and proposed exchanging my jackets and trowsers for a coat and other articles of dress. I accordingly looked out such things as I thought would suit me; and then fetching over my bag, concluded a bargain with the cunning Israelite who owned the shop. It was in a small and rather dark back-room that I performed my toilet, and was metamorphosed from a sailor into something of a dandy. I now sported a white shirt with collar erect, and a new black silk neckerchief tied in a bow, highly polished boots, and a coat resplendent with yellow metal buttons. Thus arrayed, I sallied forth to beguile the time, till my coach was ready to start.

As the appointed hour drew nigh, I returned to the inn and ordered a glass of cold grog and a biscuit; the attendant waiter bowed me into the coffee-room, where lay upon the tables several newspapers, with one of which I amused myself for some minutes. The waiter on his return eyed me suspiciously, as if he had some indistinct recollection of my person. The fact is, that this same man had seen me on my first arrival; and had pointed out the way to the hotel tap, where putting down my bag I called for a pint of porter, and (being very thirsty) took it off at a draught. The lad who served me, as he half presented the pewter with one hand, extended the other in a way which I perfectly understood to mean 'money first!' I thereupon produced a shilling and received the change; next booked my place and paid the fare; and subsequently went out to alter my rigging.

I should not have noticed this little incident, but for the different treatment I received on the strength of my new costume; in which, with whiskers trimmed short and the beard shorn away from under my chin, neither waiter nor pot-boy fairly recognized me: yet both had an evident curiosity to know who and what I was. When the former entered to announce the coach, I rose from my seat, and, taking up my worldly goods, (now reduced to the small mahogany case containing my flute) was proceeding to secure a seat on the coach; but the waiter intercepted me, very politely asking, "If I were going to town by the stage?" I replied, that I was. "Then," said he, "you had better make haste and book yourself, as the fares are always paid at the office where the coach starts from." On my informing him that I was already booked and my fare paid, he enquired, "In what name?" I then begged to look at the list of passengers, and on his producing the way-bill, pointed to the entry 'John Brown, for London.' "Why, that place," quoth my friend, "was booked by a young sailor who came into the tap with a bag under his arm; but I suppose he's got picked up by some of the crimps, as he's not here to time." In short, I found it difficult to make the hero of the napkin believe that I was the identical individual of whom he was speaking.

During this dispute, the passengers beginning to interfere were joined by the coachman: and, as the talk grew loud and fast, the landlord of the inn was attracted to the door. This worthy, after hearing what the waiter had to say, jumped to the conclusion that I was an impostor: and began to throw out broad hints about the neighbouring pump,—whilst, all in readiness for the fun, post-boys and ostlers stood grinning in anticipation of a sentence.

Just at this momentous crisis, the thought struck me to interrogate the lad who served the pint of porter already mentioned; for I now saw the necessity of explaining to the company how the mistake had arisen. So, after telling them that it was not my intention to go to sea again, and that I had exchanged my clothes in consequence, I called the pot-boy from among the outsiders, and questioned him as to what took place when he served me with the porter in the tap. I mentioned his holding back the pot, until he bagged the shilling which I had put upon the table, and also described the change as consisting of a sixpence, and three-pence in coppers; amongst which were two farthings, one quite new and bright, the other very old and scratched across the head.

The boy said at once—"Yes, that was the change;" he had marked the farthing himself with the point of his knife. I now took the coin in question from my pocket; and on seeing it, the lad readily exclaimed—"That's the farthing, sure enough!" Upon this evidence I was acquitted, and allowed to take my seat behind the coachman. We then started without more ado, being already ten minutes behind time; and in crossing Rochester bridge, I took a silent leave of salt-water, at the same time thanking God that I was once more at liberty.

During the journey, I fell into conversation with a gentlemanlike passenger, who sat next me on the right hand. I soon learned from his talk that he had been in the navy many years; at first as captain's clerk, and ultimately as purser; but on his ship being paid off he had left the service, as at that time of course many others were doing. He was very communicative; whilst *I* talked without reserve, and amongst other things asked if he was well acquainted with London. He answered, "Yes, very well." He had, it seems, been apprenticed in the city to a chemist, but not liking the confinement, ran away, entered the navy, and served some time before the mast. Eventually, however, he wrote to his friends, through whose interest he got an appointment, and was now going home for the first time since his departure; having been nearly the whole of his long term of servitude on foreign stations.

As we approached London we became more friendly; and when the coach stopped, my fellow-traveller asked me where I intended to put up for the night. In truth, I hardly knew; and my companion suggested that I might accompany himself to the 'Shakespeare tavern.' I thought I could not do better: so giving the coachman his accustomed gratuity, we started for the hotel; a porter carrying the gentleman's portmanteau, and I bearing my humble flute-case. On our arrival we were shewn into a comfortable room: the fire was burning brightly, and the place being lighted up with gas (then but recently introduced) wore a brilliant and imposing appearance. My new acquaintance rang the bell, and ordered some broiled ham, with eggs, coffee, and toast; of which we both ate heartily.

Our meal despatched, as we chatted comfortably over the fire, the proprietor of the establishment entered. He was a fine portly man apparently about fifty: there was a freedom mixed with politeness in his manner and address, that could only have been acquired by long habit and constant intercourse with society; his ready answers, and the knowledge he displayed on various subjects, convinced me that he was a thorough man of the world. My new friend, too, was a man of good education, and possessed a fair amount of book-learning; but was by no means a match for mine host. It mattered not what the subject: whether love, law, physic, divinity, theatricals, or trade, he handled each and every topic like a master; and, to crown all, he appeared to be gifted with a wonderful equanimity and self-control.

I sat enjoying the discourse till near ten o'clock, when our entertaining host withdrew. Upon rising to go, he shook hands with my friend and then with myself; and, seeing that I was a younker, gave me a fatherly pat on the head in acknowledgment of my deserts as a good and attentive listener. Thus ended what to me was really a never-to-be-forgotten treat. After another glass of grog I began to feel sleepy, which my friend perceiving, at once rang for slippers and a boot-jack; and as soon as we had disencumbered ourselves of our boots, a chambermaid appeared with lights, who leading the way upstairs pointed out our rooms on the next landing,—the doors of which were numbered consecutively 5 and 6.

I received a candlestick, and bidding my companion good-night, retired to my own apartment. Here, after shutting the door, I secreted my money betwixt the bed and the mattress, directly in the centre, and then quickly turned in. But oh, what a difference 'twixt this bed and the one to which I had been so long accustomed! Only the night before, I slept upon a hard flock mattress, that did not yield to my weight any more than a plank; and here I was all at once smothered in down. I had quite forgotten such things: but was now in an instant transported back to childish days, and the train of though tthus induced kept me long awake, ere at length I yielded to the influence of the drowsy god, and slept soundly till the servants were stirring in the morning.

I turned out of my soft nest about eight o'clock, and rang for my boots, thinking to take a walk into Covent Garden before breakfast. I dressed hastily, and when about to put on my coat was struck with its black appearance; for my purchase was, as I thought, a *bottle-green* with bright buttons: instead of which, the rascally Jew had palmed upon me a vamped-up rusty *black*, a regular 'Petticoat-laner' only fit to convert into a rag-mop. Just fancy yourself, reader, in my place! What was to be done? I would not have been seen by the servants in the house for any money; yet how was I to get out unperceived? Thus in a regular fix, I presently remembered that my friend had left his great-coat hanging on a peg in the room below. In a twinkling I slipped downstairs, unseen of any: and, borrowing the welcome garment by way of disguise, started in search of a tailor's shop,—determined never more to deal with the peoples.'

I proceeded straight on to the Strand, and soon found

a ready-made clothes shop, where the articles were ticketed in the window. Casting my eye upon a dark-blue coat marked at three pounds ten shillings, I went in and desired to look at it; upon which a boy who was dusting the things in the shop, called down the kitchen stairs—'Master, you're wanted!' Up then came a foxy-headed, tallow-faced little man, with a hump-back: *minus* neck-cloth, his breeches unbuttoned at the knee, and his stockings hanging over his slippers. I no sooner pointed to the blue coat in the window, than he jumped upon the counter with the agility of a cat, and bringing forth the article asked me to try it on; saying he thought it would fit. I took care to pull off both the coats I had on, *together;* lest he should get sight of my black with gilt buttons: so completely was I ashamed of having been taken in.

When I had tried on the coat, it fitted to a hair; and having also gilt buttons, would not be noticed as differing from that I had worn the night before. After paying the money, I confessed how I had been swindled by the Jew. The rusty black was now withdrawn from its concealment, and the little man indulged in a sarcastic grin at my credulity. However, as if to relieve me from my embarrassment, he bid me five shillings for my 'bottle-green-black,' as he wittily termed it; an offer which I readily accepted, being only too glad to get rid of such a thing at any price. Having thus finished my business, I made the best of my way back to the hotel, and returned the great-coat to the peg with unspoken thanks for its use. All had been accomplished without my being noticed by the servants, who were busily engaged on their own work.

Feeling now somewhat at ease after the annoyance I had experienced, I sat down by the fire and read the morning paper till my friend came downstairs. 'Bless me!' said he, on consulting his watch, 'it's getting on for ten o'clock; how still the people are in this house! I might have slept till dinner-time, and I suppose you are waiting for breakfast. However, we'll ring the bell and order it in directly;' which was no sooner said than done.

The breakfast being placed on table, we made short work of it, (for my friend had to be at the Royal Exchange by eleven), and then took our way towards the place where men of all nations meet for purposes of commerce. As we approached this centre of the world's mart, the great thoroughfares teemed with thousands of human beings all anxiously pressing forward, as if their very existence depended upon a single second of time. My friend having transacted his business at the Exchange, we walked into the Mansion House; where sat the Lord Mayor, with a massive gold chain suspended from his neck, dispensing justice.

Here was presently put into the dock, a poor, ragged, and sickly-looking boy, apparently about thirteen years of age: the charge preferred against him was for picking a gentleman's pocket. The prosecutor was sworn; and the evidence being conclusive, the prisoner was committed for trial. A most heart-rending scene ensued; the mother of the boy rushed forward, and raising her hands in an attitude of despair, begged piteously for mercy. She wore a widow's cap and mourning dress somewhat decayed, and her countenance bore witness to great care and trouble; it would be impossible to describe that poor mother's agony of grief, as she followed her child on his removal from the court. The sight made me turn faint, and at my request we took our departure; my friend saying, that he too had seen enough misery in that short space, to serve him the remainder of his life.

Passing along Cheapside, we stopped at a pastry-cook's, and there saw a play-bill announcing the *Stranger* for that evening, with Charles Young and Miss O'Neill in the principal characters, and Liston also in the cast as 'Peter'; all of whom I had heard mentioned, but had seen only Young. We in consequence agreed to visit the theatre, and in the meantime finished our ramble and returned to dinner at the hotel.

It was about six o'clock when we again sallied forth, and betook ourselves to Drury-lane. The doors of the house were already besieged by a dense mob pushing and squeezing for precedence; however, after some delay, we managed to get a tolerable seat in the centre of the pit, and patiently awaited the rise of the curtain. The performance soon commenced; and each favourite actor on coming forward was welcomed with a hearty greeting; but on Miss O'Neill's making her *entré* the shouts were deafening. She was truly a magnificent creature, perfect in form, and endowed with features over which she seemed to exercise a complete mastery; as she did also over the feelings of the audience.

I had never witnessed so consummate a display of art and nature blended: and as I sat rapt in wonder at her extraordinary powers, the tears stealing down my cheeks, I chid myself for being so foolish. But on looking round, I perceived that the entire audience was as much moved as myself; yet all this effect was produced without any apparent effort. In silent admiration I watched this gifted lady's performance to the close,—and then turned to my companion, who had been all the time as much absorbed as myself.

Upon my observing, that I never witnessed anything like this, he replied: 'Nor I—excepting Mrs. Siddons, who was grand beyond expression; but this play is not to my liking, nor is 'Mrs. Haller' a part calculated to shew off the powers of a great actress. I should like to see her in 'Lady Macbeth,' 'Belvidera,' 'Mrs. Beverley,' or any great part devoid of the morbid feeling that is exhibited throughout the entire of this play.' We staid some time longer, and saw a portion of the farce: but feeling little interest in the business retired before the conclusion, and reached our hotel in time to take supper; after which, being joined by mine host, we spent a pleasant hour till bedtime;—and so ended my second evening in town.

On the following morning I, by special invitation, accompanied my new friend to the northern outskirts of London, where his parents still lived in a very comfortable style. Delicacy prevented me from being present at their meeting; but I was subsequently introduced to the family circle, and spent a very pleasant day in the society of the old couple and their newly restored son. The evening was far advanced ere I shook hands with my generous acquaintance, and bidding him goodbye, took the road for London; studying, as I walked along, how to shape my future course.

The amount of my worldly possessions was three-and-twenty pounds, which I had left in the care of the landlord of the hotel, with the exception of some loose silver. This sum, in any case, would not last long; and there were besides some articles of which I stood in immediate need. Thus pondering by the way, I reached my destination: and, on entering the room where we had taken breakfast, found the landlord seated along with several customers taking their grog and discussing the topics of the day. The host gave me a nod of recognition; and ordering a glass of cold grog, I listened for a while to the arguments advanced by the different speakers; two of whom were still engaged, when I retired, upon a knotty point, which I think they might have argued till doomsday without arriving at a satisfactory conclusion.

My long walk had somewhat tired me; and I slept soundly till eight in the morning, at which hour I rose and went out to purchase a shirt, as the one I had on began to get dingy. Having done this and got shaved, I returned to the hotel, put on my clean linen, and descended to the coffee-room to breakfast. This was soon provided: and having finished my repast, I paid the bill, received back the cash entrusted to mine host's care, and departed with my parcel under my arm, which contained one shirt, a pair of stockings, and the before-mentioned flute case.

CHAPTER II.

BIRD THE WAGGONER—MY MOTHER'S RETREAT—A FAMILY REUNION—LEADENHALL LINGO—THE PRIZE RING—I DETERMINE TO RESUME MY OLD TRADE.

As I had not written home since I left, nor heard any tidings of my family, it struck me to enquire at the Cambridge waggon-office in Bishopsgate-street, as being the most likely place where to get the information I desired. So with a light step and buoyant spirits, I wended my way through densely crowded streets, until I arrived at the establishment of which I was in search.

Here entering, I asked by name for one of the waggoners whom I knew well, as he lived within a stone's throw of my father's house when I was a little boy: besides which, we used to send sometimes a hundred porkers a-week to London by the waggons belonging to the firm. On being informed that I should find my man down the yard, I walked on, and soon perceived him engaged in loading a waggon. There was no mistaking the person; for he stood about six feet four inches high, and weighed twenty-four stone. He was perhaps as fine a man as ever walked the earth,—being particularly upright, with a good-natured countenance, and ruddy complexion; and, whilst exhibiting the proportions of an elephant, he was equally docile and good-tempered.

Approaching this mountain of a man, I saluted him with—'Good morning, Mr. Bird!' For that was really his name, however inappropriate it might appear. Hereat he started, and looking at me with amazement cried,—God bless me! it reminds me of the voice of one long since dead:—'pray what's your name?' 'John Brown of Barnwell,' I replied. 'Bless me,' he again ejaculated, 'I thought it was Corney himself come to life again,'—'Corney' being an abbreviation of Cornelius, my father's christian name. So soon as this fine old fellow had descended the ladder, which trembled under his weight, he seized me by the hand, and gave it such a vice-like grip as I never felt the luxury of before or since. 'Come,' said he, 'this is my luncheon time: a piece of bread and cheese and a quart of porter will just serve me right; for I have been at work since three this morning upon nothing but a pint of purl with a toast sopped in it.'

Adjourning to the tap, he ordered a quart of porter, and at the same time asked me what I would take. I said, I should be happy to drink with him. 'No, no: that won't do! A quart is my allowance,' he observed—'call for whatever you like for yourself, and I shall be proud to pay for it: never mind the expense!' I did not stand in need of anything, having made a hearty breakfast: but to please him ordered a glass of stout. When he had finished eating, my old friend began to question me as to where I had been; saying, that I was given up for dead long ago.

I told him that my history was too long for present narration; but that I had been on board a man-of-war, and had just returned. 'God bless me!' he said, 'how surprised your poor mother will be to be sure; I was talking to her only this day week, when she was saying it was very strange that she could never hear what became of you; and that you must have been either kidnapped or taken away by the press-gang. She looks strangely altered: one misfortune after another, the coldness of relations, and the difference of circumstances have pulled her down sadly.'

As I listened to this conscience-stirring recital, my speech was held in abeyance, and unwelcome tears rolled down my cheeks. The narrator went on to say that, two years since he had removed my mother's goods to London, and that she was now living in Shoreditch, keeping a general shop. Hearing this, I anxiously requested her address, which he at once gave me: when, after thanking him heartily for his kindness, I took my leave, and with altered feelings pursued my way, ashamed of the disobedient part I had played.

Thus musing upon past follies, I walked listlessly along, in doubt as to the best way of introducing myself. On nearing the number of the house to which I had been directed, the name appeared over the door. I stopped first by the shop-window, and looked in; but seeing no one, approached the doorway. This was directly opposite a little back-parlour, where stood the old eight-day clock with the name of 'John Dison, Cambridge' inscribed on its dial. Hence, after waiting some little time, I ventured stealthily to the inner door: and on looking round towards the fireplace, there sat the poor old woman counting up coppers, and packing them in five-shilling papers: at the same time moving her head from side to side, so as almost to keep time with the pendulum of the clock; a sort of habit which I have observed in other persons who had seen a great deal of trouble.

As she did not look up from her work, I stood for some time watching her, but presently drew back, and stepped heavily on the floor, which awoke her attention; and she got up (as she supposed) to wait upon a customer. At this moment I walked into the room, and taking off my hat said—'Mother, I have come back again!' The poor heart-broken old creature fell back in her chair, and swooned away, having all the appearance of death. Frightened at the result of my abrupt address, and hardly knowing what I did, I ran into the kitchen, dipped a basin in the water-butt, and with a wet cloth bathed her temples. For two or three minutes I really feared she was dead; when, as I frantically exclaimed 'Mother, mother!' and squeezed her hands in despair, she gave a groan that seemed to paralyse my heart. I thought her soul had taken flight, and left its frail tenement of clay.

Just at this critical moment, an old lady entered who lived next door. Hearing an unusual noise, she had come in to enquire what was the matter; and seeing me standing there leaning over, as she supposed, the corpse of her neighbour, demanded who I was and what I was doing. 'For heaven's sake,' was my earnest entreaty, 'get some immediate assistance! I fear that I have unintentionally caused the death of my mother.' The new comer, now understanding the nature of the case, applied a smelling-bottle to my poor mother's nostrils, rubbed the palms of her hands, and tried every means in order to restore her to consciousness. After some minutes of painful suspense, the fainting woman began to evince symptoms of returning animation; she at length opened her eyes, and then burst out into a flood of tears accompanied by tones of anguish such as would have melted the hardest heart.

Shocked at the scene I had so unwittingly provoked, I now knelt before my parent, and begged pardon for the sufferings I had inflicted; I promised to support and protect her to the end of her days, and vowed that my future conduct should be a grateful atonement for the wrongs she had endured. Whilst I thus endeavoured in the most soothing and endearing terms to comfort her sorrow-stricken spirit, the poor woman could hardly be made to believe my presence a reality; but fancied she was labouring under some fearful delusion. By degrees, however, she became somewhat calm; and, on seeing her sufficiently restored to bear questioning upon a subject that I myself approached with fear, I enquired about my brothers and sisters.

The eldest, it appeared, was well placed as foreman at a butcher's in Leadenhall market; the next, a girl, was living at Sydenham as a lady's maid; but when I came to ask after the third (a boy two years younger than myself,) it was some time before any answer was forthcoming. At last, in bitter grief, our common parent informed me that he had been drowned whilst bathing in Hackney pits. Here, in attempting to dive, his head stuck fast in the tenacious clay: nor did they succeed in finding the body until the following afternoon, when it was borne home on a shutter, followed by a concourse of neighbours who had been aiding in the search.

This calamity, added to my unaccountable absence, nearly destroyed my poor mother's reason. For a long time, to use her own words, she 'went about distracted,' and frequently got into trouble by stopping young men in the street, in hopes of recognising me. 'Since your father's death,' she added in conclusion, 'my afflictions have been greater than I could bear.' And truly, her features bore strong evidence of the fact; her once fresh and beautiful countenance had sunk down into a fixed and settled expression of grief; twenty years of an ordinary existence could not have wrought such a difference. My return however, as she observed, although it gave her system a terrible shock, had removed a heavy load from her mind: for my mysterious disappearance haunted her night and day.

I gradually talked her into a more cheerful state of mind, until drawing a bunch of keys from her pocket she unlocked a cupboard, and producing a bottle of Port wine, said—'That has been there many a long day; and little did I expect to uncork it for you.' She thereupon handed me the bottle and a corkscrew, adding—'I am not so strong as I was.' I soon drew the cork, and after handing a glass to my mother, drank to our future happiness. She heartily responded; and as I began to converse in a more lively strain, touching old chords that had lain for years unresponsive, a smile dawned upon her countenance; the lamps of her eyes were again lit up; and her generous soul shone forth in its pristine beauty,—for she was an incarnation of all that was good and noble.

Bye-and-bye, the clock announced her dinner-hour. The old lady now rose quite cheerfully to lay the cloth; the viands were not of a very sumptuous nature, yet seemed the sweetest morsels I had tasted for years; and recalling the words of Solomon, that 'bread eaten in secret is pleasant,' I felt as if the measure of my content was full. Having made a hearty meal, and thanked God for all his mercies, I leant back in the old arm-chair to take a short sleep, feeling like a hard-pressed hare returned to its covert.

After about an hour's repose, I brushed myself up, and proceeded in search of my brother, under promise to return by six o'clock to tea. These, I believe, were the happiest moments of my existence; when my heart was gladdened with the anticipation of seeing him, whom of all created beings I loved best. Often in my suffering and affliction have I thanked heaven that my brother had no part therein: and prayed that he might be protected from the shoals and quicksands of life.

Arrived at the entrance into Leadenhall market, I repaired to the Half-moon tavern hard by; and going directly upstairs, ordered a glass of grog, at the same time requesting the waiter to let me have pen, ink, and paper. I then wrote a note to my brother addressed to his place of business, and on asking the waiter if he could send some one with it, he replied—'Certainly, it's only just round the corner, and if the boy is not in the way I'll take it myself: but I know the person to whom it is addressed very well, and it is just possible that he may be in the parlour below, as he generally comes in about this time to smoke his pipe for half-an-hour.'

In less than five minutes, I heard some one come

running upstairs, as I stood with my back to the door examining the portrait of Nelson which was hanging upon the wall. The new comer looked round, to ascertain who had required his presence; but when I turned to face him he recognized me at once, and with a half-suppressed scream exclaimed—'Good God! is it Jack?' Overcome for the moment, the tears started from the poor fellow's eyes, when seizing his hand, I begged him to be calm; for the waiter was standing by the door, and I did not like that any one should witness an exhibition of weakness betwixt us. So hushing him to silence, I smothered my own overcharged feelings, until our first sensations had subsided.

My brother then began to question me as to where I had been, and why I had not written home. I answered that he should know all in due time, as the tale was too long for instant telling; but it might suffice for the present, that I had just been paid off from the navy. Having both recovered our equanimity, we entered into lively conversation, and spent about an hour together: at the expiration of which time, a messenger arrived, saying that my brother was wanted. We therefore shook hands, and agreed to meet at eight o'clock, at home.

My mind now felt at ease; I had got through the most painful part of the business. When I reached home the old lady was reading her Bible; but as I entered the room she closed her book, and laying aside her spectacles, observed that I had returned in good time. Tea was soon ready, and during the meal my mother enquired how I had found William; saying that he was a tender-hearted fellow, very different from myself, and always had been from a child. To this I assented, observing that it was better it should be so, as we were not both destined to play the same part in life. I have before said, that I often thanked heaven, for inasmuch as the heaviest part of the burden had fallen to my own lot!

My brother was four years older than myself; and had felt the sad reverses that overtook us more acutely than my years permitted; independently of which, he had been petted and admired both at home and abroad, for he was indeed as handsome a youth as the eye ever looked upon. Those who remember him will own that I do not exaggerate; and there are many living, both here and in London, who knew him well. But beyond all this, he was brave and amiable in the very highest degree.

It was a source of exceeding gratification to me, after all my wanderings and hair-breadth escapes, to be the means of restoring some degree of happiness to those who had long mourned my absence; since uncertainty as to my actual fate was worse than any reality could have been. For when those most dear to us have passed this mortal goal, we bow with submission to the will of heaven, and time closes the wounds of our afflicted spirits.

As we lingered over our simple repast, the poor old creature gave me an account of her troubles and difficulties during my absence, which indeed were almost more than frail humanity could bear up against. However, she now at last seemed to be in a happy mood, and when the tea-things were removed, handed me the Bible, saying—'When a boy, you were considered the best reader in the village, and I should much like to hear you read again.' I at once opened the book, and my eyes fell upon the thirty-ninth chapter of Genesis, beginning with—" And Joseph was brought down to Egypt." I was always particularly fond of this most beautiful history, and therefore read it through with great care to the end, finishing with the last verse of the fiftieth chapter—" So Joseph died, being an hundred and ten years old: and they embalmed him, and he was put in a coffin in Egypt."

During the time I was reading, I had frequently to stop and wipe the tears from my eyes before I could proceed, which has always been the case whenever I have read this affecting narrative; I could see also that tears were chasing each other down the furrowed cheeks of my mother. When I had finished, she was pleased to say that I read a great deal better than when she last heard me.

It was now getting on for eight o'clock: and as we expected my brother, the old lady brought out the tobacco-jar that belonged to my father. It was a black oblong earthern vessel, mounted with a negro's head; upon the production of which I could not refrain from a hearty laugh; for I used to fancy, when a little boy, that this 'nigger' was a merry devil, since he always appeared to be grinning at me. My mirth was irresistibly excited by the resuscitation of feelings that had slept for years; and even at this distance of time, I can laugh at the old conceit.

Just as Bill made his appearance, my mother was seized with an immoderate fit of laughter, in consequence of some ludicrous comparisons I had made in descanting

on the 'nigger's' physiognomy; upon which he observed:
—'I perceive, master Jack, that you have not left off
your boyish tricks.' 'How is it possible,' I replied,
'with such a subject as this before me? here's a mouth
for a hot cross bun!' 'Ah,' said my brother, joining in
the laugh, 'you've a happy knack of making fun out
of nothing.'

Having once got into the vein, I continued keeping
my small audience in a roar, till my mother holding
both hands to her aching sides begged me to leave off.
I obeyed, declaring at the same time that not a doctor
in Christendom could devise better medicine than mine,
of which about three doses a-day, taken every four hours,
would beat all the prescriptions of Æsculapius and his
disciples. But having made up my mind to be happy
for the evening, I now related some of the comic incidents I had met with in my travels: which being quite
new to them, the night passed pleasantly away, until
the clock striking one, reminded us that it was time to
retire.

My brother had to be in Leadenhall by six in the
morning, but it was about eight o'clock ere I was called
downstairs to breakfast. I found all in readiness, and
after taking a cup of coffee and some toast, set out to
visit the market according to previous engagement. I
was not long in finding the shop, where Bill was giving
directions to five or six men about hanging up the
different joints. This process I watched to its completion; when, all being now prepared for the morning
customers, we withdrew to a noted house in the market
called the 'Rose and Crown.' Here I first made acquaintance with the celebrities of Leadenhall.

They were generally a larking saucy set of fellows, and not at all particular as to whom they practised their jokes upon. They used an unintelligible jargon, which was arrived at by spelling words backwards; for instance, they would in their slang call a fine woman—'*an enif namow*,' and a fine man—'*an enif nam*.' Thus by reversing the order of the letters, they made out a sort of language which no one understood but themselves. I was once looking at the pictures in a shop window, where two of these jabberers were making observations in their unknown tongue, when a man with a sunburnt countenance, having the appearance of a traveller, asked them what 'anguage they were speaking: to which they replied,—'Llahnedael.' 'What's that?' said the stranger. 'Why *Leadenhall*, to be sure, you fool!' roared one of these unlicked cubs, (they were mere boys with trays under their arms, having been to deliver meat), whilst the stranger shook his head and walked on; butcher boys are assuredly the most saucy knaves in the world.

I used to go frequently at night, when the time for closing shop arrived, to smoke a pipe with my brother at the tavern above named, where most of the respectable men in the market met to spend the evening. Here indeed was a goodly company; the conversation was rational, and time passed pleasantly; one night in the week was fixed for a 'free and easy,' when some excellent songs were sung. It was here I first heard that fine room-singer, Prinn, well known at most of the concert-rooms at the east end of the town; he was then a very young man, possessing a most powerful voice.

About this time the prize-ring was at its zenith: of which the London butchers were generally enthusiastic patrons, and some of them first-rate boxers; indeed, many respectable men practised sparring, both for exercise and with a view to self-protection. By persons unacquainted with this science, it has ever been condemned as being of a low and brutalizing nature. But such is not the case; for the rules of the art are framed in strict accordance with honour; and nothing can be better calculated to inspire a man with true courage and a love of justice. That many low-lived blackguards are acquainted with the principles of self-defence, is a melancholy fact; but that circumstance does not touch the art itself. If anything, it rather shews the necessity for every man being armed with knowledge to repel an attack of this kind, when made by some dastardly ruffian, as has too frequently occurred. But it is commonly observed, that bullies are for the most part cowards, and rarely attain to a perfect mastery in science.

My brother was well acquainted with all the first-rate pugilists of the day; and, being an amateur of no mean pretensions, was much respected by the fraternity. Thus he often visited the houses kept by such men as Cribb, Belcher, Harmer, and his particular friend and brother 'steel,' Peter Crawley, than whom a more inoffensive and kind-hearted man never breathed. I often accompanied brother Bill: and, being thus introduced, was treated with great civility. Peter was particularly fond of the game of draughts; and as I had acquired a tolerable knowledge of this harmless amusement, we frequently played together. He was at that time a mere novice; but I have since heard that he became an excellent hand, and that few players could beat him.

I had now to begin the world as it were a-fresh, and

my resources being by no means ample, I resolved to try my old trade once more, feeling assured that I should soon regain a tolerable degree of proficiency. Having made this determination known to my brother, he introduced me to a countryman of ours, who kept a shop in Fenchurch-street. The 'old man' gave me, in the first instance, work of the most ordinary description, with advice to put myself under a first-rate workman for instruction. This I well knew was the best course I could take, and my employer at once offered to shew me where some of the best workmen in the city were to be met with; stating at the same time, that five pounds was the usual charge in such cases.

As we went along, my companion gave me a brief sketch of his boyhood. He had been put out by the parish to the village shoemaker at Histon, three miles from Cambridge; but being badly treated by his master, he ran away one morning in his shirt-sleeves, and tramped up to London by the side of one of the stage-waggons—being allowed by the driver to get up behind, and sleep under the tilt at night.

By the time he finished his yarn, we had reached our destination, which was 'Green Arbour Court.' On arriving at No. 12, my old friend knocked gently, when the door was opened by a woman of about thirty, of fair complexion and irreproachably neat appearance, whom I understood to be the landlady. She being informed of our business, called her husband, who came down immediately: and being told what I wanted, said—that one of the lodgers was going to leave on Saturday; and that, if I thought proper, I could take his place. He also added, that an excellent workman occupied the next seat, and would no doubt undertake to do what was required.

This was one of many houses in the same quarter which are occupied entirely by shoemakers. We were shown by the landlord into a room on the second floor, having a window extending the whole length of the front, which admitted an excellent light; here sat the man who had been just recommended, and after some little talk on the subject, we concluded an agreement: the terms being, five pounds to be paid on the Monday morning when I commenced work. Having settled this business, I went to the tool-shop and purchased an entire new kit, which I had packed up, and took home under my arm.

I now informed my mother of the arrangements I had made: on which the ever anxious old creature expressed her hope that I should be a good boy. Being naturally of a sanguine temperament, I said laughingly, 'Fear not, mother, I shall be somebody yet;' for although externally volatile, and jocular even on serious matters, I possessed as great a depth of feeling as most persons of my years.

I had made up my mind to the accomplishment of one object—and that was to be one of the first workmen in the world! I felt quite certain that I possessed the capabilities: and proud in the conviction that a first-rate mechanic is the most independent man in society, I set about my task with an ardour not to be put down, nor crushed by obstacles however great. 'There's no such word as FAIL' was now my motto; and when Monday morning came, I started hopefully in pursuit of my object.

CHAPTER III.

I RE-COMMENCE WORK—A SLIPPERY TUTOR—MY RESCUE BY ARCHIE M'GILL—THE BITER BIT—CIRCUMSTANCES IMPROVE—AMUSEMENTS OF THE PERIOD—A SET-TO WITH 'BARNEY AARON'—THE JEWS' QUARTER—'RAG FAIR'—ANECDOTES.

PROCEEDING direct to my employer's, I found the master at his board getting work ready for his men, several of whom were in the shop when I entered. 'There,' said he, pointing to a set of stuff lying on the floor and ready tied up,—'take that; you will see the directions written on the soles.' So taking up the lasts and materials, I repaired to my new lodgings, and there found the man with whom I had agreed for instruction. On handing him over a £5. note, I asked for a receipt; but he said he could not write. I consequently took from my pocket a piece of paper, and having written a receipt requested him to affix his 'mark,' calling upon the landlord to witness it.

This done, I spread my kit, put my stuff into the shop-tub,[1] and addressed myself to begin. Having then

---

[1] Appropriated for soaking the 'stuff'; the shoemaker's wax is also generally deposited here, to be kept out of harm's way when not in use.

tacked on the inner soles, hammered and prepared the rest,[1] and cast off my threads,[2] I set about sharpening up my awls and getting my tools into working order. Here was an extraordinary change! During the last four years, I had led a life of the greatest activity, which rendered me very unfit for this sedentary employment. At the commencement indeed, I suffered perfect martyrdom; the pains in my back and loins, arising from the bent position in which I was compelled to sit, became nearly insupportable; and almost every half-hour, I was forced to leave my work and walk about the room till the agony subsided; my hands too became dreadfully sore, and the skin peeled off my fingers, which made me wince at every stitch.

In this state of misery I nevertheless persevered, though scarcely earning salt; but what rendered my position still more pitiable and disheartening was that the fellow, to whom I had paid the five pounds, evaded rendering me the services for which he received the money.

Had I not been well seasoned in the school of misfortune, I should now have sunk under the pressure of my feelings; yet day after day I worked on, though in despair of ever accomplishing what I so ardently desired. As I had frequent occasion to complain of the injustice of the paltry knave who had taken my money, loud and angry words ensued, which could be heard distinctly in the attic above by a strange recluse who abode there.

[1] Outer soles, heel-pieces, lifts, welts, &c.
[2] Waxed hemp, or flax, used for sewing and stitching the 'uppers' to the bottom leather.

This individual held converse with no one, and crept up and down stairs like a mouse; but it was well known that he was the most beautiful dress-shoeman in the metropolis.

It happened one day, while I was upbraiding my pseudo-instructor for his dishonesty, that the door of the room flew open, and a man of noble and commanding figure entered. He appeared about forty years of age, stood nearly six feet high, shewed a profile not unlike that of the 'Iron Duke,' and (what was rather remarkable) wore a pig-tail neatly tied with black ribbon. The visitor without further ceremony discharged a burst of such withering sarcasm at the chap-fallen wretch, as made him shrink into very small proportions. Then turning to myself he spoke in the most compassionate terms, and concluded by offering to instruct me gratuitously. He at the same time demanded instant restitution of the money I had paid: telling the tallow-faced impostor that there was a way to make him refund the cash he had so dishonestly appropriated, and that his conduct was worse than that of the highwayman, who at all events hazards his life for the robbery he commits.

By this time eight or nine other men that were lodging in the house had gathered together, who one and all expressed themselves disgusted with such a piece of bare-faced villany. But nothing could prevail upon the sordid wretch to yield up his ill-gotten spoil;—so destructive a species of insanity is avarice! And seeing that there was no possibility of getting the money just then, my newly found friend proposed that I should take my tools and work up to the garret; an offer which I was only too glad to accept. When I had removed my things, which took but a few minutes, my new shopmate proposed to go at once to the Court of Requests, and take out a summons against the fellow who had robbed me. It being no great distance we soon reached the place; where, on stating my case, the summons was granted, and we were told to appear before the Commissioners, with our witnesses, at twelve o'clock on the following Wednesday.

The summons was served in due course, and had the effect of frightening the knave; especially as the master for whom he worked, happened to be one of the bench, and thus he feared getting into disgrace. The wretch now came sneaking to our door, and offered to give up half the money; to which my staunch friend replied, 'No, he shall have no truck with you,—if he will be persuaded by me,—as long as my name is Archibald M'Gill!'—and then in the most peremptory manner commanded him to go down.

I now felt myself comparatively happy. I soon discovered that my new shopmate was no common man, and that his mind was stored with all kinds of knowledge. He was in truth a philosopher of the most extraordinary capabilities; he studied mathematics, and made telescopes for amusement; he forged tools and prepared them for use, which he sold to other workmen at a good price; he also turned out some fine specimens of cabinet-work, such as tea-caddies, ladies' work-boxes, looking-glass frames, and various other fancy articles. I have now in my possession a small work-table of his manufacture, which he gave me before I was married, thirty-five years ago. Whatever he attempted he could accomplish with the greatest facility; yet all this amount of talent was cribbed up in a garret nine feet by six, and barely high enough for the man to stand upright in. The furniture of this 'crow's-nest' consisted of a turn-up bedstead, a small German stove, a cupboard standing on the floor with a flat top which he used as a bench to plane his work upon, and the two shoemaker's seats which we occupied when at work. In this cock-loft I passed twelve months of intense application.

But to return to the case we had in hand, concerning the five pounds. Wednesday morning arrived, and we repaired, together with our witnesses, to the Court of Requests. The cause was almost immediately called on for hearing: when, having stated the nature of my complaint, I was asked by the bench if I had any witnesses. My landlord, and one of the men who was present at the altercation, stood forth, and corroborated my statement: whereupon the court adjudged that the five pounds should be returned, and that defendant must pay the costs. At this termination of the proceedings, we left the court well pleased; and on arriving at our lodgings I requested my new shopmate to take the money. He however refused; saying, that what he had promised voluntarily, he would perform gratuitously; so after thanking him for his kindness, I went steadily on with my work.

The next morning we were informed that 'five-pound Jack,' as they had now christened him, had 'got the sack': and it appeared that, on entering his master's shop on the previous evening, the latter (who, as already mentioned, was one of the bench when our case was decided) had ordered him off the premises, declaring he would not have such a dishonest scamp in his employ.

Nor were we long troubled with the discomfited rogue's presence. Shame and ridicule soon rendered his position unbearable; and one day, during the absence of the rest at dinner, he packed up his kit and walked. Thus the fool lost five pounds, a good shop of work, and the esteem of his fellow-men, by one of the most disgraceful tricks that overweening selfishness ever prompted.

As time rolled on, I gradually improved, and feeling some degree of confidence in my abilities, requested my employer to put me on better work (as I was scarcely earning money enough to buy food); at the same time telling him, that my work was quite as good as that of other men. To this he very civilly assented, and expressed himself desirous of lending me every possible assistance; he at the same time spoke in flattering terms of the progress I had made in so short a space.

From this date my prospects began to brighten; my work was of a lighter nature, my earnings were nearly doubled, and I began to feel myself progressing steadily on towards the goal of my ambition. Men of higher pretensions may ridicule the idea of an ambition so humble as that of being a first-rate bootmaker; but I can positively aver that it requires the greatest patience, together with a most ready wit and skilful hand, to arrive at that distinction. I at all events, for the accomplishment of my purpose, worked night and day, allowing myself only sufficient respite for meals and sleep. But I achieved my aim! For within twelve months of forming my resolve, I was acknowledged to be the best workman 'on the shop,' and received for my work sixpence a pair more than the other men. This is a thing very unusual in the trade, and would have caused great dissension had it been known; as although the sum named appears but trifling, it added three shillings a-week to my income.

I soon began to accumulate comforts of all kinds, such as new clothes and good linen of the best quality; and as top-boots were very fashionable at the time, I made myself a pair of the best that were ever turned out. In short I felt no small degree of pride and satisfaction, in knowing myself to be as well equipped as any man I met on the king's highway; and being now at the height of my desire, with earnings sufficient for all wants, I determined to see a little of London life.

I accordingly visited the Theatres, went to balls and concerts, attended 'free-and-easies,' and stored up every species of practical knowledge that fell in my way.

Thus for instance I became acquainted with a young man who had been in a French prison, and from him learned fencing and single-stick. I was also constant in my attendance wherever the first boxers of the day assembled, and had many a set-to with the best of the light weights: such as Dick Curtis, Jack Randall, Barney Aaron, and other heroes of the day. I was always an enthusiast at whatever I undertook, and thus soon achieved a proficiency in the 'science' that is rarely attained.

It happened on a certain occasion, that I was particularly requested to attend a gathering for the benefit of Aby Belasco; it was at a house in the Jews' quarter. About this time Barney Aaron aforesaid had become all at once a new star in the P.R., and feeling elated with his success grew very saucy; so much so that his own people desired to see him taken down a peg. To this end it was pre-arranged by his particular friend Aby, that I should go down for the purpose of putting on the gloves with the intended victim, who was at that time a stranger to me. In prosecution of this design, after I had been in the room some time, Belasco (who acted as master of the ceremonies) came up to me, and asked if I would set-to, at the same time introducing Barney. I had been apprised beforehand, that if I bested him in light play he would lose his temper; but as he knew nothing of my powers, such a thought never entered his mind; for no man possessed a greater share of self-confidence.

Having stripped and put on the gloves, we shook hands (as is usual in such cases), and stepping back threw ourselves into an attitude of defence. My opponent soon began to make play by trying to put in his left: which I parried, and quick as thought planted a gentle tap on his proboscis. However, he seemed to fancy 'twas all a mistake, and tried it on again; when a second time, I returned upon his sneezer before he could stop. At this the byestanders began to laugh, and Barney's 'mother' began to rise. A few more taps, and—the old woman being fairly up—in he rushed, letting fly left and right, goaded to madness by the laughing and jeering of the 'peoples'; for the spectators were mostly Israelites. I now found it necessary to hit in earnest, which I did—and entered some puzzling interrogatories upon his frontispiece. But my opponent still kept striking out, though retreating, until his head came in rude contact with the mantelpiece; when I dropped my guard, and regained the centre of the floor amid the shouts and laughter of the assembly. A few spots of blood being visible on the gloves, Aby came forward and in accordance with the rules requested us to take them off, with which we at once complied; and thus ended an amusing incident.

From this time I became much acquainted with the Jews, and went frequently to Duke's-place to play at draughts and cribbage with them. They are generally very well behaved people, and remarkably witty. I used to attend their harmonic meetings, where I heard some excellent singing; and often on a Monday afternoon, I would stroll through Petticoat-lane, where their 'Rag Fair' is held daily from two to four o'clock. This is perhaps one of the most filthy, yet curious scenes ever witnessed; old clothes of every escription may be seen, which have been gathered from every street and alley in the metropolis. Some of the collectors are laden with faded and soiled brocaded-silk dresses and court suits brought from the mansions of the nobility, whilst others sweat under the weight of an immense bag, crammed with a miscellaneous store gathered from the foulest dens in Whitechapel, Shoreditch, and St. Luke's. Such an accumulation of rubbish is not to be met with in any other part of the habitable globe.

Their method of doing business is to get as much as they possibly can for an article, but to take the smallest profit rather than keep the goods on hand. The Jewish maxim is, to turn their money over as often as they can; and this is the secret of their immense gains. Many very wealthy Jews have begun life with a small box scantily stocked. They generally take to business when young; starting 'upon their own hook' at fourteen years of age, or even earlier. If one of the fraternity meets with a bargain beyond his means, he will pay a deposit, and then go to three or four others, who are always ready to club their money together to complete the purchase. This done, they sell out and share the profits; nor do they experience any difficulty in this mode of doing business, as they always know where to dispose of the property, no matter what the nature of it.

The Jew is trained from his childhood to know the market value of every description of goods; this is his *trade*, in which he is just as regularly instructed, as are watch-makers, carpenters, and all others bred to any particular business. It is most marvellous to see the extraordinary transformations that take place in some of their women. Whilst engaged in business they look so ragged and dirty, you would think they were the poorest creatures in existence. But see them dressed for a ball, or the theatre,—they appear like duchesses, arrayed in satin and resplendent with jewels!

There is one excellent trait in the Jewish character which does honour to them as a people; they provide for their own poor, both old and young; and that in the best way possible. All those capable of doing business, are furnished, at nominal prices, with a stock of goods manufactured for the purpose through the aid of a fund raised by subscription. Thus young beginners gradually advance, from selling pens, pencils, sealing-wax, and other trifles, to become merchants in a large way of business. This system is clearly of an elevating character, and tends greatly to enhance the respectability of their people; whilst, at the same time, it keeps down pauperism. Surely this is much better than shutting up the poor in bastiles maintained at great cost, to consume the hard earnings of an industrious community; besides, it is carrying out the true spirit of Christianity far more faithfully than we do ourselves. The Jew in all his business transactions is keen as a razor; he can judge of his customer at sight, and asks a price for his wares in accordance with the opinion he entertains of the person with whom he is doing business.

I one day roamed as usual through the fair, and gazed on the indescribable quantity of articles scattered around,—some hanging upon the walls, other displayed in stalls, and the remainder thrown in different lots upon the pavement; the proprietor of each lot standing or lying down beside his precious stock, the greater portion of which appeared hardly worth picking off a dunghill. Here, as I moralised on the quaint scenes around me, and speculated on the many-coloured phases of human existence, a ridiculous occurrence took place. A young woman of genteel appearance was examining some muffs, which lay on the stall of a crafty looking Jewess; and after taking up several in succession, she came to one of jet-black hue with the most glossy surface I ever beheld; it was indeed so rare and beautiful a thing, that it might have tempted many a lady. But I particularly noticed that whenever the young woman attempted to turn the muff round to examine it, the quick and subtle Jewess snatched the article from her hand and coaxed it as a lady would her lap-dog, saying: 'What a peautiful ting, vat a fine closs! How nish it feels: tare never vas such a peauty!'

All this time, the Hebrew matron kept fast hold of the object, so as to prevent the girl from minutely inspecting it. Ultimately, however, a bargain was concluded (the price being eighteen shillings), and the cunning vendor most adroitly slipped the muff on to the hands of the simple purchaser, who walked away with, as I thought, some sort of misgiving. Prompted by curiosity I followed to watch the sequel. As soon as the girl had turned the corner leading into Houndsditch, she stopped to examine her purchase; and with feelings of consternation discovered, that the side so cunningly placed next her person was entirely devoid of fur, having just the appearance of bad parchment. The victim now turned back, with some vague hope, no doubt, of getting her money returned; but I knew too well how the matter would end. The Jewess of course had vanished, goods, stall, and all; and upon enquiring after her, no one seemed to know any such person. So the poor dupe went away, *minus* her eighteen shillings.

Shortly after this little incident, as I was looking about me one day in company with my landlord (who was also a brother of the craft), a Jew boy accosted us: and knowing by our appearance and aprons that we were shoemakers, offered two pairs of shoes for sale. These were quite new, and apparently of excellent workmanship; indeed, having each taken one in hand to examine, we saw that they were first-rate articles; and, the price demanded being less than half their value, a bargain was soon struck. Satisfied with our purchase, we returned home, fancying we had done a pretty good afternoon's work; then having taken tea, as was our custom on such occasions, we went upstairs to resume work. On sitting down to begin, I took up the shoes we had bought, to compare the fellows, and was struck with amazement to find them all *left* ones. This at once accounted for their cheapness; since they were of no use, excepting to a man who had lost his right foot. Such an acquisition would have been absolutely valueless to persons not in the trade,—but with us it mattered little; we fitted up a last, and making four *right* shoes to complete the four pairs, sold them to a dealer in Northampton goods: thus getting out of a bad bargain, without either loss or gain. I mention this to shew that the Jew always has his wits about him.

On another occasion, whilst passing one of the dirtiest and darkest shops in the lane, I perceived a labouring man trying on a coat, and the dealer particularly attentive in helping him on with it. When the yokel had got his arms through the sleeves and pulled up the collar, the Jew seized a handful of the back, and let it slide through his fingers gradually, till the man got the coat fairly buttoned; nor did the other even then release his grasp, but smoothing the garment down the back with the disengaged hand, exclaimed—'My got! there never was such a peautiful fit—it shets like a glove!' The unsuspecting clown paid the price demanded, and walked away with the coat under his arm. How puzzled he must have felt, when next trying it on! The coat must have been at least six inches too large for him round the chest.

Another droll case was that of a young man from the country, who came to lodge in our house, and to receive instruction in his business, as is customary. He was attired in a velveteen shooting-coat and corduroy trousers, in fact, quite a rustic suit, which looked rather odd in the streets of London; and some of the wicked boys consequently 'chaffed' him to such an extent, that he determined to sell or exchange this dress for a more suitable costume. Thus resolved upon assuming a more fashionable appearance, the youth made a bundle of his clothes, and adjourned to Petticoat-lane for the accomplishment of his purpose; which he effected to his own entire satisfaction. On his return, he untied the bundle and produced a glossy green coat with bright yellow buttons, quite new, a pair of white duck trousers, and a smart light vest—the whole intended for a holiday suit. The succeeding Sabbath arrived in due course: the sun shone beautifully bright, and not a cloud was to be seen, when our dapper hero sallied forth, proud as a peacock, to visit his sweetheart, some six or seven miles out of town.

But as the day wore on, clouds began to gather; and towards evening the rain fell in torrents. Our friend had started on his homeward journey, but a short time ere the storm set in, and was thus caught in the midst of it on the open road, far from any place of shelter. He was of course drenched from head to foot; and instead of returning in a green coat and white trousers, his coat had been washed *black*, and his trousers and boots dyed *green!* But the crowning glory of this ludicrous picture was the 'human face divine'; the grotesqueness whereof surpassed all that imagination ever painted. As he hurried to get through the rain, the perspiration ran down his face, which, it seems, he had ever and anon wiped with a pocket-handkerchief already saturated with the green stuff that had drained from his coat. The poor fellow was now quite overcome, and tears began to streak his truly verdant countenance. It was impossible to refrain from laughing; but pity mingled with the feeling, and pleaded for the simpleton, who appeared almost heart-broken.

After the feelings produced by his first appearance had subsided, we assisted him in taking off his wet things: and having got some warm water and clean towels, he washed from his person the filthy dye, which had soaked through his linen, and made him green from head to foot. Then putting on some dry clothing, he became somewhat reconciled; and as his family was in tolerable circumstances, the loss he had sustained was not of much importance.

CHAPTER IV.

A LARK WITH AN ISRAELITE—'TIPPY BOBBY'S' COURTSHIP—THE LABOUR-MARKET OVERSTOCKED—'OLD BIDDLES'—I COMPLETE MY PROFESSIONAL EDUCATION, AND RESOLVE TO LEAVE TOWN FOR A SEASON.

ON the following morning, as we sat at work and laughed over the event of the previous day, the cry of 'Clo! Clo! Clo!' was heard nearing the house. This proceeded from one of the Jew collectors; he was an elderly man with an enormous beard. The thought struck me that I would call him up; so putting my head out of the staircase window, I hailed Moses, and requested he would come upstairs. Feeling disposed to have a bit of fun with the Israelite,—as he raised the door-latch to enter the house, I at the same time, with my apron, blocked up the one square of glass that afforded any light; thus making the staircase dark as pitch. The old fellow came on feeling his way, and grumbling at every step, as he kicked his toes against the stairs. Arrived on the one-pair landing, he went groping about for the turning of the second-floor staircase, but soon became alarmed at his position; and we could hear him soliloquizing to himself, ejaculating, and muttering broken sentences, such as: 'My got! vat a hell—plooty tieves—day meansh to murder me—here's a plashted plashe to get into!'

All this time we kept calling out, 'Come up, old fellow!' until at last the Jew's fears overcame him, and he cried out lustily for a light, asking if we intended to murder him. Thinking we had carried the joke far enough, I now opened our door, which threw a good light down the staircase; and addressing him very civilly, said that I had 'got a bargain for him.' Still in a state of trepidation, and panting for breath, he cast a sharp look round the room as if to ascertain if we were what we really appeared,—and then with a countenance deadly pale, asked leave to rest a bit.

Upon this I handed him a chair, the only one in the room, such articles of furniture being superfluous to shoemakers; and as soon as the old man had recovered his breath and partially dismissed his fears, I drew forth from a lumber cupboard a bundle containing what was once a suit of black,—though its components had become sadly dilapidated by time and use, and were sorely depreciated in value. These articles being spread before him, he exclaimed with an expression of rage and disappointment: 'Is dis vat you prought me up tese tark sthares for to buy? a pundle of racks fit for noting but to preak up—why it vill hartly make a rack mop!' I replied—'Of course they are a great deal the worse for wear;—just say at once what you'll give for the lot?' Vell den, at a vord, I shall kive you eightpence, tat's all, s'help me Got! take 'em or leave 'um.'

After some little chaffering, the Jew having three or

four times risen to go in feigned anger, he at last made an exit, leaving the door open to light him downstairs; but when he had descended a few steps, I called him back and said he might take them away. Hereupon he returned, and after cramming the clothes into his bag gave me a half-crown to take the eightpence. Pretending to have no money I offered to go below and get change: to which he with some degree of hesitation assented, saying—'Vell den, make hashte, and ton't keep me here all tay!'

Just as I reached the bottom of the first flight of stairs, I threw down the piece of money, so that the sound might be distinctly heard in the room above (having left the door open for the purpose); and after a while, pretending to search for it, I muttered to myself loud enough to be heard above, 'It must have gone through this crack!' there being, in fact, an opening betwixt the boards. Hearing what I said, my shopmate called out, 'Have you lost it?'—and I replied, 'Yes, it's gone through this crack.' 'Vat crack, you plashted tief?' said Moses; 'I'll fetch an officher, by got, if you don't kive me my shange!' In vain I tried to pacify him by declaring that it was safe enough, that the coin had fallen into the cellar among the cinder dust, and that I would have it sifted in the morning and give him the change the next day when he came his round.

This cool treatment drove the Hebrew into an ungovernable rage; he called me all the 'tamd tieves' and 'schamps' he could lay his tongue to: but finding that the money was not forthcoming, swore by his father 'Abraham' that he would fetch an officer, and take me before the Lort Mayor. Affecting to be frightened at this threat, I begged that he would not do so,—but wait, while I would try to borrow the money. Then rushing downstairs and knocking at the landlady's door, I beseeched her in the most earnest tones to lend me *one-and-tenpence!* Hereat she burst into a convulsive fit of laughter (for she had been listening to the fun), but at length called out, loud enough for the Jew to hear, 'No! I've got no money.'

Having arrived at this stage of the performance, I ran upstairs in breathless haste, and asked my shopmates if they could raise one-and-tenpence amongst them; but both the Jew and myself were doomed to disappointment: all we could muster was fourpence-ha'penny. This sum I proffered, swearing to pay the balance on the morrow. 'Vat!' he exclaimed, ''tis ish atting inshult to inchurry; py got, I will ket an officer tirectly!' Hearing this threat, I bade him be gone, for a heartless and merciless Jew; but so soon as he had got safely on the second flight of stairs, I again closed the door, making all dark as night; and at the same instant rolled a lapstone[1] down the top of the staircase, which went bump, bump, bump down the steps, and so frightened the Israelite that I believe he fancied some evil spirit was after him. Being in utter darkness, and overcome by his fears, he sat down on the stairs and cried 'for Got shake' to be let out, 'and he would forkife the tebt!'

As we had now reached a climax, I went on to the

---

[1] The lapstone, as the term implies, rests on the workman's knees; and acts as an anvil, when he has occasion to use his hammer. 'Sticking a knife through a lapstone,' is a cant phrase for abandoning the 'trade' in favour of some other business.

landing and removed my apron. When the light shone down upon the old fellow, his eyes beamed with responsive gladness, and he cried out—'Ah, I shee it all! Tis is von of your callows tricks; vell, never mint—kife me de shange and let me go apout my pisness.' After a little persuasion, I prevailed upon Moses to come upstairs again, telling him it was only a piece of nonsense. By degrees he became quite reconciled; and when instead of change, I returned him the identical half-crown entire, he seemed quite delighted, and all offence was mutually forgotten. Being really desirous of resting a short time, he asked if he might smoke his pipe. 'Oh yes!' was the answer, 'we all smoke here;' so, as he produced a short black pipe, I handed him my tobacco canister, and reaching the tinderbox from under my seat, struck a light. In those days there were no lucifer-matches; and as we heated our irons over a lighted candle, tinder was an article in constant demand. As the old Jew sat smoking his pipe, I went below and sent for a quart of porter, which I presently handed to our guest, who was much pleased with his entertainment.

During his stay he gave us a brief sketch of his history, shewing how he began life when a boy, and leaving home with little more than a mother's blessing, had travelled on foot almost all over continental Europe; suffering at times intense privations, and misery almost beyond human endurance. He nevertheless amassed considerable wealth: but, through the agents of the Inquisition in Spain, was deprived of all he possessed, and narrowly escaped with his life. It was indeed a tale of sorrow; and as he proceeded, tears stole from my eyes; which the old man perceiving, took me by the hand, and said—'Hold, my young friend! You have made ample atonement for the little trick you put upon me, by the kind sympathy you accord to the bare recital of my misfortunes.' On rising to go, he shook hands with me, saying he would call as he passed on the morrow. He did so; and continued to do the same for nearly three years, excepting at the times set apart for religious observance.

Towards the completion of the specified period he complained of feeling poorly, could not relish his pipe, and occasionally missed a day or two, then a week; and at last we seemed to have lost him altogether. One morning whilst at work, I heard a fresh voice crying 'Clo! Clo!' I instantly jumped up, and opening the window, enquired for my old friend. The stranger informed me that he was dead; and asked in return, whether I was the young shoemaker with whom his predecessor used to smoke his pipe. Upon my answering in the affirmative,—'Well then,' said the new comer, 'he bade me convey to you all that he had to dispose of in this world—that is, his blessing: and his advice—that is, to treat all mankind as brothers. Now (he added) I have discharged the obligation that the old man solemnly put upon me; and having done so, I wish you good morning!' Then turning round, he recommenced his dolorous cry of 'Clo! Clo!'

Amongst our fraternity was one of the most extraordinary beings I ever met with; he was about five feet in stature, with a florid complexion, hair nearly white, and a mouth expressive of the most entire self-satisfaction: for so conceited an animal never came under my notice. He was a sort of Beau Brummell in his way, and would never go to shop with his work without dressing himself in a fresh suit from head to foot, even to covering his snobbish paws with light kid gloves. The fellow was a perfect libel on humanity; his conceit and impudence rendered him so obnoxious as well as contemptible that every one felt disgusted at his conduct; the more so because, as a craftsman, he was the veriest 'botcher' that ever handled a tool.

This poor abortion took it into his head to make love to a young woman, whose father kept an eating-house in the neighbourhood, and was reported to be tolerably rich. Unknown to the family, the wretched dandy by stealth insinuated himself into the good graces of the unsuspecting girl, who very foolishly, without consulting her parents, encouraged his advances and answered his stupid love-letters. However, the young woman's father by some means discovered the correspondence, and while deeming it advisable to forbid the swain's visits, at the same time maintained a strict watch over his daughter.

The exasperated ape now had resort to every species of annoyance and insult, that his weak brains were capable of imagining. In the evening, when the old man was busy serving his supper customers, this fellow would collect a mob of boys in front of the shop, and as each customer entered, he would call out—'Now, old leather-lip Jack! serve that ere customer with a good notch of pudding; give that 'un two penn'orth of sore-leg soup; and this here 'un a plate of roast pork, off the pig as died o' the measles!' Then followed an invitation to the by-standers, to join in three groans for 'gallows old Jack.' Thus night after night did he play the fool, to the intense annoyance of his victim; nor did the persecution end here.

The old man being a dissenter, used to go every Sunday to a chapel in Sloane-street, Chelsea, upon which occasions his daughter accompanied him: and the tormenter having watched for their coming out, would then walk by the girl's side the whole distance, occasionally pressing her arm, and making her laugh to the parent's great disgust. Still, as it was Sunday, he bore all with Christian fortitude for a long time; however, as there are times when patience ceases to be a virtue, so it proved in this instance.

One evening, as they were returning home, the fool, emboldened by the father's passive bearing, requested the daughter to take his arm. The elder's indignation was now fairly roused: and being a powerful man six feet high, he seized the little imp and threw him into one of the pens in Smithfield, where the party chanced to be passing at the time. In the scuffle, the wretched Beau's hat flew one way, and his gold-headed cane another: the latter being picked up by a younger daughter of the old man, and carried home unperceived; for it was quite dark at the time when this ludicrous scene occurred. Next morning this valuable trophy was returned to our hero, accompanied with a note threatening legal proceedings, if he did not desist from his unmanly persecutions.

But instead of feeling ashamed of his dirty work, the fool was gulled into a belief that the old man would be glad to give him a sum of money to desist. Acting upon this suggestion, he writes a note to the father, offering for twenty pounds to give up the girl's letters, and never again trouble the family. We all felt assured that the old man would take no notice of such a dirty missive, and therefore concluded to write an answer ourselves as if coming from the party addressed. This was accordingly done, the purport of the communication being, that *twenty* pounds was too much; but if he thought proper to take *ten*, that sum should be paid him.

No sooner had the scrub received this letter from the hands of the postman, than in breathless haste he came running upstairs, and flourishing the precious document aloft, exclaimed—'Look here! I've got the old rascal; here's his signature, though it can hardly be made out; the old devil has spelled every word wrong,—what damned stuff of writing! Never mind: he offers me ten pounds, but I'll make him glad to give the twenty! Look here—it ain't 'the cobbler's boy' now; he writes 'Mr. Smelt.' Oh, I'll give it him, I'll worry his life out, if he don't hand over the twenty pounds. It would be silly to abate my demand; I'll have the whole or none.' Having arrived at this determination, he despatched a second epistle expressive of his mighty will.

After a short consultation, we agreed to accede to his demand, and wrote an answer in strict accordance with his desire; requesting at the same time that he would come on the following afternoon, at four o'clock, to sign a document drawn up by a solicitor for the occasion; and to receive the money, on giving up the letters which he possessed. He was also warned to take no notice of any one who might be in the shop, but to walk through into the little parlour and sit down.

On the following morning our friend occupied the window, anxiously awaiting the postman's knock: and when the anticipated reply arrived, evinced his exultation by laughing and jumping about like an hysterical monkey. The prospect of receiving so much money elated him beyond all possibility of attending to business; and most part of the day was spent in polishing his jewelry and performing his toilet. About ten minutes before the appointed time, he was ringed, pomatumed, and scented to the highest pitch of dandyism; reminding me of the old song of 'Tippy Bobby as he walked through the lobby;' the more so, as the fellow was sometimes called by that name.

Thus equipped, he sallied forth to conclude the important business. Arrived at the shop, and perceiving a customer taking a basin of soup, he walked through into the little back room, as directed. This room was chiefly used by the *élite* of the old man's customers; and catching a glimpse of the visitor as he hurried through the shop, the proprietor called out to his daughter who assisted in the business—'Mary, see what that customer wants!' The girl stood as if petrified, well knowing who it was: upon which the old fellow, who was very crabbed and irritable, himself opened the door to ascertain what was wanted.

A truly unexpected sight met his gaze. There was the evil demon of his house comfortably seated before the fire, in superb array, with an immense frill sticking out from the front of his shirt. This last display of puppyism so exasperated the elder, that he seized hold of the excrescence, and tore it from the intruder's breast; at the same time bellowing with stentorian voice,— 'What do you want here?' The silly goose replied, 'You sent for me.' 'Aye, aye,' retorted the enraged old man,—'Mary, open that door!' Then catching up the uninvited guest by the collar, he kicked him into the street, and set the dog on his heels,—of which however the ejected party made pretty good use, by running away as fast as he could, pursued by a mob of ragged boys, who hooted him like a pack of hounds to his cover.

As he rushed in, panting for breath, we were sitting at tea; and perceiving the disordered state of his dress, I compassionately enquired what was the matter? With a diabolical expression of countenance, gnashing his teeth, and uttering a fiendish growl, he at once assailed me with the grossest epithets in the vocabulary of slang. But ere I could resent this behaviour, the master for whom I worked entered the room, pretending to be entirely ignorant of what had taken place; although he had been apprised of the proceedings, and had actually witnessed the process of ejectment from a public-house opposite.

After some little persuasion, the dandy was prevailed upon to go in company with my employer (who was a liveryman of the city) to ask an explanation of the old man in regard to the disgrace inflicted upon him; but just as they had got outside the door, my shopmates could no longer contain themselves: and burst into an immoderate fit of laughter at the dupe's credulity. Hearing this, he returned, and sitting down disconsolate, continued for some hours to brood over his disappointment. Having subsequently indulged in the sulks for a whole fortnight, at the expiration of that time he packed up his kit and bolted.

About this time the labour-market began to be overstocked, in consequence of so many men having, at the close of the long war, been discharged from the army and navy. Most of the inferior mechanics were thrown out of employment; and amongst their number was the unhappy subject of the foregoing anecdote. He, being much reduced in circumstances, became morbidly disaffected towards the government, and joined the radical agitators of the day, who travelled from place to place exciting the people by their oratory.

At length our hero was arrested for seditious language, and sent to prison; but finding that he was a half-cracked, hair-brained simpleton, they discharged him with a caution as to his future conduct. Hence, sinking by degrees, he became a miserable wanderer about the streets, picking up a few halfpence by exhibiting white mice in a cage; his principal covering being an old sack with a hole in the bottom to put his head through, and the corners cut off to make arm-holes. Thus equipped he strolled about by day, and slept wherever he had a chance at night. On an occasion of his being recognised in this garb by an old shopmate, the latter called out—"I say, Bobby, what sort of a 'cut' do you call that?" The poor creature's vanity was galled, and he consequentially replied, "I ain't half so bad off now as some people; there's Poll Barton ain't hardly got rags enough to cover her!"

After living some time in this destitute state, his intellect, which was never very strong, gave way; and he was sent to a lunatic asylum, where his miserable existence terminated. Had this foolish fellow taken as much delight in work as he did in dress, he might have passed through life in comfort and good repute. But there is a great amount of alloy in man's composition, and the best of us are but fragments and atoms—the sweepings and refuse of nature's workshop!

The landlord of the house where I lodged, was an extraordinary instance of money-getting at any price. He used to 'tan' all the materials that passed through his hands: that is, exchange the soles and heels for inferior stuff of about half the value; thus alike robbing the customer, and ruining his employer's credit. He resorted to every possible means to obtain money, and would buy or sell anything, from a church to a mousetrap; he would also lend cash on any sort of property, at usurious interest. He was a second edition of 'old Biddles,' the miserly shoemaker in Bishopsgate-street, who died worth more than half a million.

The first-named worthy, even after he had accumulated great wealth, lived in a miserable state of independence, having but one room, which served for parlour, kitchen, and sleeping-place; and this, in a dark and filthy alley. The consequence was, that his wife died of a malignant fever engendered by the impurities of the neighbourhood, and accelerated by his unaccountable parsimony. At this period, he had houses in various parts of London; besides land and other property in the country. It was certain also, that he possessed a great amount of money; though where it was deposited no one knew.

In this fashion he lived a few years, but being one day taken suddenly ill, he lay for a time half insensible, until attacked by a fit of delirium; then, jumping up in bed, he roared out—'I'll appeal to the public!' and falling back with his face on the pillow, (as if ashamed of the part he had played in life), with one convulsive groan, finished his miserable career. The money he had amassed at his soul's cost, could never be discovered. He left behind him one son, who took possession of the houses and lands: but could never find any document leading to the discovery of the cash.

Having now finished my education in this seat of professional learning, the resort of English, Irish, Scotch, and Welsh, (the greater part of whom were inveterate fuddlers), I made up my mind to visit my birth-place; once more to breathe my native air, and to gaze on the unforgotten scenes of childhood. Confident in my own powers as one of the best workmen of the age, I felt assured of being a welcome acquisition to any establishment in the trade; besides, in country towns, first-rate mechanics were, at that time, very rare.

Having arranged with my employer, he expressed himself sorry at my leaving; and very kindly promised me that I should have my 'seat' of work, whenever I thought proper to return. He at the same time jocularly said, that a country town would be too small to hold me long. After bidding him good-bye, I returned to my lodgings, packed up my kit, and had my chest conveyed to the waggon-office under direction, 'to be left at Cambridge until called for.' I passed the remainder of the day in company with a few of the best of my shopmates: for there were amongst them men of rare talent, and some who would have graced any situation in life. Towards evening, I went to my mother's and took tea, according to arrangement; for she had some time since been apprised of my intentions.

The old woman was looking happy; and seemed proud of her 'aggravating scapegrace,' as she used to call me when a boy. I was now in the flower of manhood, well looking, well dressed, and (considering the disadvantageous circumstances in which I had been placed) tolerably well informed. But if I enlarge on this head, it will be suspected that I contemplated entering for a fellowship at a certain College, where each of the elect is required by statute to be—*bene natus, bene vestitus, et moderatè doctus.*[1]

The hour of eight, proclaimed by our old eight-day clock, interrupted the usual after-tea confabulation; reminding me that I had made an appointment to spend the evening with my brother. The same every-day circumstance on this occasion also brought to mind an incident of my boyhood. Somebody had informed the governor that I was in the habit of going on Sunday afternoons, seeking birds' nests, along with a boy in the village who sold matches. I certainly was guilty; and to make a repetition of the crime impossible, I was on the very next Sabbath condemned to watch this very clock, subject to the condition, that *when it stopped, I might go!*

I kept guard patiently for about twenty minutes; when it seemed to me, as if the hands of the clock had ceased to move: so putting my ear to the keyhole to ascertain the fact, I discovered that the clock had really stopped. Upon communicating the discovery to my father, he exclaimed with astonishment—'WHAT!' I said: 'Father, the clock has stopped.' He then unlocked the case door, and found, sure enough, that the clock was

[1] 'Well born, well attired, and *moderately* instructed.' It was many years later, that I first heard of this quaint proviso. However, as regards the two first attributes, at the period under notice, I freely confess to having entertained a sufficiently comfortable opinion of my own claims.

run down;—upon which he turned round, and said to me smilingly: 'You may go.'

And now, taking this opportunity to remind the old woman, that Time was man's best friend after all, I bade her good night, and wended my way towards the Leadenhall *rendezvous*, where I arrived just as the room began to fill. A chairman having been already appointed at the last weekly meeting, business soon commenced: and some excellent songs and recitations were given. In the course of the evening, the chairman called upon me for a song; but I told him that this was one of the little things, unhappily, not within the range of my accomplishments. 'Well,' said he, 'perhaps you will favour us with a recitation?' This I essayed, and gave the 'tent scene' in *Richard the Third*, to the entire satisfaction of the company; and to the utter astonishment of my brother, who knew nothing of my theatrical predilections.

From this time I rose a hundred per cent in his estimation, as he knew perfectly well that I had received but little instruction. Whenever he heard others recite, he would say—'Very good, but nothing to my brother Jack!' Of course, some little allowance must be made for brotherly partiality; he was a kind-hearted fellow, and our misfortunes in childhood had endeared us more strongly to each other; he was (as heretofore mentioned) my senior by four years; but I always felt as if I were his elder brother, and would take any amount of beating to screen him from punishment. Having spent a pleasant evening, we took our leave of the company; and upon arriving at Bill's place of residence, parted with mutual good wishes, and the invocation of heaven's blessing upon our several endeavours.

CHAPTER V.

I RETURN TO CAMBRIDGE—'HOBSON'S CONDUIT' AND 'HOBSON'S CHOICE'—I ENCOUNTER MY OLD ENEMY—MEETING WITH MY GRANDMOTHER—BARNWELL—THE COLLEGE WALKS.

WHEN I reached home, the old woman was sitting up for me. But it was getting late; and, knowing that she must feel tired, I went directly to bed, telling her that I should start by five o'clock, as it was my intention to be in Cambridge the next evening.

I had no sooner got comfortably ensconced under the bed-clothes than I fell asleep, but awoke exactly at the time I purposed. Dressing quickly, I knocked at my mother's door to bid her good-bye; but to my surprise, found her already up, and breakfast too prepared. The kettle was steaming beside the fire, and a plate of toast on the 'footman' before the blazing coals, the whole constituting a most appetising arrangement. Having made a truly comfortable meal, I rose to depart: and, after taking an affectionate farewell of my mother (not without some tears on either side) started on my journey, —a pedestrian one, from choice. The distance was just fifty-one miles: and, in order to accomplish this in one day, I purposed walking each mile in a quarter-of-an-hour by my watch. Encumbered with nothing but my walking-stick, I bounded along light as a deer; enjoying the bright and beautiful banquet, in which Nature appeals to the senses of all created things.

As I emerged from the dingy forest of chimneys, the sun shone forth in dazzling radiance, imparting a vivifying influence to all around. Insects hummed and buzzed in the air; birds carolled forth their grateful notes; and cattle lowed in the fields: as if sending up one universal song of praise to the God of day! How different were my feelings when last I traversed this road, a poor and helpless boy! But let that pass; my path lies onward. Vehicles of every description drove past me, from the donkey-cart to the four-in-hand; but I felt no wish to ride. I could walk well, and delighted in my strength and speed; for nature had bestowed on me a cast-iron frame, furnished with muscles and sinews of elastic steel. It would be impossible to describe the pleasurable sensations I experienced through this day's journey.

Having reached Ware (rather over twenty miles from London), I halted at a small neat-looking inn, where I took some bread and cheese and ale; after which, feeling all the better, I pursued my journey: doing every mile to time, as I had resolved on starting.

Nothing occurring to detain me on the road, I got to Melbourn, a distance of forty miles, by four o'clock. Here, when a boy, I had often stopped at the 'Dolphin' whilst going to and fro between Cambridge and Royston; and now I entered the house in order to take some refreshment. Just at the same moment, the landlord came in from the fields (for he was both publican and farmer) calling for something to eat and a cup of tea; in which latter I was civilly permitted to join him.

This slight refection disposed of, I again set out to complete my day's work, and marching on at the old pace reached the well-known 'Green Man' at Trumpington, just as the clock struck seven. I stopped here to rest, and brush the dust off my clothes and boots; and then, after taking a sluice at the pump and a glass of ale, walked steadily on towards that ancient seat of learning, from whose portals have issued some of the greatest men that this or any other country ever produced.

The last rays of the departing sun were gleaming on the Cantab's landmark,[1] as I paused beside the perennial stream that supplies the town with water, and invoked a blessing on the memory of honest THOMAS HOBSON.[2]

---

[1] The pinnacles of King's College Chapel. This beautiful edifice is the first object conspicuous in approaching Cambridge, from whatever direction.

[2] For a further account of this Cambridge 'Worthy,' see *Spectator*, No. 509. Mr. Hobson combined the occupations of carrier and horse-dealer. His memory is preserved in two facetious Epitaphs by Milton. The 'Hobsoni Lex' is also the subject of an elegant Latin Epigram by Vincent Bourne; and there is another, said to be of considerable merit, in the collection of Latin verses entitled *Lusus Westmonasterienses*. Hobson died, in 1630, of sheer *ennui*, when compelled to intermit his periodical trips ''twixt Cambridge and the Bull' (in Bishopsgate) on account of the plague then raging in London. Thus, as Milton further says—

'Too long Vacation hastened on his Term.'

The celebrated Conduit was opened in 1614; but the original building, which stood in the Market-place, has been removed to the corner of Trumpington-road, near the spot described in the text; its place being supplied by a handsome fountain of mediæval architecture.

Wherever the English language is spoken, nearly every one has heard of 'Hobson's choice'; but everyone does not know the origin of the saying. The local tradition is, that the worthy projector of the Conduit, was also the first man who let out hack-horses to the Cambridge students, furnishing them at the same time with whips and boots. His way of conducting business was rather novel; the horse whose turn it was to go out, always stood nearest to the stable-door, having been shifted from stall to stall, until it occupied that position. So soon then as a customer entered, there appeared before him, 'Hobson's choice—*that or none!*' Thus even to dumb animals did the old horse-dealer evince the same benevolence, which he so bountifully exercised towards his fellow-men.

Presently starting from my reverie, I walked on and entered the town, noticing the most prominent objects as I passed along. There stood the Addenbrooke Hospital, a monument of eternal honour both to the original founder, and to later benefactors: on the other side stands the oldest college in the University, called Peterhouse, then presided over by one of the most humorous and kind-hearted old men[1] that ever lived. Nearly opposite is Pembroke, another ancient foundation: and a little further on, I recognised St. Botolph's church, up a passage by the side of which I used to go to school.

Passing on by King's college and Great Saint Mary's, I turned towards the Market-place, and proceeded to the

---

[1] The late Dr. Barnes, who, at the period of his decease, had nearly attained the age of one hundred years.

'Town Coffee-house,' to get a lodging for the night; having by this time done enough for one day's work. I found that I could have a bed; so being snugly seated after my long walk, I indulged in a pipe and a glass of grog; and betwixt nine and ten retired to rest, well primed for a sound sleep.

As I opened my eyes next morning, the well remembered chimes of St. Mary's clock proclaimed the hour of eight: and by the time I had descended into the little bar-parlour, the landlady was preparing breakfast. This influential personage I saluted with a 'Good morning, madam!' to which she replied courteously, and asked if I would take breakfast.

I without further ceremony assented; and drawing a chair to the table, proceeded to make an excellent meal. During our repast, I hazarded several enquiries about persons resident in that quarter, including the landlady's own husband, whom I had known well. He indeed was on intimate terms with my father, and used to come frequently and smoke a pipe with him; but what made me remember him more particularly, was that he had given me many a penny, when I was an apple-munching urchin.

As we still conversed together, the kind hostess enquired my name; observing at the same time that *I* seemed well acquainted with the names of the people in the neighbourhood. Upon hearing the two monosyllables that composed my patronymic, she sprang from her seat, and seizing me by the shoulders, looked into my eyes; as if to see whether the word impostor was written there. She believed that I had long since perished at sea; and there was such an indescribable expression of wonderment in her looks, that I could not refrain from laughing. Upon this, the landlady at once exclaimed, 'I'm satisfied! That laugh has convinced me that you are the son of my old friend,—than whom no more honorable man ever walked the earth!'

Well pleased at hearing such an unqualified eulogium upon my father's memory, I thanked her, and with difficulty restrained the feelings that rose within my breast. For I remembered that the subject of such warm praise had never laid a finger upon me in anger, nor even reprimanded me in harsh terms: but always seemed to bear in mind that he was once himself a boy; a consideration for which I have ever cherished a holy and grateful reverence. If the best feelings of our nature will not bind a man, curses and stripes are useless.

Having finished my breakfast, I went to the waggon-office to look after my luggage, which I soon perceived standing amongst a miscellaneous quantity of goods that had been just unloaded. Producing a duplicate of the address, and paying the charge of carriage, I was allowed to remove my property, which was presently deposited in the safe-keeping of my friendly hostess. I then again sallied forth; intending to stroll round the town; and, at the same time, to 'occasion' the principal shops.

The first that I entered was an old-established place of business, working principally for the Colleges; and, although it was in long-vacation time, the proprietor would have set me on (being from London) but for the interference of his wife, a little sharp-nosed, hungry-faced old woman; who, in the most insulting terms, asked me,—'What I had run away from London for?' Indignant at her insolence, I left the shop, and passing on, enquired at others that lay in my way. But the same answer was given at each—'We've nothing to do.' In fact, they seemed somewhat surprised that I should ask for work at such a season.

After trying all the principal houses to no purpose, I gave it up for a bad job: when the thought struck me, that I would just go and look at the old shop where I was apprenticed. On nearing the window, I perceived that the place presented a scene of utter destitution. A few children's lasts, and about half-a-dozen old shoes were strewn upon the show-board; and there sat my hypocritical tyrant of a master, botching an old shoe, and to all appearance, in a state of great misery.

Having gazed on this deplorable wreck for some minutes, I walked in, and asked if he had any occasion for a 'boot-man'? The question seemed to come upon him like a clap of thunder: for he jumped up as if electrified, and, staring at me with his lack-lustre eyes extended to their utmost stretch, dropped his jowl,—exhibiting a most capacious entrance to his starved and wolfish maw. Again I put the question; and then in a state of hesitating bewilderment, he drawled out—'No, no!' I turned to leave the spot, satisfied that retributive justice had avenged my wrongs and sufferings.

Just at this moment, a man entered the shop who had seen me in London, and now told my old employer who I was. The latter however disputed the information,—saying, that it was impossible, as I had been drowned at sea. In order to convince him, I was requested to return, which I did: and on my again entering the shop, the master asked if my name was John Brown, and whether I was his apprentice of that name. Upon my answering in the affirmative, he stretched his lantern-jaws to their fullest extent, saying: 'We heard that you were dead long ago—that you were drowned at sea.'

I replied: 'I might have been either drowned or hanged, for aught you cared,—*you*, who drove me forth by cowardly persecution to almost certain destruction, brought about by your hypocrisy and villainy. Know further, to your confusion, that (although you tried to brand my name with infamy), I stand here proud in right, and acknowledged one of the first mechanics in the British empire. The same strong arm that knocked you down, has held me up, and sustained me through every difficulty.' Having said thus much, I left the canting hound, and turned towards my native village: which, however abused by the world, has still some charms for me.

As I passed each well-remembered object on my way, early associations crowded on my mind; and the scenes of childhood rose again before me—visions of innocence and happiness. Arrived at the abbey, I stopped to survey its crumbling walls, and note the ravages of all-devouring time.

Things were much altered since I was a boy; many of the old buildings had been pulled down, and the whole fabric was fast approaching dissolution. Where were the people gone that spread the feast at harvest-home,—where was the flock of a thousand sheep, and where the wellknown shepherd with his crook,—where too the merry sunburnt faces that assembled at shearing time? Those scenes have passed away; enough only is left to tell of former prosperity; but the old church[1] is hastening to decay; and many of the elders of the village have gone to their long home. Everything seemed marvellously changed in a few short years.

Thus pondering over Time's conquests, I approached the door of my grandmother's cottage, where the old dame with spectacles on nose sat mending stockings. After asking some indifferent questions, I introduced myself by degrees, and ultimately told her who I was. Never shall I forget the eagerness of her scrutinizing eye, the expression of her fine old countenance. It would be impossible to describe how she endeavoured to trace the lineaments of my altered features; until at length, looking into the corner of my eye, she discovered the 'mother's mark' that was stamped there at my birth. And being now fully satisfied of my identity, she hugged and wept over me as over her first-born.

But so soon as the instinctive yearnings of affection had somewhat subsided, the old lady reproved me in earnest terms for the disobedient course I had taken. I could offer nothing in extenuation, but begged pardon and promised that my future conduct should be a fair atonement for the past. So we were presently reconciled, and the good dame brought out home-made wine and cake: and seem well pleased, as I gave her a brief

---

[1] The ancient Church of St. Andrew, Barnwell, in consequence of the increased population having been found totally inadequate for the wants of the parish, the present parish church (Christ Church) was built by subscription and opened in 1839. The old church was fast succumbing to the ravages of time, until the noble exertions of the 'Cambridge Architectural Society,' seconded by the liberal contributions of the University and Town, rescued it, and restored it to its ancient beauty.

account of my 'travel's history'; and when I had concluded, she thanked God in fervent accents that I had escaped so well.

Desirous of looking round the village, I now resumed my hat and set out to visit the people, every one of whom I knew. But no one recognized the boy in the man; all trace of my former self appeared to have been wiped from the tablets of memory, and a feeling of desolation came over me.

Almost weary of my task, I called at a cottage door at the extremity of the village, where my poor birds'-nesting companion the match-boy used to live. He had a brother who was both deaf and dumb, and partially idiotic; but I had no sooner opened my lips to speak to his mother, than this creature ran to me like madness let loose, evincing his delight in the wildest antics. Turning me round to examine me all over, then jumping and dancing, crying and laughing, he fawned upon me as a faithful dog would upon his master; and by his motions made me understand that I used to give him bread-and-butter in former days.

This occurred at that calamitous period during the late war, when the best bread was one shilling and tenpence-halfpenny per quartern loaf. At that time many of the poor people's children were half-starved, and often have I cried for a slice of bread-and-butter to give to my poorer playmates. The cravings of my own stomach would not have made me solicitous; the greatest luxury of my life has been the administering to the wants and necessities of my fellows.

Returning from my ramble through the village, I paid a visit to the tombs of the forefathers of the existing generation, and read over the quaint epitaphs on their gravestones now partially obliterated by time: but when the sun's altitude informed me that the old lady's dinner hour approached, I returned at once to the cottage. Here I found the cloth laid; and in about ten minutes the board was steaming with some rough-jacket suet dumplings—a food to which I was always very partial. Off these, and pickled pork, greens and potatoes, I made an excellent dinner; finishing with a cup of the old lady's home-brewed.

The cloth being removed, my grandmother requested me to read a chapter; for I was always considered by her, a great card at my books, however great a trouble in other respects. Having complied with her request, she expressed much satisfaction: and going into the adjoining room, took from her stays a twenty-pound note, which she presented to me by way of dessert,—saying, it would serve to help me through the long vacation. Well pleased with this generosity, I thanked her most heartily, as may be supposed.

The reception I had met with, together with the old lady's present, made me feel quite happy: and when she withdrew to look after her dairy and cows at milking time, (a business which would occupy an hour or more), I with a light heart set out to look through the Colleges, and once more admire the well-remembered walks, than which nothing can be more picturesque.

Here giant avenues form a magnificent arch of foliage overhead, a beautiful and most welcome shelter from the mid-day sun, through whose intervals one may catch glimpses of ancient and noble buildings, in one or other of which some of the greatest spirits that ever adorned the realms of science, art, or song, have consumed the midnight oil. In traversing these consecrated paths (for to me it seemed,—aye, and still seems,—hallowed ground), I experienced a sort of superstitious awe. The solemn quietude that reigned around, filled me with holy and reverential feelings; but it was in a cheerfully contemplative mood, that I slowly retraced my steps.

CHAPTER VI.

MY PROGRESS AT CAMBRIDGE—I WIN HONOURS, AND OTHERS WEAR THEM—THE DEAN OF ST. JOHN'S—I GET DISGUSTED —THOUGH NOT FOR WANT OF GOOD FRIENDS—A 'MILL' IN JESUS LANE.

THE sun-dial in Trinity great Court now indicated that it was time to return, if I wished to partake of the old lady's tea. Emerging from the College gate, I met one of the master-bootmakers whom I had 'occasioned' in the morning; but neither thinking nor caring much about the fact at the moment, I was in the act of passing him: when he accosted me, and asked, whether I was not the person whom he had seen in the early part of the day. Upon my replying that I certainly had called upon him,—'Well,' said he, 'this is a bad time of the year; I cannot give you full employment: but if you think proper to make a pair of jockey-boots, I will give you out the stuff this evening.'

This was just my object; for I felt well assured that one specimen of my handicraft would be sufficient to gain me a permanent standing. My intending employer behaved with remarkable civility, and aided me to procure a lodging: after which he gave me out the materials and lasts, with instructions as to substance and the style of boot he required. Having deposited these at my new lodging, which was not more than a hundred yards distant, I made the best use of my legs, and got back to Barnwell just as the old lady was preparing for tea.

I of course informed her, that I had so far succeeded as to have a fair chance of shewing the trade a specimen of those abilities upon which I justly prided myself. I did not suffer more than one hour to elapse, ere I went to look after my chest, and get it removed to my new lodgings. This done, I spread my kit, wetted my stuff, and tacked on my inner soles ready for the morning: and, having thus set everything square to begin work, took another stroll through the streets.

Passing by St. John's College, I saw a man standing in the gateway, in whose countenance I recognized one of my old schoolfellows; and one too with whom I was always on good terms. Without ceremony therefore I introduced myself, and was recognised with great cordiality, but at the same time with some surprise; for my former companion had also heard the rumour that I was drowned at sea. After mutual congratulations and a few words of explanation, he invited me to the buttery to take a *size*[1] of ale, which was handed to us in silver cups, as is customary at all the Colleges.

My friend held a situation in St. John's College: and

---

[1] A somewhat arbitrary liquid measure,—perhaps, on an average, about three-fourths of an imperial pint. At the College Hall dinners, 'a sizing' implies a portion of soup, sauce, vegetables, pudding, or any other delicacy extra to the regulated fare,—which the cook supplies to individuals on private account.

as he had some little duties to perform, I left him under promise to meet about nine o'clock at the celebrated 'Red Bull,' which was frequented by the princes of the road (the most despotic monarchs that ever held the reins of government), and by all the sporting characters of the neighbourhood. At the hour named I entered the room, which was crowded to suffocation; in fact, all was one dense cloud of smoke.

Here were the great betting men making up their books for the ensuing Newmarket races. 'Five ponies to one on the field!'—'Done, Sir, done!' 'I'll take a hundred to five against the Bee,—who'll bet me a hundred to ten against the Ant?' 'I'll take the field at four to one,—who says done?' 'Two to one offered?' 'I'll take that.' 'You're on one hundred even on the field?'—'Done, Sir, done! in five places.'

The books made up, a confusion of tongues ensued, rivalling the discordance of Babel. The company were the *élite* of Cambridge society; jolly fellows enough in their way, but rather different from any set that I had as yet been acquainted with; time, however, reconciles us to all things. After spending the evening at this provincial Tattersall's, I bade my friend good-night, and retired to my new domicile.

On the following morning, I rose and commenced work as the clock struck seven; the sun shone beautifully bright, and the day wore on pleasantly. By six in the evening, I had completed my task, which, after making myself spruce, I took to shop. Here I was requested by the proprietor to make some pumps and dress-shoes for the window,—just to fill up my time when there were no boots ordered. He would give me, he said, as much work as I thought proper to do, until term commenced: and then, I might have all the boots I could undertake.

This suited me very well; as I had come down partly for a holiday, and to enjoy the benefit of my native air. I soon discovered that my employer knew but little about boot-making; in truth, he was a *barber*, who had somehow crept into the trade, and by craft and cunning had succeeded in appropriating other men's knowledge to his own advancement. I was afterwards informed, that if a first-rate workman chanced to enter the town, Mr.———— would not fail to secure him by hook or by crook; thus his work was always turned out in better style than at the other shops: and he ultimately succeeded in getting the first business both in town and university.

When it became generally known that my employer had obtained the services of the best workman yet seen in Cambridge (and that man a native of the place), it was truly wonderful to witness the eagerness of the people to get a pair of boots of my handy-work. Business rolled in from every quarter, and kept on increasing till the October term began, when we became completely inundated with orders; so much so, that I had to write to London requesting some of my old shopmates to come down for the winter.

I was now required to attend shop, in order to cut out the work, and to conduct the business, which had grown far beyond the limited knowledge of the 'outside 'barber-ian' my employer. What added to this unprecedented popularity, was the fortunate circumstance of a visit by the Duke of Sussex to the University. Through the interest of his valet Mr. Blackman (who was indeed a black man) I was introduced to the notice of His Royal Highness, who gave me an order for dress shoes and pumps.

Now the Duke had a very large foot: so I got a couple of blocks in the rough, and made him a pair of lasts as true to the form of his foot as it was possible to accomplish. This done, I selected the most beautiful materials for the purpose; and turned out such work as the trade pronounced 'fit for the glass case.' I had now reached the crowning point of my ambition; the Royal arms were granted to my employer in consequence of this last success; and all went on swimmingly. But as all the customers came to *me* to give their orders, Mr.—— grew jealous of my rising fame, and (as knaves will do) judging others by his own measure, arrived at the conclusion that I intended to supplant him in his business.

I soon perceived by my employer's treatment of me, that his narrow mind was labouring under some hallucination; and resolving at once to snap the slight thread that bound us, I told him that I should leave at Christmas. He asked where I intended going; and I said, most likely to London, as I had seen nearly enough of the country. This seemed in some degree to appease his perturbed spirit, and to allay his unfounded suspicions. However, at the end of term I left him,—a fact which soon transpired.

In about three days from the time that our connection was severed, just as I was packing up and preparing for town, a message came from Mr. Baker, then dean of St. John's College, that he desired to speak with me: to which I answered, that I would wait upon him within five minutes. I knew very well where the dean 'kept,' having supplied him with a pair of lasts and half-a-dozen pairs of shoes during the term.

Being forthwith admitted, I made my obeisance, and asked his pleasure. Mr. B. then said,—'We have been ill suited with a shoemaker to the College, and after due consideration among the seniors have arrived at this conclusion, namely, to offer you the appointment together with the situation of chapel-marker (the only one now vacant), with an understanding that you shall be preferred to the next best place that falls in: and also, that whatever funds you require to carry on our business shall be advanced to you.'

After expressing my grateful thanks for this truly generous offer, I informed the dean with sincere regret, that I had accepted an engagement in London, where I was to have a hundred a-year, and a per-centage upon all goods sold out of the shop: and I was positively bound to be there, and to enter upon my duties, on the following Monday. Mr. B. then, in the most flattering terms, assured me that the society would be much disappointed: as they had been well pleased with my services and attentions during the short time I had ministered to the comfort of their *understandings*. In conclusion, he hospitably insisted on my swallowing two glasses of most excellent port-wine; and then, with a hearty shake of the hand, bade me farewell in the following words: 'God bless you, and prosper your endeavours! I had hoped to have been the means of laying the foundation of your fortunes.' I could not suppress my feelings at such disinterested kindness, and in half-stifled accents took my leave.

Descending the old-fashioned staircase into the spacious court below, I met my old schoolfellow, to whom I also said good-bye; being engaged to spend the remainder of the day with my grandmother, and start the next morning by coach.

I next got my chest conveyed to Marsh and Swann's waggon-office, settled with my landlady, and then turned towards my native village, to take a farewell of the old lady. She indeed would fain have had me stop where I was: and tried to induce my compliance by offering me money to start in business; but I had no present inclination to enter upon the responsibilities of life, feeling assured that a man should first get married, though for that state I considered myself as yet too young.

After urging all she could to no purpose, granny observed that I was still the same self-willed boy as ever, and must take my own course. But she added, that at all events I had two days yet to spare; for it was now Wednesday, and, not needing to be in London till Saturday, I might as well spend the remaining two days with her. To this request I could not but accede, and this trifling concession pleased the old lady; she well knowing my unyielding nature, when set upon the accomplishment of any special end.

Everything within the range of her means was now brought into requisition in order to render my short visit agreeable; her best home-made wine was produced; tarts, cheesecakes, and custards sprung into existence like mushrooms; and a fire was made in the best parlour. Had I been a prince, no hostess could have spread the board with a more profuse liberality. During this brief interval I ran over some of the most amusing incidents of my youth: over which my aged relative laughed heartily, and seemed happy as bright-eyed innocence.

Thus occupied, time flew on with rapid wings. Whilst my grandmother was engaged in her afternoon's duties on the Thursday, I had walked into Cambridge to say good-bye to some young folks, whose acquaintance I had made during my short residence; and from some of them I learned, that a party had been formed for the next evening, for the purpose of bidding me farewell: upon receiving which intelligence, I accepted their kind invitation with grateful feelings.

On my return, I found that the old lady had completed her work in the dairy; and was sitting by the fire reading her large Bible, with my namesake's commentaries. She now laid aside her book and prepared for tea: after which, between reading and conversation, we passed a pleasant evening until bed-time; when before retiring, I took care to mention the invitation I had received for the next day; to which the dame raised not the least objection.

Awaking at six in the morning, I could hear my grandmother's cheerful voice humming a hymn to the accompaniment of her cans and milkpails as they rattled in the dairy: and on going downstairs, I found her busied in straining the milk from the pails brought in by the boys from the cow-lodge. As I had performed this duty myself when a boy, I went into the lodge to look at the stock, which was in fine condition. One of the boys being about to milk a fine brindle cow, I requested him to allow me to do the job;—so taking the pail and stool I commenced, but had scarcely got seated and laid hold of her teats to begin, when, feeling a strange hand, the animal in an instant threw round her leg and swept John Brown, pail, stool, and all into the grain pit,—to the great delight of the boys, who generally pride themselves on the management of their cattle.

Regaining the house, and telling the old lady of my mishap, she laughed heartily, saying—'You are not the first by many, that old Brindle has kicked over.' However, I had taken no harm beyond being partially smothered in grains; so I soon brushed my clothes and put myself in order. Then taking a stroll by the river, and visiting the haunts of my childhood, I returned to find breakfast all ready, and the old lady waiting my arrival. But a continuance of this monotonous kind of life would soon have driven me melancholy. I had always been accustomed to some sort of active employment, and excitement was essential to my very existence. Nevertheless I made out the day as cheerfully as I could, until the hour arrived for visiting my young friends, whom I found at the appointed *rendezvous*, a gay and goodly company.

As I entered the room, they all rose and surrounded me with hearty greetings. The scene would have been a study for an artist; the young men were in their best attire, the females appeared as 'when unadorned adorned the most,' with the fresh bloom of health upon their cheeks, and in the pride of flowing ringlets of auburn or raven hair,—whilst artless smiles and laughing eyes made up a picture that Apelles might have been proud to sketch. Wine and cake were circulated, songs and tales were introduced, merry games were played, and hilarity tempered with discretion reigned over the joyous throng. Thus minutes flew with lightning speed; and the hand upon the dial all too quickly indicated the hour of nine.

Supper being now announced, we retired to another room, where the table was spread with viands that would have satisfied the taste of an epicure. We partook of the good things set before us, and then returned to make the most of the short time that remained to us; for the nearer the hour approached for breaking up, the swifter the moments passed, until at length the clock struck eleven, announcing the time for departure. All was now hurry scurry; bonnets and shawls were soon donned; and the youths having arranged about escorting the fair ones to their several homes, again pressed forward to shake hands with me,—one and all bidding me a hearty adieu!

It fell to my lot to take charge of one of the girls who lived but a short distance off, in the direction that I was going; but I was not fated to reach my journey's end without an adventure. Just as we turned the corner into Jesus-lane, we met three undergraduates in their caps and gowns: and in passing, one of them said, 'Don't go with him, girl, he's a snob!' Whereupon I retorted, 'You're a tailor!' This sorely offended my gentleman's dignity, and, his friends laughing at the same time, he ran after me, asking if I could fight; I told him, 'No: nor could I see the slightest cause for fighting.' However he insisted that I should fight.

By this time his friends came up; to whom I appealed, and asked them if he was not the aggressor? He called me 'snob,' and I replied by calling him 'tailor,' which I thought made us fairly quits. His friends stood by apparently enjoying the fun, whilst I tried in the most good-humoured way to allay their associate's choler. But it was all to no purpose; he still insisted that I must fight: and finding him so determined, I at last said: 'Well then, just allow me to see this young lady to her home (only a few doors farther on), and I pledge my word to return, and give you such satisfaction as you seem to think called for in this stupid brawl.'

Having seen my fair partner to her door, I asked permission to leave my great-coat; and this done, walked back and met the three coming towards me. I was not now in the very best humour, for I considered that the young woman had been grossly insulted by the unmanly remark addressed to her in the public street. I felt not the slightest doubt in my own powers single-handed; but it was just possible his friends might interfere, and do me some serious mischief.

Upon coming up to them, I asked if my adversary was still bent on compelling me to fight in such a ridiculous quarrel, and at so late an hour. Nothing however would satisfy him—fight I must: so finding all my endeavours useless, I appealed to his friends, as gentlemen and men of honour, since I was compelled to this business, to pledge themselves not to interfere with either.

To this proposition they at once assented: which little preliminary settled, I took off my hat and coat, he his cap and gown, which we hung on some palisades in front of a large red-brick house next to the Crown inn. We had only the faint light of a lamp to aid our operations; the night was dark, and the town still as death; there being at this time neither watchmen nor police to interfere.

We then threw ourselves into attitude, and the battle commenced by my opponent's rushing in with mad impetuosity: I avoided his assault by stepping back, and then, with my left, planted a smashing hit on his right eye, which made him stagger back a few paces, until he went down in the mud like a bag of sand. A great deal of rain had been falling for some time, and the road was like a batter-pudding. When my antagonist came up again half smothered with mud, he seemed more cautious, and tried his hand at out-fighting.

Presently he let fly with his left, which I parried and caught him bang in the mouth: when again he measured his length in the mire. Nothing daunted however, up he jumped, and rushed at me like an infuriated bull; but this time I stepped aside and caught him under the ear; which blow sent him reeling against a high brick wall. Here he stood about a minute to recover himself, when he came up apparently distressed and panting for breath. Thus we continued on till the sixth round, when I sent out my left with terrific force upon his nasal organ: and planting my right straight to the mark, caught him in the wind, which doubled him up, in vulgar phraseology, 'like a dog in a coal-box.'

Feeling convinced he was hurt, I went to his assistance, and lifting him on his legs asked if he had any further occasion for my services; to which he faintly answered, 'No.' We then walked to his friends who were sitting on the coping of the palisades, and had been silent spectators of the fight. No men could have kept their word of honour more sacred; for which I made them my grateful acknowledgments. They both shook me by the hand and complimented me upon my conduct and prowess, saying that throughout the whole affair I had acted nobly; and concluded by inviting me to their rooms to take some wine. This I most respectfully declined, but shook hands with my antagonist, and advised him never again to insult strangers; as it was just possible he might catch a tartar.

By this time he had recovered, and now informed me that he had been taking lessons in the art of boxing of some professionals who came down from town, and had been here the whole of the term; and that they had told him that no man without science could beat him. 'That,' I said, 'may be true; but it does not warrant you in picking a quarrel with an inoffensive person for the purpose of shewing off your knowledge of boxing.' I observed at the same time, 'that all the different styles of fence were invented and established for man's protection, not for his destruction.'

'Besides,' I added, 'the laws thereto appertaining are based on certain strict principles of honour, which you have unquestionably violated in this case; now, take my advice never again to engage in fight without having some just cause of quarrel. Thus, at least, you will always come off with credit, if not with victory.'

When I had delivered this short lecture, he was quite solicitous to know who and what I was, and where I lived. But I told him it mattered not, for I was off to London on the morrow. Then bidding them all good night, we parted excellent friends.

I now put on my hat, and hanging my coat over my

arm, walked to the door where I had left my charge. She was sitting up with her mother, anxiously waiting my return; and when I entered the room, the old lady asked me how we had settled the quarrel, as her daughter had informed her all about it. In a few words I described the scene, which rather pleased her, as she said; for when herself a young woman, she never dared stir out of doors after dark, as those young collegians went about in gangs, and played most abominable tricks upon females, if they caught them in the streets at night. Nay, it was a common practice with them to break open the doors, where a family was sitting quietly by the fire-side.

All the protection they had at the time, was that of the proctor, which was but little, for he could not be in all parts of the town at the same time. Thus the rioters pursued their game with impunity, whilst the inhabitants lived in constant dread of their nightly visits. 'But,' continued my informant, 'a great change has taken place within these last fifty years: the population is much larger, and the young men of the town have frequently turned out, and given the offenders a terrible beating.' She remembered one handsome young man having his nose chopped clean off his face, and knew of many others who were maimed and crippled for life, in what were called the 'town and gown' rows; but, thank God, they were beginning to die away.

After wiping the mud from my boots, washing my hands, and plaistering up a cut knuckle, (it had come in contact with my opponent's front teeth), I bade the mother and daughter good-bye, and having not more than a mile to go, soon reached home. I was provided with a key,—so unlocked the door quietly, and went up to bed without disturbing the old lady; who no doubt had retired punctually as the clock struck nine, her custom through life.

CHAPTER VII.

BOUND FOR LONDON—A FACETIOUS JEHU, AND AN EXTORTIONATE PUBLICAN—SYDENHAM AS IT WAS—HEROES OF THE RING—I ASTONISH MY NEW EMPLOYER—THE SNOB'S FEAST—ADRIFT AGAIN.

NEXT morning, after breakfast, I took an affectionate leave of my truly loved and respected relative. As I quitted the house, it was just half-past nine o'clock; and the coach would start at ten. I had thus half-an-hour to walk a mile and a-quarter, which would leave me some minutes' leisure.

When I arrived, the men were putting-to the horses, and the coachman was tieing a lash on to the thong of his whip. As I approached, he recognised me, having seen me at the Red Bull, the usual rendezvous of the 'Knights of the whip,' of whom a more dashing specimen never shaved a turnpike-gate. As the box-seat was not taken, I was invited by the driver to occupy it: Jehu being pleased to say, that he should be happy of my company. I jumped up accordingly, and as it was cold weather, found the apron a very welcome protection.

Entering by degrees into conversation, I found that my companion had collected a great stock of quaint and witty sayings, which he brought out at intervals. There was something very amusing about this man; in fact he let fly his arrows at every person and every thing that tickled his fancy; no matter to him whether the subject were old or young, lame, deaf, or blind. We met a little crooked hump-backed fellow, remarkably thin, and bent like a hoop:—'Halloa!' sung out my facetious companion, 'I say, old friend, did you come straight from home?' 'Yes, Sir!' replied the man. 'Well then,' was the rejoinder, 'I can only say that you've got cursedly warped on the road!' At which sally the deformed little man flew into a great rage, and stood gesticulating and bawling after the coach till we descended a hill and lost sight of him.

When we stopped to change horses, coachee demanded 'a glass of brandy-and-water, with a cinder in it'; but I, having no taste for such luxuries, requested to have mine cold *without*. By the time we had drank our grog, the team was in readiness, snorting and pawing the ground, evincing their eagerness to start. We again mounted the box, the driver gathered up his ribbons, and drawing his horses together, at the word 'all right' and a crack of the whip, we started off in gallant style. This was considered the perfection of travelling in those times, although we were six hours going to London, a distance of fifty-two miles.

About half-way betwixt Cambridge and London, the passengers were informed that twenty minutes would be allowed for dinner; but I should think that ten minutes of the time had elapsed before the victuals were put upon the table: and ere the sharpest set of teeth could have masticated sufficient to satisfy the most moderate stomach, it was announced that the coach was ready to start.

Three or four elderly persons had scarcely eaten a mouthful, but they must pay notwithstanding. One hardy looking old fellow, with a Yorkshire accent, and having the appearance of a cattle-dealer, very deliberately cut a round off the loaf, and taking two slices of beef which were on his plate, doubled the bread and put the meat in the middle: saying that if he hadn't time to put it in his stomach, he had time to put it in his pocket. Which he did: at the same moment throwing down the money, to the consternation of the waiter, who seemed to fear that the rest of the passengers would follow his example. However, they contented themselves with securing the pieces of bread that were ready cut, together with some morsels of cheese, and hurried off grumbling to take their places; and well they might grumble, for a more knavish and dishonest trick was never practised.

When fairly on the road again, I asked the coachman if *he* had got any dinner; for he did not enter the passengers' room,—'Oh, yes,' he said, 'mine is always ready to the minute.' I asked why ours was not ready at the time also? That, he answered, was quite another thing; they used to be punctual at one time, but the landlord was nearly ruined by it during the war, when provisions were at famine prices, and some hungry customers used to eat enough to serve them for the next day. So he adopted the plan of putting them on short time, as the only means of retrieving his losses: and now makes it pay 'tolerably well.' This I could easily believe.

As we bowled merrily along, my friend seemed on excellent terms with himself, and his 'fifty mile of females,' as he jocosely expressed it; nodding, winking, and smiling at individuals of the sex, as they peeped over the blinds to take a glance at the passing vehicle.

At last we entered the big town, and were absorbed into the never-ceasing din and bustle of its eager and busy population. Here it required all the driver's skill and attention to thread his way through the maze of vehicles, which was every now and then brought to a dead lock; arresting all traffic until the course could be cleared. On arriving at Cornhill, I alighted: and, after giving the coachman his accustomed fee, went direct to a noted coffee-shop in Leadenhall, in order to get some refreshment; for I had made but a sorry dinner at the liberal host's table, where the coach stopped on the road.

Having satisfied my appetite, I walked through the market to see my brother: and as soon as he was at leisure, we adjourned to the 'Rose and Crown' to take a glass together. I gave him a brief history of my sojourn and doings in our native place, with which he seemed well pleased; but, as his time was particularly precious just then, we parted, promising to meet on the morrow and spend the day in company.

I next repaired to my new place of business, and announced myself: whereupon my employer expressed much satisfaction, saying that I had arrived most opportunely; for the man whom I was to succeed, was unable to get the work finished that was required to be sent home that night; the morrow being Sunday.

Hearing this, I took off my coat, borrowed an apron, and turned to in good earnest; the result of which was, that, to the utter astonishment of my predecessor, I had everything treed up and sent home to the customers by nine o'clock. So delighted was the master, that he expressed himself in the highest terms of commendation and invited me into his private room; where I partook of a fine rump-steak, and some of the best stout I ever tasted. After this, I looked over the order-book, and put the measures in readiness to commence business on Monday morning.

This despatched, I took my leave, and anxious to see my mother, went straight to the old lady's dwelling. Here I found her busy as a bee, weighing up and serving out all sorts of small groceries; for this was a very poor neighbourhood. As soon as I entered, she came round from behind the counter, and with a bland smile of welcome, requested me to go into the little room at the back of the shop, saying, she should soon be at liberty. During the time she was engaged, I wrote to my grandmother; giving a short description of my journey to town, and thanking her for the kind treatment I had received at her hands. I had just concluded this epistle, but not yet subscribed my name, when the old lady came in, and was gratified by my adding a few lines at her dictation, before the letter was posted.

It was now time for supper; though ours was a very humble repast, consisting of bread-and-cheese and a pint of porter. But what of that? How many have been prematurely sent to their long home, by luxurious living, for one that has died of homely fare! 'Hunger may starve: but excess is sure to kill.' Our meal over, a pipe supplied from my old friend the 'nigger'-headed jar, a glass of grog, and the relation of my late Cambridge adventures, sufficed to occupy me, and to interest my willing listener until midnight; when I retired to bed, and feeling rather exhausted, soon fell asleep.

The clock was striking seven next morning, as I turned out and prepared to receive my brother, who was expected to breakfast about eight. He arrived true to time, and clean as a new pin; his dress was a dark blue over-coat with braided collar and silk buttons, tight pantaloons and hessian boots with tassels; and he looked altogether as smart as any soldier that ever figured on parade. After a hearty breakfast, we agreed to walk to Sydenham, to see our sister, who (as I have before mentioned) lived there as lady's maid in the family of an old general officer.

It was a dull foggy morning when we started; but as the day wore on, the mists cleared off, and it became tolerably fine. We soon found ourselves in a beautiful part of the country,[1] interspersed with gentlemen's seats isolated in gardens encompassed by high walls, and having every appearance of security and comfort.

Upon our arrival at the house where our sister lived, we were ushered into a neatly furnished room, and supplied with fine old ale, and excellent home-made bread

---

[1] This, it must be remembered, was many years before rail-roads were in vogue, or the Crystal Palace dreamed of. The immense increase of buildings has obliterated many former characteristics of Sydenham and its neighbourhood.

and Stilton cheese; and then she introduced us to the presence of her mistress, who had expressed a desire to see the visitors. Here, upon paying our respects, we were asked many questions, to which we replied as pertinently as we were able: and after an interview of half-an-hour, the general's lady dismissed us with a complimentary observation regarding our manners and bearing, and graciously desired that we should enjoy ourselves during our stay.

We were eventually shewn over the spacious premises, including garden, stables, etc.,—and everywhere found evidence of good taste and liberality. Were it possible to satisfy the inordinate desires of man, this place, with an adequate revenue, appeared well calculated for the purpose. But I have learned from observation and experience, that human cravings have no limit. Having spent a most pleasant and satisfactory day, we requested that our grateful thanks might be conveyed to the lady of the house, for the kind treatment we had received: and after taking leave of our sister, wended our way homewards.

It was towards eight o'clock, that feeling somewhat tired after our walk, we reached my brother's lodgings. Here, however, a judicious application of towel and brush soon fitted us for the *rendezvous* of the sporting men about Leadenhall, a place much frequented by the first pugilists of the day. The conversation of these heroes was not of the most refined character; neither was it so uninteresting or irrational, as many honest persons might suppose. For although the parties spoken of might lack book-learning, some of them beyond doubt possessed a great amount of worldly knowledge, and sound common sense; qualities, in my estimation, of the highest value.

In saying this, don't let me be deemed an advocate for prize-fighting. Were it in my power, I would put a stop to such brutalizing work at once; but the 'art of self-defence' should be preserved and taught by competent masters. For well assured am I, that the more courageous a man is, the more gentle will he also be. But man was not formed by his Creator, and furnished with such powers of strength and action, to be passive as woman. He was ordained to protect the latter, (as also for the protection of those dearer to her than her life's blood), to subdue the elements, and to bring his race to a proper state of civilization, which crawling cant and hypocritical bigotry can never accomplish.

On Monday morning, after an early breakfast, I started to enter in earnest upon the duties of my new situation. Previously to my arrival, the 'trotter' had swept out the shop, cleared down my cutting-board, and placed my knife and measures with the order-book ready for business. After requesting his attendance round the premises, to shew me where the different materials were kept which I required for my use, and selecting such things as I needed, I commenced cutting out and fitting up stuff for the men. All this should have been done on the Saturday; but as the poor fellow whom I succeeded had been ill a long while, everything had got considerably behind-hand, and the men in consequence had lost their time; which fell very heavy upon them, as they for the most part had families to support.

The book being full of orders, I selected those that took the least time to give out,—with a view to set the men to work as quickly as possible. Thus, having the aid of the apprentice (whom I set to cut linings, tie the stuff together, and write directions on the soles), I managed to find every man in work, if he pleased to begin, by eleven o'clock. This was certainly one of the great achievements of my professional life.

By-and-bye, my employer arriving from his country house, looked round with evident signs of dissatisfaction, and then turning to me, enquired: 'Have you got nothing ready for the men?' I hereupon called his attention to the order-book, and pointed out the different orders I had already cut and given to the closers. The master threw a glance over the entries, and with a look almost approaching disbelief, exclaimed: 'Well, this is what I have never seen approached!' Turning then towards his private room to put aside his great-coat and whip, he said: 'You had better let the men have the bottom stuff,—so that they may get it fitted, tack on their inner soles, and make their threads, as that will forward them an hour each.' I replied, that with the assistance of the lad, this had been done already; upon which, without another word, he retired to his room and sat down to his books.

I now proceeded with all the back-standing orders, and by the end of the week had got the business into good working trim: so that my own duties assumed a perfect regularity, and were easily discharged. Things were so managed, that the proprietor scarcely troubled himself about the business; the men too were kept well employed, which made a great difference to their families.

When I had been installed about a month, our employer gave the workmen a dinner, or (according to their rule of living) it might have been rather called a supper, as it took place at seven o'clock in the evening. As is customary on such occasions, he occupied the chair himself, and requested that I would act as vice on the occasion.

All being properly arranged, and the board groaning under substantials, roast, baked, and boiled, the entertainer offered up a short grace: after which, we began to cut down the mountains of food placed before us. Slice after slice disappeared in rapid succession, until the round-of-beef that I was carving was reduced to a mere ghost of its former proportions; and nearly every joint on table shared the same fate. A second course then made its appearance, in the shape of jolly plum-puddings, of which all ate heartily, almost to repletion; nay, one poor fellow so overgorged his stomach, that we thought he would die. However, being carried into another room and receiving medical aid, he so far recovered as to be able to walk home, where he remained three days in bed.

In the meantime, after his removal, the table being cleared, we indulged in mirth and song, keeping the revel up till midnight. In the early part of the evening there was some excellent singing; but towards the finish, nearly all became oblivious; and, like the heroes of Burns's song, 'Willie brew'd a peck 'o maut,' they fell beside their chairs, and lay till daylight peeped in upon the inglorious scene. The 'governor' retired about eleven, leaving me to preside over the goodly company, which I managed to endure till their eyes were sealed close as oak,—save those of one who was lying on his back, fancying he was still joining in the chorus, and calling for more punch.

My company having now reached a state of unconsciousness, I went up to bed: having secured one in the house, so as to be ready for business in the morning. Thus ended this feast of the brothers of the gentle craft; but when I came downstairs in the morning about eight o'clock, some of them were in the tap still under the influence of last night's debauch.

On entering the shop I found the apprentice sweeping up, and putting the lasts, trees and other things in their proper places; the trotter had not yet arrived, at which I did not much wonder, he having been one of the party overnight: for although he went away in pretty good time, I felt assured his head would feel disordered in the morning. I had myself been particularly careful as to the quantity I drank. Yet the smoke, noise, and late sitting conspired to make me feel heavy, and quite unfit for my ordinary work: as I could not bear to lean my head over the cutting-board.

I therefore resolved to take a walk in the park, and get rid of the fumes that clung about my brain. After an hour's ramble, I returned, took a glass of brandy, and felt able to get through a portion of the business in hand. But the poor men did not get over their eating and drinking for three or four days, and the covetous fellow who stuffed himself with plum-pudding, was ill for some time; so that, upon the whole, I regretted exceedingly that the 'governor' ever gave them the treat at all.

By degrees however we resumed our regular way of business; and all went smoothly, except that my employer caught a severe cold, which brought on a painful and incessant cough. His case became gradually serious and at length hopeless; he was compelled to take to his bed, and (to my great regret) died, in about eleven months from the time of his first seizure. The deceased was only thirty-eight years of age,—a fine-looking man, well educated, and possessing an excellent temper, with an extraordinary share of good feeling and common sense.

He left to deplore his loss, a widow and four children; the eldest only eight years old, and the youngest eighteen months. But as his private property amply sufficed to bring up the family, and to maintain the widow in comfort, it was soon resolved upon to dispose of the business. This determination was intimated to me one morning soon after the funeral, by the widow's brother, a gentleman of distinguished appearance and courteous manners. He informed me, that the concern would be advertised for sale; and civilly added that he had strong reasons for recommending me to the purchaser, whoever he might be. I thanked him, and said I would conduct the business until I left, with greater care, if possible, than if it were my own.

Having expressed himself perfectly satisfied, my visitor bade me good day,—saying he would call on Saturday morning, and give me a cheque for the amount that I required to pay the men. Thus things went on for three weeks; at the end of which period, an old gentleman with two sons accompanied my late master's brother-in-law, to look over the stock and premises. Having examined everything minutely, they requested to look at the books; all of which I shewed them. These were the order-book, waste-book, day-book, ledger, and measure-book,—in which last I had set down, upon an inch scale, the exact size of every customer's foot and leg, with a full description of the shape—noting bunions or corns, broad thick toes, or long and thin, with all the peculiarities my observation had supplied me with; to which were added instructions how to make an unmistakeable fit.

I had also numbered the lasts of every customer, and entered them both in the order-book, and in the measure-book, together with the names of the closer and maker, in ruled columns opposite; or in a line with the number of the lasts. By this system, goods could be manufactured and sent in perfect confidence to any part of the habitable globe: even after twenty years' absence, by making allowance for the alteration which always takes place in the foot, at about forty years of age. When I had explained my entire system of management, I took from a drawer under my cutting-board, a memorandum-book made of cartridge-paper, containing the address of every customer to the shop, during the time that I had conducted the business; thus putting them in possession of knowledge quite indispensable in every new undertaking of the kind.

Within a week from this time, the old gentleman called again, and told me that he had concluded the business: and was owner of the premises, together with the entire plant, from the present date. Now it chanced to be a Saturday, and my time was up at nine o'clock in the evening; for all situations of the kind, in the trade, are held upon a weekly tenure. I went through my day's work as usual: and when nine arrived, the new proprietor called me into the counting-house, and paid me my week's wages, together with a per-centage upon all goods sold out of the shop, in accordance with my original agreement.

He then offered me two pounds, as a gratuity for what I had shewn him; and at the same time expressed his thanks for my system of measuring, and book of the customers' addresses. I told him that he was perfectly welcome to the little services I had rendered; but as these clearly fell within the time for which I was paid, according to agreement, I begged to decline taking more than my wages. Being further pressed, I told him I had ere now been driven to great straits: but would never take alms, when I had ample means at my disposal.

Thus ended a service of fifty-eight weeks. The next thing was to pack up my sizestick, pinchers, and round knife adapted for cutting out: these being the principal tools used by the individual termed in the trade a 'clicker.' Having wrapped these in paper, I bade the old gentleman good night, and retired.

When I reached home, my mother had already prepared my evening meal: for I was always punctual, being desirous of giving her no uneasiness by irregularity. After supper, I changed my clothes, and walked to Leadenhall for the purpose of arranging with Bill about spending the next day.

When I arrived at my brother's place of business, the shop was crowded like a fair, inside and out; the gas-lights were fluttering in the wind, and the men cutting up and throwing the meat into scales to be weighed. He in the meantime called out the weight and price; which were booked by a clerk sitting in a small raised counting-house. This bustle continued about half-an-hour; the hurry of the day was now drawing to a close; and seizing a favourable opportunity, I went in and spoke to Bill about the morrow. Having agreed about time and place of meeting, I bade him good night, and went direct to a house in the city frequented by the most respectable men of my own trade: where they usually met on a Saturday night to smoke their pipes, talk politics, or sing a song.

As I was well esteemed by the trade, and had not seen them for a long time, they all rose and gave me a hearty greeting. There is nothing more grateful to the feelings than being well received: and more particularly so, when you endeavour to merit such reception. It matters not whether prince or peasant, the feeling of gratification is the same. There is nothing so priceless as a good name; 'it is the immediate jewel of the soul.' I have ever found it of inestimable value, have prized it beyond all earthly treasure, and have not been wholly unrewarded.

Soon after my arrival, the landlord (to whom I was well known) entered the room, and, remembering what had been done on some former occasions, brought in the rum bottle, and requested us to 'splice the main brace.' This nautical usage I had introduced when I first used the house, which seemed to tickle the fancy of mine host, as he thought it meant splicing a rope; the natural inference a landsman would draw, more particularly if he had heard of 'tacks' and 'sheets,' 'hallyards' and 'braces.'

There is no time so rationally spent as that in the company of respectable, sober-minded, and sensible men;

persons possessing the advantages of a more refined education would hardly guess what an amount of knowledge and book-learning is to be met with amongst the members of my ancient trade. It is certainly very singular: but I have met with nothing like it in men of any other calling; and I think the fact can only be accounted for, by the sedentary nature of our employment, which is a natural inducement to thought. After enjoying a pleasant hour with these humble philosophers, I shook hands with them cordially, and bade them good night; promising to meet again on the following Saturday. By the time I got home, my mother had just closed shop and finished business for the week. We were both of us pretty well tired, and glad to seek repose.

CHAPTER VIII.

THE TWO STUTTERERS—THE 'FUDDLERS'—'TRYING THE BOOT'—THE RIVAL 'ROOKS'—THE DOG STEALERS—'KING HOBDEL'—SKITTLES—FEMALE PUGILISTS—THE STOURBRIDGE FAIR CATASTROPHE.

ON the morrow, at the appointed time, I sought my brother at our usual *rendezvous*. I had not been long in the room when three or four young men entered, all of whom I knew to be salesmen in the market; and in a few minutes we were joined by others, making ten in all. It was now arranged that we should pay a visit to a sporting doctor at Stoke Newington, who, being a bachelor and a patron of the P.R., had on a former occasion invited us to spend an afternoon with him whenever convenient.

All being agreed, we started off full of life and spirits, and upon our arrival were shown into a spacious room looking out on a beautiful garden. Here we were soon joined by the doctor, a fine muscular young man of about eight-and-twenty, who, notwithstanding his 'fancy' predilections, enjoyed an excellent practice. We met a hearty reception; wine and tobacco were introduced, and we enjoyed the fleeting hours to our hearts' content: our host being replete with tale and anecdote. The evening indeed passed swiftly: it was nine o'clock when we took our departure, and by this time we had all had sufficient to drink; insomuch that two or three of the party could not walk so steadily as they should have done. Hence a most untoward occurrence took place.

Just as we approached Kingsland-gate, we met three young men, who apparently like ourselves had been out spending the day: and it happened that one of our party and one of theirs had the misfortune to run against each other. Being both (curiously enough) stutterers, and both partially inebriated, each thought that the other was mocking him; so from stammering they came to blows, and a regular fight ensued.

Our man got the worst of the round, and being picked up, said to Jack Gracey, one of the best light weights in the kingdom, 'I s-s-say, Jack, th-th-this fellow's too m-much f'' me.' 'Very well,' said Jack, who was his second, 'in the next round *I'll fall down with you*, which, it being dark, nobody will notice; then *you* pick *me* up, and set me on your knee.' This being done, Jack went in and floored the poor fellow opposite to him; who fell as though he had been shot.

Upon coming up again, he perceived that they had been ringing the changes upon him, and stammered out: 'Th-th-that aint the m-m-man I've been fi-fi-fi-fighting with!' 'No,' retorted the other, 'I'm d-d-d-damned if it is—h-h-he's a b-b-blessed sight b-b-better m-man than I am!' When it came to be explained that both the combatants stuttered, we all had a hearty laugh,

R

shook hands, and parted good friends. Thus ended what might have been an unhappy business.

On the morrow I took a turn through the town visiting my old shopmates; several of whom dedicated the day to its patron saint.[1] A prize-shoe was to be exhibited at the sign of the 'Crispin' in Grub-street, kept by old Cochrane, a sporting Irishman, and father to Ned O'Neil's wife, who was a very beautiful and well-behaved woman, as you would meet with in common life. It was proposed that we should pay a visit to the place, and examine this extraordinary piece of work: as it was reported to be the most delicate specimen ever turned out by the hands of man; the name of the maker was Robert Jones, a Welshman. But it will be necessary here to explain how these things are managed.

If perchance ten or a dozen of the fuddling fraternity meet at a public-house, they will spend every farthing they possess, in order (as they term it) 'to try on a boot'; that is, to get the landlord to give them eight or ten guineas for a prize-boot for exhibition to the 'trade.' The landlord receives a shilling from each visitor on a certain day appointed for the show; and every visitor on payment is entitled to a glass of gin. If the gang do not succeed in 'getting on the boot' the first day, they go round recruiting, and make up as large a regiment as they can muster. Then on the next day, after selling their cabbage[2] and pawning their kit to the

---

[1] Saint *Monday*. This is a holiday extemporised by artisans, whose Saturday night and Sunday excesses incapacitate them from resuming their ordinary labours on Monday morning.

[2] Scraps of stuff.

men of whom they purchase their grindery,[1] the original set pay a second visit to mine host: and commence business by ordering half-pints of gin, pots of porter, pipes, tobacco, &c. Two or three stragglers then drop in and join the company; presently a second bevy arrives, and the tap-room is soon crowded to suffocation.

At this stage of the proceedings, the landlord is applied to for a larger room; who, thinking he has got some rare customers, shews them into a spacious apartment used for various purposes, such as dinner-parties, benefit-clubs, Druids, Knight Templars, Odd Fellows' Lodges, or any other gatherings that favour his business. Should the landlord be a little green, the bait is soon taken; they begin to talk about the intended removal of their 'shop's-meeting' from its present place of assembly to some other house, and promise Boniface their interest in the matter: telling him they can command votes enough to carry any measure they think proper to propose. If this lure succeeds, the bird is quickly in the trap; articles are drawn, and a deposit paid.

Thus they keep up the fuddle, until the boot is drank out; the article is sometimes really made, and sometimes not: for perhaps the man engaging to make it goes on tramp to Liverpool, Manchester, Oxford, Cambridge, or any other part of the world,—leaving the general victim a legacy of 'walked chalks,' such as was never before seen upon his tally-board.

Towards evening we arrived at the 'Crispin,' where this marvellous shoe was to be exhibited. Having paid our shilling, and taken each the accustomed glass of gin, we proceeded to the further end of the room, where

---

[1] Small necessaries required by the workman in his business.

stood the 'father' with his precious production cradled in a hat-box, carefully bedded on a silk handkerchief, with which it was ostentatiously wiped before being handed for inspection. After a thorough examination, I could not but pronounce it the most delicate and beautiful piece of mechanical work of the kind, that I had ever seen. The forepart, or edge, of the sole did not exceed the substance of a sixpence, with which I compared it; the stitching, which was as fine as the work in the finest shirt-collar, and true as copper-plate, was invisible on the other side; and this was composed of two substances of leather.

I offer this explanation for the benefit of those uninitiated in the mystery. As for giving an accurate description of the motley assemblage, and the clatter of tongues that prevailed on this occasion, it would defy the greatest genius that ever wielded pen or pencil. English, Irish, Scotch, and Welsh were all jumbled together, and all more or less inebriated: making up one mighty scene of inexplicable confusion. Their costumes were equally various, from the dandy in most exaggerated attire, to the ragged and dissolute 'rook,' with his toes growing through his shoes, his elbows peeping through his coat, and a most luxuriant crop of hair waving over his crownless hat.

There are two orders of 'rooks,' deriving their titles from two notorious houses used by rival factions: and there is nothing like them on earth or elsewhere. One class takes its name from the 'Crow' public-house in Moor-lane, which the founders of the order, by a little stretch of fancy, corrupted to 'Rook,' thinking that a more appropriate cognomen. This particular class are not very nice about the quality or fit of their clothes, nor whether they are their own or another person's; their suits are usually very much dilapidated, and in general without buttons, which were indeed superfluous,—seeing that they invariably brace themselves up with a long waxed thread, easily replaced when worn out. This thread passing through loops of the same material fastens under the collar of the outer garment, with a slip-noose, so that they have no trouble to undress; one pull at the string, and their entire suit falls off as if by magic.

The other class of rooks have their head-quarters at a house called the 'Gully-hole,' in Brown-bear court, Moorfields; they are called members of the pin-and-skewer, from their never using either ties, loops, or buttons. If they have the misfortune to get a rent in any part of their dress, they as soon as convenient either pin or skewer it up; thus you see them very oddly ornamented from top to bottom with alternating pins and skewers. Between these two bodies some little jealousy has existed for nearly two hundred years, and whenever they meet there is sure to be a fight.

It so happened on this remarkable day, that two worthies of opposite factions met in the room face to face,—both being a little more than half-seas over. One forthwith scowled at the other, implying, 'You are as bad a rook as I am.' The other retorted aloud, calling him all the ragged beggars and scare-crows he could think of. Most of the company knew of the fixed and deadly hatred that existed between these rival ragamuffins, and therefore prepared for the desperate conflict, by urging them on and giving them plenty of room for their operations.

Presently the fight began; away flew the bits of

shreds and patches from the pins and skewers, till the wearer was reduced almost to a state of nudity. Nothing daunted, 'Gully-hole' fought on in gallant style, and seizing 'Crow's-nest' by the head, pulled the cord that bound the rags to his carcase; when down fell all, leaving him naked as an unfledged bird. I had now seen enough of this kind of life, and determined to retire from a scene which Hogarth in his highest flights of fancy never imagined.

Being somewhat under the influence of that potent power which destroys both mind and body, and saps the foundation of every virtue by prostrating the nobler energies of man, I made the best of my way home, and feeling some small degree of shame at my state, sneaked quietly up to bed. I awoke in the morning without a headache, but on going downstairs to breakfast received a little wholesome admonition from those lips whose utterance should ever be held in honour and veneration. How many around us drink daily of the bitter cup of repentance, through having rejected a mother's counsel! There is nothing in nature so truly ugly as an undutiful or ungrateful child; but it has not been my lot to figure in this vile character. Having made a simple promise to be more cautious in future, the kind old woman expressed herself satisfied.

I now put myself in order, and started off to the Secretary of our society to enquire if he knew of a situation that would suit me; but hearing that there were many applications, and that all the good berths were filled, I determined to have a week's holiday, and amuse myself by the study of men and things as they presented themselves to me. I was not bent upon anything in particular; but merely contemplated a roving excursion, and determined to keep within the bounds of strict propriety.

Being desirous of seeing the effects of yesterday's proceedings, I went direct to the house: and immediately upon entering was importuned by a dozen or more of half-dead and stultified sots for some beer, as their money was all spent. I thereupon pretended to be without money, except sixpence and a few coppers; but this did not much matter, as they knew my credit was good with the hostess, an Irishwoman with a strong brogue, and wearing a cap that looked like a bushel basket stuck on her head. Whilst I stood talking to this quaint old lady,—after having ordered a gallon of beer for these poor deluded fellows,—a young woman of superior manners and elegant figure, evidently educated far above the vulgar walks of life, came to the bar-door, and in a prettily refined Scotch accent, enquired for 'James McDonald.'

Knowing the man, and suspecting this young woman to be his wife, I requested the landlady to invite her into the bar, while I went into the parlour to enquire for him,—there being some sort of aristocratic distinctions even among 'snobs.' When I opened the door, Mc D. was in his shirt-sleeves just taking his cue to begin a game of bagatelle; on hearing of his wife's being in the bar, the poor fellow, though partially stupid with drink and sitting up all night, turned pale as death, and informed me that he had been induced to allow one of the party to pawn his coat to pay a bet that he had lost at cards. I at once said: 'Give me the duplicate: go into the kitchen and wash; and in five minutes I will be back with the coat.' Within ten minutes he was ready to meet his wife, who was only too happy to see him safe and well. This was a remarkably steady and respectable man: only on this occasion had he transgressed, and placed himself in this unhappy dilemma. Hence, on bidding the pair good-day, I felt well pleased with the part I had played in this business.

During this time several poor squalid creatures came after their drunken husbands; some children too sought for their fathers: but, oh such husbands and fathers! Rags and misery seemed to be their only inheritance. Sickened with this scene of mental and bodily debasement, I took my leave, as civilly as I could, to avoid being assailed by these madmen in such choice expressions as they coin or cull, in order to express their scorn of everything in the shape of common decency.

Turning into Chiswell-street, I observed on the opposite side of the way several men (whom I had often seen in different parts of the town) leading poodles fantastically trimmed, and ornamented with red collars attached to a blue riband. As I felt desirous to know something of the habits and manners of these people, I followed their steps, thinking they were going to some place of *rendezvous*. Keeping on their track, I saw them enter a public-house, the sign of the 'Queen's Head,' in a narrow alley leading from Golden-lane to Goswell-street,—a locality abounding in intricate and difficult turnings, whose occupants appear to be as completely secluded from the rest of London, as if they had dwelt in a dense forest.

The party entering the house passed through a back-door into a skittle-ground; I halted at the counter, where the landlady, a good-looking flashily dressed young woman, apparently not more than three or four-and-twenty, sat talking to a man with whom I had frequently 'set-to' in different parts of the town. This individual had a smooth and oily tongue that would have deceived Satan himself; there was nothing low in his manners, dress, or general appearance, which was that of a respectable gamekeeper; but I afterwards found out that he was George Hobdel, king of this notorious fraternity of dog-priggers.

Their system, in order to avoid detection, is to receive dogs stolen by their agents in the provinces, and send them on a migration tour: exchanging them throughout the country in every possible variety of direction. Fancy dogs were mostly reserved for the London market: and valuable sporting dogs sent as far from home as possible to one of the firm's respectable agents,—who, if the purchaser was at all inquisitive, very politely shewed a written card giving the late owner's name and address: for the dealer 'made it a rule never to receive dogs without such a warrant, as the practice of stealing them had become so prevalent of late.' Upon enquiry, the village or seat turned out a myth, and the 'late owner' never had any existence, save in the inventive imagination of king Hobdel.

After taking a glass of porter, this gentleman civilly invited me to look over his kennels, where dogs of every size and variety were to be seen, each chained so as not to be able to interfere with his neighbour. His menage consisted of two old cottages, which served equally for both his family and canine friends. Having looked over this filthy place, and feigned to be interested in the sight of the half-starved animals,—the stench being enough to poison a regiment of Hottentots,—I walked with him into the skittle-ground: and, being in such respectable company, was very politely asked to play at skittles, a game at which the gentlemen present were what is called 'sharps.' I consented: and each man now put in a 'piece,'—a knife, button, penny, sixpence, or anything else,—which articles are thrown up in the air; and the persons owning the two pieces nearest each other, on their falling to the ground, are partners against those owning the two furthest apart. The game is generally played two out of three; each player knocking down the pins in as few shots as he can, and throwing till they are all down, or counting one for the last pin standing. At this game, as well as at many others, they play 'three poll one.' This is managed by the 'sharp' who has the novice for his partner always contriving to lose the game, generally by one pin: so that if they play for money the 'green-one' only loses, and the other three divide the spoil in private.

I was well up in this business, and took no notice of their crafty proceedings, but played on till we lost six rubbers: then declaring myself tired, paid one-and-sixpence to the waiter (being my half of the loss), leaving the same amount to be paid by my 'sharp' partner. He very considerately offered to 'play off': that is, for one or the other to pay the whole of the reckoning; but as I declined playing any longer, they, to their sore mortification, had to pay sixpence each: and what added to their chagrin was the not being able to 'get on' a bet of a single shilling.

Sitting in the open space, smoking my pipe, and conversing with my acquaintance, the potent disposer of the canine species, I observed amongst the company (which had increased considerably) several females, young, good-looking, and smartly dressed in a peculiar flash style; they also wore large gold ear-rings, and had their hair parted and laid smoothly back from their foreheads. On a form in one corner of the ground sat a most wretched spectacle of human misery, blind and wrapped in filthy rags, scraping on an old fiddle; beside him sat a something that might once have been a woman,—but was now so transformed by filth and dissipation, that it was almost impossible to determine to what species such a creature belonged. Quarts of porter and half-pints of gin disappeared in quick succession; the girls and half-drunken men danced reels and jigs in supreme confusion, screaming and distorting their bodies into every imaginable posture, and setting every rule of order and decency at open defiance.

Just as this scene was at its height, a girl rushed into the midst of the bacchanalian crew, and seizing one of the dancing girls by the hair, twisted her round with all the fury of a maniac, using at the same time such language as I had never before heard from human lips. Presently they were parted, a ring formed, their hair and bosoms tied up, and a regular fight ensued: each combatant being seconded by brutal things called men. The abomination of this display transcended all I had ever witnessed, and far surpasses my powers of description. After fighting for more than half-an-hour, one of the poor creatures lay stretched upon the ground lifeless as a corpse; and in this state they carried her away (as I was informed by Hobdel) to her wretched home, a brothel in one of the alleys close at hand. At the outset I was about to interfere to prevent this inhuman scene, but was cautioned by the man I was talking with, who told me that if I did so, he would not give a farthing for my life.

The day was now drawing to a close: I withdrew quietly, fearing lest in their madness the wretches might attack and murder me: for their greatest delight seemed in the indulgence of their savage passions. Disgusted with the depravity I had witnessed, and sorry that poor humanity should be so degraded, I traversed the streets in a state of mental abstraction, wondering how, in a civilized and enlightened country, such things should be suffered to exist.

In this state of sorrow and perplexity I reached home, to find my poor old mother labouring under a rheumatic paroxysm, with which she was at times afflicted. I presently sat down and read several chapters in the Bible, which was always a source of great gratification to her: and after supper we enjoyed a long talk over by-gone days. The old lady seemed to live her girlhood over again: recalling in graphic terms the feasts and fairs, the Christmas holidays, birthdays, and harvest-homes, at which she had assisted, where innocence and freedom unrestrained shone through the laughing eyes of jocund youth,—and even age itself would join the throng, to lead its grandchild through the mazy dance.

Then lapsing into a graver mood, she described a frightful tragedy which occurred at Stourbridge-fair, when some heartless villains raised the cry of 'Fire' in the old wooden Theatre: when the building was crowded with country people, who had sought this annual mart in order to lay in a stock of requisites for the succeeding twelvemonth. She told how in the confusion some were trampled to death, and others maimed for life; some had their pockets cut from their sides, and gowns torn from their backs; how shawls and shoes were purloined, and rings forcibly torn from lacerated and bleeding ears.

Several of the poor bruised and wounded women were brought into our house, the doctor being sent for and every assistance rendered; their hurts having been dressed, and such restoratives administered as seemed necessary, they were then put to bed. Ours being a large old-fashioned farm-house had sufficient accomodation for a good many: and the parish constables, or such authorities as existed at the time, sent a proportionate number to each house. I can just remember seeing the women lying on the floor as they were brought in, and the doctor, with my mother and servants, dressing their wounds and carrying them up to our warm beds—from which we had been removed; and sat huddled by the fire, all wrapped in blankets; for the night was cold, as the event happened on the 27th of September.

Although my mother was a remarkably strong woman, this heart-rending scene affected her for a long time: and even in the recital, so many years after, tears rolled down her cheeks at the remembrance. Some indeed of the victims were relatives of hers, who had come from Linton and St. Ives to spend the day, and pass the night in dancing, as was the custom of the times. For these she had provided an ample feast; my father had selected the best joints, with ham and tongue; while puddings, pies, tarts, and custards were in great plenty. All was in readiness, waiting the arrival of our guests, when a cry of lamentation reached the hearing of the people in the village, although the theatre was full half-a-mile off. Frantic screams reverberated through the darkness, striking consternation into every heart; presently a crowd surged onwards,—whence emanated despairing cries, some calling in vain for husbands, others for wives, brothers for their sisters, and sisters for their brothers: whilst little children crying for their parents were taken up and carried by charitable neighbours. Such an awful catastrophe can be better conceived than described. This atrocious massacre was supposed to be the work of London thieves, who had resorted to the fair for the express purpose of reaping a plentiful harvest: however, the precise truth is not known—and most likely never will be.[1]

---

[1] "During the performance at the theatre at Stourbridge fair, on the 27th of September, a cry of fire arose in different parts of the house, which was exceedingly crowded. Although the manager and performers assured the audience that the alarm was without foundation, and tried every persuasion to obtain order, a general rush took place. Several persons scrambled down or threw themselves from the upper boxes and gallery into the pit. Some fell down the gallery stairs, and in the rush to get out three girls and a boy were thrown down in the crowd and trampled to death. Many other persons were violently bruised. It was supposed that the cry was got up by parties whose object was plunder. J. C. Hindes, the manager, offered a reward of one hundred guineas for the discovery of the miscreant, who however escaped detection."—*Cooper's Annals of Cambridge.* See also the *Annual Register*, under date September 28, 1802. The Play being performed, was the Comedy of *A Bold Stroke for a Wife.*

CHAPTER IX.

SKETCHES IN LONDON STREETS—SADLER'S WELLS—BROWN THE COSTERMONGER—OLD FRIENDS—BILLIARDS—A SET-TO WITH PADDY—THE TWO WEDDINGS—A ROMANCE IN REAL LIFE.

I HAD no business to demand my attention on the morrow: and, scarcely knowing how to pass the time, started forth to make my observations upon the endless variety of human countenances that are constantly succeeding each other in the main thoroughfares of the great metropolis. What an immense study is here presented; what pages to be read,—if we might judge by that index, on which some have affirmed that every passion and feeling of the soul is stamped with unerring truth,—indelibly cut in unmistakeable characters.

Here insolent PRIDE comes striding along, thrusting all meaner things aside, attended by watery-headed VANITY in holiday attire: stealthy AVARICE, with hollow eye and sunken cheek, casting suspicious glances round on every side, sneaks craftily with cautious steps: then bloated, blear-eyed DRUNKENNESS, with poisoned lips, reels by, infecting the air with burning and typhus breath: next the common THIEF, whose eye endures not to meet the light in his fellow-man's; for well he knows that the brand of shame is burning in his own: and thus conscience-stricken leads a coward's life, rather than earn his daily bread by manly labour. Now heart-broken SORROW, with pallid cheek and wasted form, struggles through the shifting mass: and here ghastly POVERTY, in well-brushed threadbare garments, shuffles on his path with soleless shoes, and vest tight buttoned to the chin, to hide the want of linen underneath. Behind him stalks a common gaol-bird, the genuine London 'Rough,' a character at open feud with all the decencies of life. Behold again, the sleek and oily HYPOCRITE, with every feature set to an air of godliness, walks the earth, looking with contempt upon the fallen sons of Adam, and cheating himself into the belief that he can impose upon his Maker as well as deceive mankind. Close upon his heels, scarcely less steeped in vice, comes the painted BAWD, (who has long since parted with all the more delicate attributes of her sex), seeking, like Satan, whom she may devour.

The ruined SPENDTHRIFT next occupies the scene, bent on inveigling some greenhorn into the den of thieves where he himself was plundered of his all. For he once possessed beautiful estates, and the title of a baronet: but now spends his nights in a loathsome hell, and shares the plunder of such victims as his craft entraps. He has disgraced a long line of noble ancestors; has brought his mother's grey hairs with sorrow to the grave; and now hastens to his own end, diseased, despised, and loathed by all mankind.

Returning from my tour of observation, and taking a retrospective glance at the varied phases of many-coloured life that had passed before my vision as in a panorama, gliding by like a fairy scene by moonlight, I reached home in time for dinner, which (as eating is to me nothing more than an act of necessity performed to sustain the body, and keep the mental powers in a healthy state) I despatched in a very short time: and after a brief nap, proceeded to Dalston to visit two young women from Cambridge, from whom I had received an invitation to spend the afternoon. When I arrived they introduced me to their family circle and visitors, in all a goodly company. Having spent the afternoon very pleasantly, and taken tea, the girls expressed a wish to see 'Sadler's Wells,' it being their first visit to London.

I at once agreed to be their convoy: and starting in good time we crossed Kingsland-road and proceeded through Rhodes's fields and past the 'Robin Hood' to the theatre, where Grimaldi's ever welcome 'Here we are!' at that period astonished the gaping cocknies: making amends for all the squeezing and pushing to gain admission. The entertainment was divided betwixt scenes on *terra firma* and at sea: the water at that time being let into the theatre from the new river; so that mimic fights took place with floating ships, magazines blew up, and all the incidents of a sea engagement were presented to the audience. At the conclusion of the performance my country lasses retired, well pleased with the novelties they had witnessed: and on reaching their place of sojourn, an excellent supper awaited us. In short, ere I again took my leave daybreak was at hand.

At last however I bent my steps homewards; but

proceeding along the road leading into Kingsland I heard, from some distance a-head, sounds indicating distress. Making therefore all the haste in my power, I soon came up with an old man, who was crying bitterly about his daughter; the said damsel being right in front of us, arm-in-arm with a young man. Upon enquiry, I learned that the old man had requested the girl to go home, and that the young fellow had consequently struck him. When we came up with them, I demanded how he dare set at defiance the father's authority, and add insult and outrage to an act of wrong; at the same time insisting that the girl should be allowed to go home with her legal protector.

Hearing this, the dastardly knave approached in fighting attitude; but as soon as he came within distance, I shot out my left arm, and sent him to his mother-earth. Having then seized the girl's wrist, I consigned her to her father's keeping: and next made a shew of taking my prostrate friend's name, which seemed to frighten him. The fellow was some time in regaining his perpendicular, and a more cringing coward I never looked upon. I was therefore content to threaten him with a warrant to answer before the magistrates of the district for his unmanly conduct, and pursued my journey homewards.

On the following day, having no particular object in view, I called upon a few members of the craft; most of whom were busily employed trying to fetch up lost time, which can only be done by working early and late. Here, comfortably seated on the only chair in the room, I smoked a short pipe, and talked over the merits of the prize-shoe, and the various incidents connected with the late gathering of the 'knights of the lapstone,' from every quarter of the metropolis. The number of visitors, I was now informed, had amounted to upwards of fifteen hundred; giving a profit to the landlord of something like seven pounds, besides what he gained by the sale of spirits and beer, which was no trifle.

Whilst thus engaged, the well-known voice of my namesake, a distinguished costermonger, reached our ears, crying, 'greens and turnips'; and as his appearance was always the prologue to a bit of fun, I threw open the window, and saluted him with—'Hallo, my friend! what, they've let you out again, eh? How long have you been in *college* this time? You'll get a pretty good education if you keep on! How many times a-week do they flog at your school?' In a second up went the costermonger's hat, off came his jacket, and he was in a fighting attitude in less than half-a-minute.

'What's the good,' I resumed, 'of your getting into a passion? You know you were shot in your hinder parts for stealing cabbages: and wasn't you forced to wear your wife's petticoats for more than a fortnight,— and didn't that happen at the time when your daughter Jemima was married to the clergyman,—and didn't the young members of the cloth stick you up in the middle, and dance round you with their shovels and brooms? And besides, you remember that bushel of potatoes in Spitalfields; when they washed you all over in one of their tubs, and then run you round the market to dry?' Foaming at the mouth, the incensed Mr. Brown now screamed out—'Come down here, you gallows warmint! what regiment did you desert from last?' Having got him up to this pitch, I shut the window, and left him vindicating his character to the crowd who stood by laughing at the fun. He had not got above fifty yards, when I again hailed him with—'Then you're forced to sneak off!'—and back rushed the purveyor of greens; while off went his jacket, and up flew his hat as before. But as he squared up and challenged me to fight, I coolly told him to wait till I came down: then closing the window, left the poor fellow to cool down by degrees.

After waiting some time, and finding that I was not likely to appear, my namesake walked away with a mob of children at his heels, and some of the crafty boys saying: 'they know'd it warn't true—that he'd never been in jail—and had never been shot in the stern for stealing cabbages—nor yet washed in a tub in Spitalfields, nor nothing of the sort.' Indeed, 'twas only a tale devised for the occasion,—a piece of mischief which, I must confess, does not redound much to my credit. Some time after, upon meeting him in the street, the costermonger earnestly implored me not to serve him so any more: saying that it was too bad,—as whenever he went that way the boys called after him, 'Who stole the cabbages?' After soothing his feelings with a few compassionate words and standing a quart of porter, the poor harmless fellow seemed somewhat reconciled; and, as I promised never to molest him again, he went away tolerably well satisfied: leaving me to reflect, that what is fun to the boy is death to the frog.

The time now beginning to hang heavy upon my hands, I took my leave, and started for the west-end, having formed an intention of visiting two young men, both of whom filled situations in grocers' shops. Arrived at Piccadilly, I found one of them as directed, whom I had not seen since we were boys at home; we could scarcely recognise each other, but exchanged civilities, promising to meet on Sunday and spend the day together. At parting, he informed me that my other old acquaintance had recently got married; and having some money with his wife, had started in business on his own account. I soon reached his abode, and seeing the well-known name over the door, entered the shop, expecting at least to be treated with courtesy; instead of which, the ill-bred mongrel affected not to remember whether I was myself or my brother, although we had both greatly befriended him as boys. For his parents were the poorest of the poor in our village; and often had my mother filled his belly and given him clothes, in those distressing times when children of his class often went supperless to their beds.

In mingled pity and contempt for the poor brainless thing, I left the shop abruptly, wondering at the pride and ignorance I had witnessed, and resolving to be cautious in future of introducing myself to old acquaintances; but I ought to state that this was the only instance of the kind I ever met with. I heard sometime afterwards that the upstart became a bankrupt, having cheated his creditors to a considerable amount; and, after quarrelling with his wife and parting from her, died in a loathsome state of a scorbutic disease with which he had been afflicted from his birth. This affection he used to hide as much as possible, by wearing shirt collars up to his ears, enveloped in the large cravat which was fashionable at the time. I have been told that this clumsy style was borrowed from France, and introduced into this country by the Prince of Wales, or some one about the court of George the Third. Be that as it may, the fashion has passed away with many other absurdities of that debauched and corrupt period of our history.

As I was returning through the Strand, I saw inscribed on the fan-light over an entry the words—'BILLIARDS—PUBLIC-ROOM.' I had never seen the game, and feeling a desire to know something about it, without further thought, walked through the passage and entered the room. Here I found two men contending at this beautiful game, who appeared excellent players; and several lookers-on were offering and taking bets as the game varied. My object being merely to observe, I took no part in the betting, although I might have done so, as it was not very high business; being principally half-crowns and shillings.

The match was soon finished, when the marker took away the balls, and reached down a bag containing others which he distributed to six persons. These balls, I could see, were numbered, and the game now about to commence was that known as 'Pool.' It may be said to bear the same relation to an ordinary game at billiards, as at cards *Vingt-un* does to *Ecarté*. I watched the proceedings most attentively, and soon began to comprehend the principles of this game.

When the marker was preparing to give out the balls for the next pool, I requested to be allowed to take a ball; for although I had never before played billiards, I could strike a ball with the greatest truth at bagatelle: and I knew that the utmost loss to myself would be but three-and-sixpence, even if I did not win a stroke. As I could handle a cue and strike a ball, I was not in any dread of being laughed at. It's generally said that the devil favours young beginners; so in this instance it turned out, for the balls ran so favourably for me, that I took lives enough to pay my pool. Encouraged by my unexpected success, I tried my luck a second time, but with a different result; taking only two lives, and being *minus* half-a-crown.

However I felt well satisfied. I had seen billiards and pool, which to me before were a perfect mystery; besides, I had been in company with a class of men very different from any with whom I was as yet familiar. Although by reading and observation I had formed a tolerable notion of what a gentleman should be, I now perceived that training and practice were indispensably necessary to the maintenance of that character.

There is nothing more grateful and satisfactory to an ardent and enquiring mind, than new discoveries. Every thing fresh and rare possessed indescribable beauties, and presented a boundless treat to my expanding soul. I luxuriated in contemplating the varied scenes of life, and now, entirely under the influence of this feeling, determined to dedicate as much time as I could possibly afford to the study of men and manners. There was nothing too high or too low for my investigations.

After quitting a scene far above my station in society, I returned to the dark slums of the city, and called at my old lodgings to enquire after my disinterested friend, the genius and philosopher, the recluse and philanthropist, for whom I entertained a feeling of respect approaching to veneration. Here I learned from the landlady of the house, that he had left; but whither he was gone, she could not inform me; he had paid his rent, and left suddenly. As I was very desirous of ascertaining my friend's whereabouts, I went upstairs into the room where I had formerly worked; and sat down among the men, expecting to hear some tidings of him; but to no purpose. All the information I could get was, that they thought he had gone to the west-end of the town.

During our confabulation, we had three or four quarts of porter, brought up by the landlord of the public-house not more than three yards distant; and hence ensued a little incident of an opposite nature to what I had seen in the early part of the day. At this public-house was held weekly, a 'set-to' principally among the Irish; for the landlord being an Irishman, his countrymen came to patronize him. It now happened that a burly fellow, who had been drinking just enough to make him fancy himself a hero, and render him a terror to his assembled countrymen, had put on the gloves and taken possession of the room, challenging any one to set-to. The publican knew me well, as having frequently put on the gloves there during the time that I lodged hard-by. He presently came uptsairs, and asked if I would just have a turn with a troublesome customer whom he hardly knew how to manage.

This was a business in which I always felt great pleasure, so I accompanied mine host: and had no sooner entered, than Paddy politely advanced from the other end of the room, and in a rich brogue said: 'Will you set-to, sir? by Jasus I won't hurt ye's.' 'Very well,' I said, 'if you won't hurt me I shall have no objection.' 'Oh, by the powers, sir, the devil a bit at all, at all!' Feeling assured there was little to fear,

I put on the gloves, and walking quietly to the scratch shook hands with my over eager opponent, who began hammering away right and left as if he'd got a hard day's work to perform: little considering that his arms would soon get tired. After bustling round the room, my legs came in contact with a chair which compelled me to drop on the seat; still he kept hammering away with all his might, determined to keep the advantage which he supposed he had gained, and fancying he had got it all his own way. But suddenly I slipped under his arm and bolted to the middle of the room, when Paddy came rushing after me as I had expected: and just as he came within reach I planted my left upon his most prominent feature, drawing forth an ample flow of claret, to the great astonishment of the Hibernian and the delight of the spectators, the majority of whom were Irish. The most galling part of the business was the chaff his countrymen cut at his expense, while he sat wiping the blood from his damaged frontispiece, and crying out: 'I don't like it at all, at all, and I don't like dem dat pershwaded me to it!' These little things would be of too egotistic a nature to set down, and savour too strongly of vanity: only that there are persons in every quarter where Englishmen are to be found, who know me either personally or by report.

Thinking it time to go home, I left this scene of low life, after receiving the thanks of the host and the congratulations of the company for the little amusement I had afforded them. I walked along, turning over in my mind the exterior difference I had this day observed between beings of the same species. I had by chance fallen into society such as I could not approach under other circumstances; here every man was on guard, standing sentry over his own words and actions, the countenance expressing manly dignity, the bearing erect, and every action of the body graceful. What a contrast to the poor untaught creatures I had just left, who regarded little beyond the gratification of their animal wants. It is a dreadful thing to note the remissness of the governments that allow such destructive material to accumulate unheeded: and to speculate upon the possible consequences to civilization, if they do not look better to their duties.

I had long entertained a wish to see my friend and fellow-traveller at Hampstead: so putting myself in order, on the following day I started with the anticipation of making a pleasant excursion. Just as I reached the 'Angel,' at Islington, a procession of carriages turned the corner; the postillions wearing white favours, and the parties inside being dressed in the most costly and gay attire, afforded unmistakeable evidence of the business they were upon. As I had never seen the marriage ceremony performed, curiosity prompted me to follow to the church: where I arrived before the minister had taken his place at the altar. He, however, soon made his appearance: and the bride and bridegroom with their attendants being ranged in order, the solemn service commenced.

Although the backs of the wedding-party were towards me, I could perceive a great disparity in the years of the principal actors in this important business of life; and as the ceremony proceeded, I observed that the bride trembled from head to foot, and could scarcely articulate the responses. When they arrived at that all-important point, the placing of the talismanic symbol on the finger, she fell back and was caught in the arms of her friends, whose countenances seemed to anticipate the sad occurrence. A painful delay ensued, until, with the aid of smelling-bottles and cold water, the victim so far recovered as to be able to complete the sacrifice. For sacrifice it was! Here was a sight for a noble heart to witness; here was a dreadful mockery of God's holy ordinance! When the poor drooping girl turned round, and was led by her attendant maidens towards the vestry, the resignation of despair was stamped upon her marble face: as if she had been changed from life and loveliness into stone, for violating nature's sacred dictates. Close behind her followed the hard-featured hoary-headed man, who had just been mated in solemn mockery to youth and beauty.

Can this sickening and loathsome act (I asked) have the sanction of the great Creator? And my sense of justice at once supplied the answer—'No: it's a lie, a gilded cheat, born of gross desires, and sanctified by hypocrisy.' Surely this crime shall be answered before the great tribunal of nature's God.

Ere this melancholy procession had cleared the aisle a second party was introduced by the clerk to the altar; but oh! what a glorious contrast to the preceding one! The bride had just attained the perfection of womanhood being a little above the ordinary height of her sex, her eyes were dark and penetrating, and her hair raven black, her countenance such as nature in her most triumphant mood might revel in creating; her lips were plump as cherry ripeness, and nature's untainted bloom shone upon her polished cheek; modest and serious she stood before the officiating priest, realizing my brightest visions of female loveliness.

The bridegroom was a fine young man, apparently about three or four and twenty: he was tall, with a noble brow and manly countenance; such as woman might look up to with respect, and feel proud in the performance of the sacred duties to which she binds herself by the most solemn obligations in the presence of her Maker. During the performance of the rites, the people who had followed to see them joined in the bonds of wedlock, looked on with unalloyed delight: and at the conclusion followed the bride and bridegroom to their vehicles, showering upon them blessings and good wishes for their future happiness and welfare.

As the carriages drove away, I asked an elderly female who and what the parties were, as the people appeared to be so much interested in them: observing at the same time that they were as proper a pair as my eyes had ever looked upon. In this opinion the old woman perfectly coincided, and without ceremony proceeded to give me their history in brief. The lady, whom she called 'Miss Ann,' was the only daughter of a rich builder, who had by persevering industry risen from a journeyman to be the largest contractor in that part of London. When she had attained fifteen years of age, a gentleman's son in the neighbourhood made overtures which she communicated to her parents, thinking they would be perfectly satisfied with so advantageous an offer; but the stern old man informed her at once that he would never consent to her being married to a man who could not work at a trade, whatever property he might possess.

The girl had taken a special liking to the youth, and with a heavy heart informed him of her father's determination: expecting that this would put an end to her fondly cherished hopes. What then must have been her surprise and pleasure, when her lover declared he would renounce his studies and learn a trade, or do anything that could be accomplished by man rather than part with her.

After entering into a solemn engagement to meet at the same hour, in the same place, that day three years, they parted. At the expiration of the time the girl proceeded to the appointed *rendezvous*, scarcely expecting to meet the object of her long-cherished solicitude. As she approached the trysting-place a full-grown man, in working costume, advanced, and taking her by the hand exclaimed—"I have succeeded!" Their first warm greetings over, they entered into arrangements for their future conduct.

The lover had determined to learn a trade of which her father was a judge, and he therefore articled himself to a first-rate man of the same business: in which by determined perseverance he became a competent workman. His next step was to apply to the father for work, which he readily obtained, as good hands were scarce at the time: and every evening met his affianced bride, in order to report the progress he was making in the good graces of the old man. After some months spent in his employ, he gave the latter notice of leaving in a month from that date. This was a source of great mortification to the master, as the stranger had evinced extraordinary aptitude and perseverance in getting work completed under all circumstances.

However, time progressed; the month expired. On the Saturday evening he went into the counting-house to receive his pay: and as the hour was approaching when he should be at the usual place of meeting, hurried thence to the spot. The youth now imparted to her (whom he loved with as pure and holy a passion as ever possessed the soul of man) his further intentions. 'I have done,' said he, 'all that your father required: and now, with your permission, will wait upon him on Monday morning, and ask his consent to our union.' The faithful and confiding girl assented: and having made arrangements for an interview with her parents, they embraced and parted.

The eventful morning shone forth all bright and auspicious, as the beautiful girl tremblingly awaited her lover's arrival. He at the appointed time appeared,—not in the habiliments of a workman, but dressed with the nicest care and furnished with all the appointments of a gentleman. Observing him pass the window she rose and opened the door, rather than ring for a servant. After a few minutes' conversation, she repaired to her father, and announced that a stranger desired to speak with him: upon which the old man requested her to shew him in. The business having been pre-arranged, they proceeded hand-in-hand to the presence of the stern judge, upon whose decision hung their destinies. Firmly and respectfully the lover urged his suit, setting forth his pretensions with modest dignity, and shewing how he had persevered to prove himself worthy of the father's confidence and his daughter's hand. The old man listened attentively to the end,—when, overcome with admiration at the noble and disinterested conduct of the young man, he exclaimed: 'This is the will of a higher power than man's, to which I bow.' Then rising, he took their hands and asked a blessing from that source whence alone the union of hearts is ratified.

My informant stated that 'Mr. E——,' as she called the hero of this interesting narrative, 'having been weaned from the pursuits of a gentleman, determined to improve his fortune by sticking to business: which so pleased the father of his destined bride, that he resigned the entire management into his hands, promising at the end of two years to retire, and at the same time to give his beloved and beautiful daughter in marriage. The time has just expired; and the ceremony you saw performed is the crowning point of his manly truth and perseverance. This, young man, is the cause of the demonstration evinced by the number of persons you saw both inside and outside the Church: who, from the knowledge they have of the parties, came determined to express their joy and satisfaction at the consummation of such well-merited happiness.' Highly gratified with the old lady's story and the truthfulness to nature she exhibited in telling it, I thanked her, and with the present of a shilling, bade her good-day.

As I walked away deeply impressed with the contrasted scenes so unexpectedly presented to my view, my whole soul was entranced; the painful sacrifice and its beautiful contrast were engraven on the tablets of my memory; they had become pictures, as it were, and filled choice spaces amid my cabinet collection. Whilst contemplating the first *tableau*, I ever shudder at the sight, and sicken over the details of sordid baseness, against which religion and humanity revolt, but which are quite agreeable to modern (so-called) refinement and civilization. I, for my part, prefer barbarism, so it walk hand-in-hand with nature and true affection; for what says the immortal poet?—

> "Things base and vile, holding no quantity,
> Love can transpose to form and dignity;
> Love looks not with the eyes, but with the mind:
> And therefore is wing'd Cupid painted blind."

CHAPTER X.

I RENEW AN OLD ACQUAINTANCE—BARTHOLOMEW'S HOSPITAL—ABERNETHY—THE CATO-STREET GANG—'DE MISHNER'—REAL CHARITY—'THE LORD'S PEOPLE'—THE END OF HONEST ARCHIE M^CGILL—'BARBER'-OUS PRACTICES—A BALL IN CATEATON STREET—GALLERY OF SELECT PORTRAITS.

THUS engaged in contemplation, I reached the pleasant village of Hampstead, and entering an old-fashioned public-house in the vicinity of his abode, enquired after my old fellow-traveller from Chatham. The landlord at once informed me that the gentleman would most likely drop in within half-an-hour, to take his accustomed glass of ale. As I sat conning the *Weekly Despatch*, my friend with some others entered the room. I rose to salute him, and for a moment he hesitated; but then at once recalling my face, shook me by the hand, and expressed himself glad to see me. The time since we parted had made but little alteration in *his* appearance, save that his whiskers were somewhat more bleached, and his person more plump and round.

For myself, instead of the short head of hair which was just growing again after being shaved off in hospital,

I had now a most luxuriant crop with whiskers black as coal; it was therefore no wonder that I should not be recognized at sight. Besides, having mixed more in society I had acquired greater freedom of speech, was better acquainted with ordinary usages, and was sufficiently 'up' in the leading topics of the day to handle them with tolerable fluency; all of which greatly aided my external metamorphosis. Having passed about an hour in pleasant conversation, my friend requested me to accompany him home.

On approaching the house, I perceived it was just in the same order as when I was there before: all bespeaking happiness and comfort. The door was opened by the same servant: the same little dog came barking into the passage,—but upon seeing his master wagged his tail and returned into the room, where sat the old lady and gentleman, a perfect picture of domestic ease and comfort. Being reintroduced to the old people, they expressed their surprise at my altered appearance, and gave me a cordial reception. During our conversation the old lady asked after my mother, and how she had borne the unexpected meeting. I gave a short account of my 'travel's history' since she last saw me to the present time.

When I had concluded, she expressed herself in terms of approbation of my conduct, and ended by saying, that, if I pursued the course I had so well began, she doubted not but that I should in time make atonement for all past follies. The day was spent as pleasantly as on my first visit: and when the time of departure arrived, my friend insisted on driving me into town. His chaise was light, the horse fresh and in good condition; so we soon reached the outskirts of the city, and pulling up at a noted house of entertainment took a parting glass, and separated in mutual good-will.

I had now gone through five days of my tour of observation, and on the morrow rose prepared to finish the week. Feeling a particular desire to know what had become of my eccentric shopmate and benefactor, I went to the clerk of his shops-meeting: from whom I learned that the object of my enquiry, being seized by a malignant fever, had been removed to Bartholomew's hospital. Without further ceremony I hastened thither, feeling it a part of my duty to render my old ally such assistance as lay in my power.

Entering the square of this noble Institution, I saw some poor maimed and sickly creatures crawling dreamily about, looking more like inhabitants of the other world than living and animate beings. None of these could inform me in which ward my friend was likely to be found: but on putting the question to a well-dressed man who stood on the steps leading into the building, I was by his direction shown into the spacious room where my sick friend lay with ten or a dozen others, all of whom looked ghastly and pale, and had white caps on their heads.

The place was beautifully clean, the floor and deal tables were comparatively white as snow; a card was attached to each bedstead, whereon was written the name of the patient and the doctor who attended him. The principal nurse or sister of the ward was a remarkably neat and matronly looking woman, apparently about fifty: to whom the greatest credit was due for keeping everything in such a creditable state. The under-nurses in attendance seemed to perform their duties with tenderness and care; in truth, the greatest order prevailed throughout.

Approaching the bedside of my poor friend, I would have taken his hand; but alas, he was too feeble to raise it from under the bedclothes; his fine large orbs had sunk back into their sockets; his cheek-bones projected, his temples were hollow, and his fine aquiline nose looked sharp and attenuated. His lips seemed parched and black from the consuming malady that pervaded his entire system; his tongue was no longer able to perform its office; but by following the motion of his lips, I could imperfectly understand him.

Whilst I sat beside the evidently dying man, a sudden and clattering noise issued from the passage. This was occasioned by the great Dr. Abernethy walking the round of his patients, followed by a number of students who had almost to run to keep up with him. Having heard and read a great deal about this extraordinary man, I followed to the door of the ward he had entered, for the purpose of taking a good impression of him. He was about the middle height, square built, with hard features, and had a bluff style of addressing the sick; he wore a blue coat, light waistcoat, and kerseymere small-clothes. There was a homeliness about him that gave him the appearance of a gentleman farmer; he appeared restless and impatient as he went from bed to bed visiting his patients, some of whom he spoke to very sharply; but this I suppose was only his way,—for no man could possibly bear a more excellent character.

To me, who have ever held genius and talent in veneration, as being

"Olympus high above all earthly things,"

the sight of this plain unostentatious man afforded more pleasurable feelings, than could all the gilded pomp beneath the sun. The great practitioner shortly returned, and left the building in the same hurried manner that he had entered it, followed by his pupils, who appeared anxiously to observe his every word and motion.

I remained about an hour with my fast declining friend, and then took a sorrowful leave of him,—promising to call on the morrow. My poor shopmate's case deeply affected me. I could not, indeed, but entertain the greatest regard for the man to whom I was so much indebted, for having raised me from a state of helplessness to comparative independence. Before leaving I had learned from the sister of the ward that there was not the slightest chance of his recovery; it was merely a matter of time: and that, she said, would be very short. Although I had been on such intimate terms with the departing, he never hinted even where his friends resided: and it was now too late to ask, for his power of speech was gone.

I therefore went round to several of the most respectable men in the trade, to make arrangements for his funeral. As there was no other way of defraying the expense but by subscription, two others with myself agreed to be answerable for the amount to the undertaker until the money could be collected. It is usual in such cases, and in those of sickness, to appoint two respectable and trustworthy men in the trade to visit every member: for which purpose they are furnished with the name and address of every man on the trades-books, by the clerk of each division. This is commonly done on Sunday mornings, as they cannot spare time on a week-day. No specific rate is set down; each man gives what he can afford, some being always better off than others; the amounts subscribed vary from half-a-crown to sixpence.

These arrangements completed, I repaired to the eating-house in Milton-street, kept by the old man who had been so tormented by the dizzy-brained 'snob,' as recorded in a former chapter. Here I dined with several of Thistlewood's gang, the well-known Cato-street conspirators—Davidson, Tidd, Ings, Brunt, Gilchrist, and others; this being the locality where many of them resided, and where their insane plot was hatched.

Amongst them, on this occasion, was the treacherous and cold-blooded wretch Edwards, the government spy and chief instigator of the contemplated atrocities. I well remember, after the execution of his poor deluded victims, having seen him soused with stinking water from the shoemaker's shop-tubs, as he sneaked through the narrow courts and alleys; he was a most repulsive and cadaverous looking wretch. Another of this lot was, to my knowledge, little better: being one of the most sneaking, cowardly knaves that ever disgraced the form of man; he still lives not half-a-mile from my dwelling, and imposes upon the benevolent by pretending to be religious. I will give a sample of his doings.

Some time ago there was in residence a fellow of St. John's College, a very charitable man: but one who indulged in that virtue to an admired extreme. Being in holy orders, he was accustomed to visit the poor: and amongst the number called upon this miserable trickster, who so wrought upon the good man's simple nature as to make a tolerable property out of sheer weakness. Whenever the amiable dupe of this dirty knave was seen to approach, the latter would call to his wife, 'D— your eyes, you ——, down on your knees: he e's L——w coming!' Thus did this worse than infidel impose upon his unsuspecting victim. I have been told that he has been known to go to Mr. L——w's rooms at breakfast-time, and so work upon his feelings that the good soul has allowed the knave to clear the table, and dispense with his own meal. Thus, between his hypocritical practices, and parochial relief obtained by false pretences, the fellow has managed to live in idleness for years.

Brunt was also a member of the gentle craft, but a mad enthusiast: who fell blindly into the flimsy trap set by the spies and minions of cruel and designing men in power. It was believed at the time that Lord Castlereagh sanctioned the proceedings, and paid the treacherous purveyors of treason and bloodshed; this is a sad blot upon the history of the period. Brunt's son was apprenticed to a boot-closer: the premium being raised by a subscription, towards which I gave my mite.

Having finished my meal, I left these poor deluded fellows (I had no inkling as yet of their secret schemes), and went round to several of the trade, to apprise them of the arrangements we had made for the interment of our respected shopmate; for I felt assured that many would like to follow him to the grave, as he had been highly esteemed by all who knew him.

While I sat talking to one of the men on whom I had called, in a very poor neighbourhood in the city, a sudden knock was given at the door. I turned the handle, and opened the door: which was no sooner done than a black woman entered, and upon being asked her business, said she was 'De mishner: dat she come to sabe de soul ob de nighted people, so dat de debil sant get old ob' em!' This was too much; it was so irresistibly comic, that we laughed most heartily. This was turning the tables upon us with a vengeance; we were sending out missionaries to christianize the heathen, and here a poor black woman was employed as the means of salvation in this our enlightened and christian land.

After the first impressions of this truly ludicrous scene had subsided, I felt indeed sorry to see such wretched means employed towards so important an end. Of all the maw-worm stuff that had ever come under my notice, this was the most unbearable exhibition I had ever witnessed. There was something so truly ridiculous in the poor creature's appearance and expressions, that I could not refrain from smiling: at which she flew into a great rage, exclaiming—'You won't laugh when de debil gits old ob ye!' However, finding she had but little chance of succeeding in her mission, the negress withdrew, looking something like a painted semblance of the old gentleman she quoted so freely.

There is nothing in my estimation more disgusting than hawking and bawling about religion in the public ways. I have known several of the most disreputable men that ever lived, engaged in parading their hypocrisy before the public: there is one of the worst characters that ever came under my notice, going about London as a local preacher. He was convicted of housebreaking, and sentenced to two years on the treadmill; after which he joined the Ranters: and, like a great many of that fraternity, cloaked an immoral life under the forms and disgusting mockeries of genuine piety. I had seen so much of this vile cant in my boyhood, that the bare remembrance of it awakens thoughts and feelings of indignation.

The day was fast declining and my week of observation nearly ended: so, taking leave of my brother-craft, I strolled through the great thoroughfares of the city to pass the time till nine o'clock, when I was to meet my shopmates with whom I spent the previous Saturday evening. The time having arrived I made for the place, and upon going into the room recognised several whom I had not seen since my return from the country. As I approached to shake hands with one, I perceived that he was blind. Poor fellow! it was a sorrowful sight: and what made it appear more so, he was a fine-looking man and a most desirable companion, being of a lively disposition and an excellent singer,—indeed, he had been trained in a Cathedral choir. He seemed tolerably cheerful under his lamentable deprivation; and after a time the chairman asked him to favour the company with a song, which he did: and in such a style as no untutored voice could have accomplished.

The chairman having then requested the use of a couple of plates, one of the company went round: and a collection was made for their blind friend, which amounted to fifteen shillings. This had been their custom every Saturday night since he had lost his sight: with which sum, and eight shillings per week received from his club,—besides what he cleared by selling nuts,—he managed to support his family. The company being composed of men of steady habits and good character, had nearly all departed before the clock struck twelve, at which time I left: thus finishing off the first entire week that I had passed in idleness since I was eleven years of age.

The morrow's sun shone forth in dazzling splendour; the beautiful azure canopy above seemed translucent as crystal; the atmosphere sparkled with light; and all nature appeared lulled into glorious repose. Impressed with the majesty of the scene, I, in silent admiration, did homage to the omnipotent Creator of the universe. The tradesman had forsaken his business, the tools of the artisan lay idle on the bench, the toiling millions rejoiced in their rest: all giving evidence of the wise and holy institution vouchsafed to man, that his strength and energies may be restored to their proper tone of action ere recommencing the labours of the six days wherein he shall earn his bread.

As with feelings of reverence for this beneficent dispensation I went forth to visit my dying friend, I observed a number of very poor women and children enter a narrow passage near Smithfield. Thinking they were going to some place of worship, I enquired: and was told they were followers of that miserable impostor Johanna Southcote. Being desirous of knowing something of their doctrine and manner of paying their devotions, I followed them up a ladder with broad steps which led to a spacious loft, the rafters and tiles of which were bare. A few rough deals were fixed round for seats, and a sort of pulpit (something like a sentry-box of unpainted deal) was stuck in one corner.

The priest was a tall, dark figure, apparently about thirty, having a profusion of long black hair dropping loose down to his shoulders, with an ample flowing beard descending to his breast. After offering up a prayer with much outward solemnity, he read aloud a chapter from the Bible, and then prepared to address his congregation: which consisted, besides myself, of three miserable looking men, nineteen poor looking women, and about a dozen ragged children of both sexes. His address, or sermon, or whatever he pleased to call it, commenced thus:—'My dearly beloved brethren, if you go into a Catholic chapel, they will tell you 'We are the Lord's people;' if you go into a Protestant church, they will tell you the same; and if you enter a Dissenting chapel, there is a like story; but, my dearly beloved brethren, —YOU are the Lord's people, and no other!'

Just at this moment, up came two half-drunken mechanics with aprons on and short pipes in their mouths, who seemed rather astonished at the scene before them. This unseemly intrusion quite disconcerted the man in the deal box, and brought him to a dead standstill: when one of the intruders bawled out: 'I say, Mr. Blackbeard, what sort of a game do you call this?' The preacher recovering his speech, consigned the pair without ceremony to the bottomless pit; and the congregation rose in great confusion: the old men, women, and boys scrambling and tumbling about in their endeavours to eject the unwelcome visitors. The noise reminded one of a disturbed rookery. During this hubbub I slipped out, having seen quite sufficient to satisfy my mind about these deluded people.

I now repaired to the hospital; where, as I entered the ward, the sister informed me that my old comrade's end was fast approaching. I cast a look round to the corner bedstead where he lay, and perceived his breathing to be difficult, and accompanied with a rattling noise in the throat. As quietly as possible, I seated myself upon the locker by his bedside, and watched the feeble struggles of his departing spirit. Whilst I sat indulging in serious thoughts and speculations upon the impenetrable future, I perceived the shrunken skin quiver on the bony cheeks; the eyes opened wide; and the skeleton form made one convulsive effort to rise. 'Twas nature's last struggle 'twixt time and eternity! Having closed the eyes of the departed, and offered up a short prayer in silence to the throne of mercy, I withdrew from the melancholy scene, and repaired to the undertaker to request his immediate attendance.

On the following day the corpse was borne to the humble lodgings of the deceased, deposited in its coffin, and there kept till the next Sunday: when it was followed to the grave by a great number of the best crafts of the day; for no one was held in higher estimation in the trade than poor Archie McGill. If what I am now writing should ever be published to the world, it is just possible that his surviving relatives may come to a just conclusion as to his end, which, I feel convinced, has hitherto been a mystery to them. That he sprung from a goodly stock was evident: nor need his kith and kin be ashamed of the branch thus fallen from the family tree. Although no stone marks the spot of his rest, he sleeps in good company; for his bones were laid in the same ground that is consecrated by the ashes of Milton and De Foe.

Having performed this last sad duty, we repaired to the 'Crispin' to receive the amount subscribed towards defraying the funeral expenses: when, upon putting the different collectors' monies together, we had twenty-five shillings over and above the undertaker's bill. This, it was resolved, should be divided betwixt two poor widows who had been left with families. I now took my leave of the generous souls who had given their time and means in aid of a sacred duty, and paced my way homewards in a sorrowful and reflective mood.

On the following morning I went at once to the secretary of the Clickers' Society to enquire if any applications had been made for persons wanting situations. I was informed that there was a place vacant in Cheapside: the man who held the situation having by some means lost forty pounds belonging to his employer. But this result was no matter of wonder; the fellow was an inveterate fuddler, and (worse than that) would commit any mean act in order to gratify his bestial propensity. Nothing can be more pitiful and despicable than taking bribes of the workmen, a practice of which he was guilty to a great extent. A pair of fowls for his Sunday dinner, a gown-piece for his wife,—all was fish that came to his net; and this was done to the detriment of the best workmen, who are mostly of higher character than would stoop to such degrading trickery.

However, as retributive justice is, sooner or later, sure to overtake the perpetrator of evil deeds, the powerful and unseen arm fell upon him with crushing force. His dissipated habits had always kept him behindhand; and as soon as it become known that he had lost his situation, and with it his character, the landlord seized for rent: everything was sold, and the poor wretch was compelled to take shelter in the workhouse.

On making application for the post thus vacant, I was at once approved of by the proprietor; but here a difficulty presented itself. My late master was dead and the business had passed into other hands; consequently I could not refer to my last situation for a character, which was indispensably necessary. What was to be done? The thought struck me that I would name my barber-master at Cambridge, whose fame had been raised and established by my abilities when I obtained for him the Royal Arms. I mentioned him accordingly: and a letter written in my presence was at once sent to post.

On the Wednesday following I called, expecting that an answer would have arrived: but none had been received; the next day the same; and so on to the end of the week. As all parties now began to grow impatient, I wrote to my brother, who had lately returned to Cambridge and commenced business on his own account. I requested Bill to ask the unmannerly knave why he did not answer the application for my character. The sneaking cur now made some frivolous excuses: such as, that I had been in another situation,—and that I did not behave well to him in making some boots for several of the fellows of St. John's College, after I left his shop! Disgusted at the paltry conduct of a man who had been so much benefited by my exertions, I made up my mind to prepare my kit and return to the 'seat.'

My name being well known in the city, I had no difficulty in getting work: which having procured I set to in good earnest, and determined to make the best of it. In a pecuniary point of view it made little or no difference, but in other respects being at the board was preferable, inasmuch as it was much cleaner work; and the position is also considered more respectable. However, I made up my mind to bow to the will of fate: and being young, and of a buoyant and sanguine turn of mind, I looked forward with hope to a future of glowing brightness. Although able to laugh at this folly, I could not divest myself of the feeling; and under the most disadvantageous circumstances, this peculiar influence ever possessed me.

In the winter season, after leaving work, I amused myself by attending to a set-to, or a free-and-easy, or playing at draughts or cribbage. Sometimes I would go to a dance, which the parties concerned called 'a ball.' I remember on one occasion being present at a thing of the sort, at an inn in Cateaton street; the tickets were ten shillings each. The room, which was very spacious, was lit up with chandeliers, and filled with company: a very large majority being females.

At first sight I took them for ladies and gentlemen: but after dancing about two hours, I got into conversation with a smart lively fellow, from whom I learned the true character of the charming circle. He informed me that the gay throng was made up of members of the frail sisterhood and their fancy men:

some of the latter being 'prigs,' 'smashers,' and housebreakers,—others shopmen and clerks, who spent ten times the amount of their earnings upon these fascinating sirens,—of whom many not only danced, but sang in excellent style. Some indeed possessed accomplishments that would have graced any station in life.

My new acquaintance undertook to describe some of the most prominent figures in the picture. "That tall fine creature," he observed, "with auburn hair and blue eyes, looks at the first glance like a pattern of decorum; but observe her closely: watch the motion of her eyes, and the voluptuous expression of her mouth. Although she appears a fine full-grown woman, she is not more than seventeen: but has been two years in the keeping of Captain D—— of the Guards. He has lavished upon her immense sums, which she spends upon that handsome youth with curly hair and black whiskers, of whom she is madly jealous. Were he to pay the least marked attention to any female in the room, she would seize him like a tigress; *I have seen her do it!*

"However he knows his place, and keeps it; he is the son of poor parents who gave him an education far above their means, and placed him in a merchant's counting-house in the city: but since he became acquainted with this seductive girl, he neglected his duties, lost his situation, and is now entirely dependent on her prostitution. Now observe that sprightly little woman tripping along with the lightness of a fairy. Although entirely uneducated, she has acquired the style and manners of fashionable life, but is as well known in the city as Aldgate Pump. The man with whom she is dancing is one of the most successful 'fences' in London; they live together as man and wife: and so secretly have their illicit operations been carried on, as to baffle the vigilance of the most active Bow-street officers. It has indeed been strongly suspected that, in many instances, they shared the 'swag'; however that may be, it is quite certain that our friend has never been detected, although he has been at this game from boyhood, and has accumulated considerable property.

"Mark next that elderly female with a kind of turban round her head, and a sparkling ornament in the centre; the paint upon her cheeks is so thick, you might fancy it had been laid on with a bricklayer's trowel. Those girls you see talking to her are her daughters, whose father she contrived to get transported, by secreting some stolen property about his person, and then betraying him into the hands of *justice!* Her incentive to this fiendish act, was the desire of enjoying undisturbed infamy with her paramour,—yon tall, sinister-looking fellow with a bald head; he was one of the most expert housebreakers of his time: and although tried three times at the Old Bailey, always managed to escape, in consequence of the evidence not being 'sufficiently conclusive' to convict him. The worthy couple now keep a brothel in the City-road, which is chiefly supported by the old beldame's daughters, four in number; and all have been trained to thieving and prostitution. This, you'll say, is a nice family party.

"I will now draw your attention to a character, which otherwise might have escaped your notice. Do you perceive that withered-looking hag, sitting in a corner of the room? She is the most notorious procuress in the metropolis, and has been the means of seducing more poor girls, than any of her rivals in the same hellish trade. You see the delicate child who is just now approaching her; that victim has been recently inveigled from a widowed mother, who is very poor: she will ere long be sacrificed to some rich debauchee.

"It is extraordinary what sums of money this devilish woman gets by her abominable traffic. The net in which she entangles her victims, is cunningly and elaborately wrought. Whenever she sees a girl likely to suit her infernal purpose, some pretext is devised for entering into a conversation,—in the course of which, every species of corruptive art and seductive allurement, are dexterously employed; or, failing to succeed alone, she calls in the aid of her retainers,—two or three girls elegantly attired, and kept as decoys,—who fire the weak imagination of the doomed one with the most enchanting prospects. If the latter be once persuaded to set foot in the tempter's den, she is lost for ever; force or fraud will achieve the rest.

"Just to complete our picture-gallery, I will lastly introduce to your notice a character as opposite to those I have described, as could be found in nature. Look to the right, and you will perceive a spruce dandy-looking fellow with black hair, curled all over like a poodle-dog: he is conversing with a dark-eyed Jewess, the daughter of a celebrated pugilist. That youth is the only son of one of the most wealthy merchants in the city: and in the common course of events, will be heir to a million sterling. He is so infatuated with the girl to whom he is now talking, that he lavishes his money and attentions upon her in the most insane manner. Poor deluded fool! The woman is fairly surfeited with his fulsome assiduity: but bears with him, for the sake of the rich jewels and costly presents that attest the sincerity of his devotion. Thus our 'Master Simple' not only wastes time and substance, but also risks character and prospects: whilst the object of his passion heartily despises him, and bestows her favours upon a swain of her own tribe."

Having concluded these interesting delineations, my lively informant prepared to take his departure. The morning was now fast advancing; so as I had seen enough of this congregation of 'pleasant vices,' I also retired: and, after walking along with the stranger as far as Finsbury-square, bade him good night, with thanks for the information he had given me. I soon reached my lodgings, which were close at hand; but the novel scene I had witnessed, together with the graphic sketches of my stranger acquaintance, continued to occupy my thoughts. And the moral of my reflections was,— that vice, however gilded over, is still a hideous monster; in which conviction, I resigned myself to that power that 'must delight in virtue.'

CHAPTER XI.

WORKING DOUBLE TIDES—THE IRISH 'COCK AND HEN' CLUB—ROUSE'S CONCERTS—THE 'WAKE'—I FIGURE AS A WITNESS AT GUILDHALL—THE RESULT—AN ENTERTAINMENT—THE BOOT-CLUB.

WHEN I rose to begin work, the morning was on the wane: so that all my energies were needed to accomplish twelve hours' work within ten hours—a very natural consequence of last night's amusement. However, as it had ever been with me a rule to 'will the thing and do it,' by making the hand obedient to the mind, I finished my task within the time; and arrived at shop before the clock struck seven—the hour appointed for giving out stuff. Had I been later, I must have been without work the whole of the next day, which would have been a loss to me of seven shillings: that sum being the wages for a pair of boots at the shop for which I worked. As 'the trade' may ask, 'What shop?'—I at once, for their information, state that I refer to the establishment of JAMES, in the old Jewry. Jones was clicker there at the time, a man well known in the trade, and who must still be remembered by most of the 'old crafts' in the city, such as my esteemed friend, Tom Moynes, the celebrated kit-maker, than whom a finer specimen of manhood does not walk the earth. There are many others still living, who remember the circumstance to which I have referred in this trifling episode.

Desirous of recruiting my somewhat exhausted powers, I now prepared my stuff for the morrow's work, and retired to rest in good time. Hence, on rising in the morning, I felt myself equal to anything that might be expected from me; the day glided pleasantly away, my task was accomplished in good time, and after going to shop and taking out my materials for the next day, I repaired to the public-house hard by. I knew the landlord very well, and was on friendly terms with him; this was what is termed an 'Irish' house, and the host, himself an Irishman, had but little indoor custom except amongst his countrymen: and they were mostly of the labouring class. I was well known to the different parties that used the place, and was invariably treated by them with great civility. There was one young man, a breeches-maker, with whom I was intimately acquainted; he worked at a shop close by, on Moorfields pavement, and happening just now to drop in, asked me, "If I had ever been to an *Irish* 'cock and hen' club?" Upon my replying that "I had not," he requested me to go upstairs: saying, that I should see some excellent fun.

The room we entered was about forty feet by twenty, rather indifferently lighted; the company was a motley gathering of choice Hibernian specimens, both male and female. Quarts of porter were circulated in rapid succession; half-pints of gin were gallantly handed round to the 'ladies,' with compliments in Irish, pure as the sweet waters of Killarney. As their hearts warmed with potent draughts of the 'cratur', they began capering about and whirling round with the velocity of spinning-wheels,—occasionally, in the course of their evolutions, giving vent to such discordant shouts, as called to mind the descriptions of an Indian war-dance.

At length the floor was cleared: and two fine daughters of the emerald isle, stepping gracefully into the centre, commenced a jig. They began to slow time, but kept on gradually increasing in speed amidst the shouting and clapping of hands, till both performers appeared wrought up to the highest pitch of frenzy; and perspiration streamed down their blowzy faces as they whirled dizzily round, urged on by the mad drunken creatures that surrounded them, until one dropped from exhaustion. This was considered a great triumph, as it was well known in their own circle that there had been a challenge between the two parties; I think my companion informed me that they were respectively from Connaught and Munster.

As the girl who had tired the other down was a great favourite, the delicate half-swipy gentlemen surrounded her: all scrambling to snatch a kiss from the lips of the victorious damsel, who had saved the credit of their province. The vanquished was taken below, and received the benefit of the pure air to be found in the skittle-ground,—for this was one of the most confined and offensive localities in London; the sign of the house was the 'Punch-bowl,' in Half-moon alley, Little Moorfields. When the girl had recovered from the effects of her over-exertion, she was brought back into the room by her friends; and singing and dancing continued till the entire group was furiously excited. One of the pot-valiant heroes smashed the fiddle, because the fiddler was too far gone and had fallen asleep, his head hanging over the back of his chair in the corner.

At this peculiar juncture, a mighty storm arose in the assembly. One Jim Donohoe was seen to kiss Mr. Pat Flannigan's wife as she came up the stairs: 'Och, by St. Pathrick,' roared out Pat, 'and is it *that* you mane, Mr. Donohoe?'—'You dirty spalpeen,' retorted Jim, 'I don't care the great-coat of a pratie for the like o' yees, nor all the Flannigans 'twixt here and Belfast, your dirty native place!'—'Och, by the powers then,' said Pat, 'just be after bringing your filthy carcass downstairs, and I'll tache you better manners than you ever larned under that bottle-nosed ould sexton of a Protestant at Mullingar: where you could never git a congregation at all, at all, if the ould woman as opened the pews happened to be sazed wid the toothache!'

'D'ye say that, ye dirty blackguard!' roared out Jim; 'faith, and I'll make ye know your lord and master from Biddy Sullivan!' Downstairs they rushed by mutual consent: and at it they went in true Irish style,—when both being drunk, tumbled against each other and fell rolling over like a couple of hogs at sea. After this splendid display of science the combatants were propped up, while they shook hands, kissed, and made it up; but in attempting to put on his shirt poor Jim was terribly bothered. The sleeves had got so entangled with the fragments of the body (which was slit into ribbons) that from what was once a shirt, it had become a puzzle of so difficult a nature that the poor fellow gave up the attempt in despair, exclaiming: 'By Jasus, although I've been a long time acquainted wid yees, I can't find the way into yees at all, at all,—any more than if we'd been strangers!' With this short soliloquy he gave up the job, and put on his clothes without the usual under garment.

Treating the late belligerents to half-a-pint of whiskey at the bar, we took leave of the interesting revellers: and strolling up the City-road as far as the Angel, on our return looked in at old Rouse's twopenny concert; the tickets for which were eight-pence, but each entitled the bearer to sixpenny-worth of grog. Here some of the best room-singers of the day were engaged; amongst them was Charley Rayner, with Bob Glendon, Joe Martin, and other celebrities of the time; there were also two brothers (boot-closers) who recited remarkably well.

The company was a mixture of both sexes, and of all ages, from sixteen years of age up to middle life; nay, even grey-headed old men and women were there, who seemed as well pleased as their juvenile companions. On a platform elevated about three feet from the floor stood a piano; at which a man presided, who accompanied the vocalists. Some of these could sing to music; but in the case of such as could not, the pianist accommodated the music to the voice, as he best might. The singers were introduced according to the programme, and announced by a conductor or master of the ceremonies; and, on finishing their allotted parts, each and all enjoyed a hearty round of applause.

Rouse, the proprietor, was very particular in keeping order during the hours of performance: and, always proceeding systematically, in the end found himself at the head of a most superb establishment. I have never seen a place of the kind fitted up with such taste and elegance; the grounds are spacious, lighted up with a profusion of gas, and ornamented with grottoes and statues; the saloon, or theatre, is commodious and beautifully adorned with various designs painted on the panels of the dress-circle, which have a very lively and pleasing effect.

But at the time when my friend and I spent our evening here, the original house yet stood. It was an old-fashioned inn, called the 'Shepherd and Shepherdess', with skittle-grounds attached, and a few ill-conditioned arbours where the company smoked their pipes and quaffed their ale. At the back part of the premises, the 'governor' had raised (what he called) 'Russian mountains,' with steep circuitous pathways, made corkscrew fashion, and running from top to bottom: down which the adventurous public travelled in chairs with considerable velocity. The charge for this amusement was something very trifling—I believe a penny, or twopence; but the numbers made it a profitable speculation. From such small beginnings did 'governor Rouse' elaborate that famous resort known to the world as the 'Eagle tavern' in the City-road.

On the conclusion of the performances, we made the best of our way home; and parted under a promise to meet again the next evening at the 'Golden Hind' in Little Moorfields, kept by one of my friend's countrymen named Murphy; where we frequently met some excellent players at 'draughts,' in which game both of us were also acknowledged proficients. Eight o'clock being the time appointed for our meeting, I repaired punctually to the little back-parlour, which was our usual *rendezvous*. On entering the room, I found my friend in serious conversation with a man whom I had frequently seen in the same place, a cooper by trade, who worked at the docks. I soon gleaned from their conversation, that the cooper was inviting my friend to accompany him to an Irish wake: which the latter declined doing, on the ground that he was engaged to spend the evening with me. To obviate this little difficulty, I was also invited; and having never witnessed this ceremony, (except as typified in the wild grief of the poor young widows on board the *Tigris*[1]) I readily availed myself of the occasion; and we all set out for the locality indicated.

The house was situated in one of the most secluded and dirty lanes betwixt Cripplegate workhouse and Fore-street, then called Featherbed-hill. As we approached the door, which was open, I perceived a number of lighted candles ranged in order, which were stuck into ginger-beer and blacking-bottles. Upon a table close to the door was a plate containing a quantity of silver coin,—into which my two friends threw a shilling each, as did I also, understanding such to be the custom: and then taking my seat on a plank laid between two chairs, proceeded to take a cautious survey of the company who were jabbering away together in their native Irish.

All present seemed of the lowest order; and in one corner sat three hideous-looking old women smoking short pipes black as ebony; it struck me they would

---

[1] *Supra*, Part II. Chap. IV.

have done well for the witches in Macbeth. Some of the younger females had washed their faces, and put on what (I suppose) were intended for clean caps; but the dresses of the entire company were neither of the finest quality nor latest fashion; and were besides, in many instances, considerably patched.

At the further end of the room was the corpse, laid out in white, and surrounded with candles, which threw a glare of light upon the sickening spectacle. The child (for such it was) had died of the most virulent kind of small-pox; the head had swollen beyond all proportion, and wore the appearance of an immense plum-pudding; the features being absolutely obliterated by the horrid disease. Two large bunches of flowers were placed on each side of the body; where sat the parents and kindred of the deceased. In the centre stood a can of beer and three or four earthern pots without handles, which were constantly being handed round,—with, at intervals, a glass of the 'cratur.'

As the liquor began to operate the talk became fast and furious: but what was said I knew not, as all was carried on in the Celtic vernacular. Just when the storm was at its height, the before-mentioned old women broke out into the most hideous yells that ever scared man or beast; the other females joined in a chorus loud enough to have awakened all the Irish that have been buried since the days of St. Patrick; the men began raving and fighting; pots and cans flew about in every direction: over went the tables, out went the lights, and lastly down rolled the corpse upon the floor to be kicked and trampled on by the bacchanalian mourners!

Of all the absurd rites connected with the idea of a

religious (!) observance, the ceremony above described is certainly about as brutal and debasing, as any ever practised by the veriest savages in creation. I sat near the door; and, having taken the precaution to put my hat under the seat, as soon as this infernal hubbub reached its climax, I made a hasty retreat, followed by my friend and by the man who had introduced us to this extraordinary exhibition. Glad as I was to escape from such a disgusting scene, I nevertheless felt gratified that I had at least witnessed something to be remembered. The frantic sounds soon died away in the distance: and finding that it was still early, I invited our late guide to return with us and take a glass of grog.

He assented, and we all three again entered the house whence we had started for the 'wake.' Here the principal room was crowded to suffocation: the reason of which was that a committee, appointed to receive subscriptions for the purpose of building a Catholic chapel in Moorfields, had been sitting. The secretary, who, not having yet put up his books, was smoking a pipe in self-defence, very politely asked me to subscribe towards the work in hand; which to those of his faith was, he said, a desideratum of the highest importance. My reply was: 'In religious matters I am no bigot; I presume all good men to be guided by those imperishable laws which our common Creator has established for the welfare of the entire human family; I therefore most willingly tender you a crown, which is as much as I can afford.' The money was received with thanks mingled with some degree of surprise: for they all knew me to be English, and as a matter of course, a Protestant.

But throwing off all the shackles that were ever forged to enslave the mind, I say with Pope—

> "For modes of faith let senseless bigots fight:
> His can't be wrong, whose life is in the right!"

As the time arrived for the company to depart, I rose to leave: but having occasion to go through the yard, I heard voices in earnest talk on the other side of the wall which separated the yard from the court adjoining. Prompted by curiosity, I looked over the wall, and distinctly saw under the archway two of the men from whom I had just parted. They were talking over the proceedings of the evening, quite loud enough to be heard by anyone passing the end of the court,—but in the most orderly and steady manner possible. One of the parties was named Kelly, a most powerful man, the strongest (I had been informed) that ever came from the part of Ireland to which he belonged; the other was named Donoghoe, a great jumper, who once cleared twenty-one feet on the level: which was considered a great feat.

All at once a sudden and unexpected attack was made upon the speakers, by two men armed with constabulary staves; who declaring themselves to be city officers, proceeded to take both into custody for a breach of the peace! Kelly was not the man to stand this sort of nonsense; but he had scarcely, with one powerful swing of his arm, swept his immediate assailant into the opposite gutter,—the official's hat rolling in another direction,—ere the notorious Tom Evans made his appearance, followed by a number of young fellows designated the 'City-road gang,' of which he was captain;

and I observed that one of the new comers took up the vagrant hat, and carefully pitched it over a high wall close at hand. Mixing with the crowd that had by this time collected, I followed the parties to the watchhouse; and after seeing them passed in, went quietly home.

Turning over in my mind the piece of villany I had just witnessed, I determined to go before the magistrates next morning and state what I had seen. Half-an-hour before the business of the day commenced at Guildhall, I went into Murphy's (the house which the two men had just left, when they were attacked and taken into custody), and found the old man in great grief, lamenting the unhappy circumstance; but dressed ready to go to court and watch the proceedings. I at once proposed to accompany him, reserving to myself the knowledge I possessed connected with the entire circumstances of the case. On entering the time-honoured hall, I perceived that the seat of justice was filled by Sir John Haymer. Barristers and attorneys sat lazily looking on, as the prisoners were placed in the dock; whilst their vile accusers stood by in all the complacency of official self-esteem. For, as the poet says: 'O what a goodly outside falsehood hath!'

The court was crowded; and as the wretched satellites took the sacred volume in their hands, swearing in the presence of their God to speak the truth, the whole truth, and nothing but the truth,—I blushed for human nature.

The evidence they gave was necessarily a tissue of lies,—not one word of truth, nor anything approaching to it, escaped their lips. When the prisoners were asked if they had any questions to put to the self-constituted witnesses and accusers, Kelly asked them: 'Why, when he and his companion were simply saying a word or two at parting, they came rushing upon them as rioters or robbers?' The dastardly knaves looked foolish; and simply reiterated the first part of the charge, namely, that the two were committing a breach of the peace: which Kelly and his friend designated as a 'wicked lie.'

The magistrate now asked the accused if they had any witness in court, to which they replied—'No: there was not a soul near when the officers assaulted them; and although within a minute from the commencement of the affray many people came up, it was impossible that any of them could speak to what had occurred at the commencement.'

Just as Sir John was about to decide the case on the evidence (such as it was) I asked the crowd to make way, which they did with great readiness; and having reached the centre of the floor, I requested to be heard: telling his worship that I had witnessed the whole transaction from beginning to end. This seemed to take the entire court by surprise,—magistrate, prisoners, officers, and all.

As soon as the buzz had subsided, Sir John asked me my name and profession, evidently mistaking me for some one in a higher position: as I wore a good suit of black, and had on a white cravat. When I told him that I was a bootmaker, he asked me whether master or journeyman. I told him the latter, and gave the name of my employer,—which he observed was sufficiently respectable.

The clerk of the court then proceeded to administer the oath and take down my deposition; and when I had concluded, a feeling of satisfaction seemed to pervade the entire assembly: a feeling too which was expressed in more than whispers of wonderment at the rascality which had been practised. The chap-fallen knaves in the meantime stood there self-convicted; their countenances unmistakeably expressive of guilt and shame, and all the accompaniments attendant on detected crime.

In a few minutes the worthy magistrate ordered the prisoners to be dismissed, and peremptorily desired the officers (whom he at once suspended) to appear before the authorities from whom they had received their appointments. They were of course dismissed in consequence: and frequently have I since beheld them crawling about, the most abject wretches in life,—shoeless, shirtless, and without food; for no man commiserated their miserable condition, after it became known that they had obtained a livelihood by wholesale perjury.

On quitting the court, the men who had been so unjustly treated, expressed their gratitude to me in the warmest terms. But I replied that they were under no obligation for the little service I had rendered them,—I had only done what I conceived to be my duty; and as their wives and friends were waiting for them outside, I bade them good day and steered my course homewards, with the intention, if possible, of fetching up the time I had lost: a matter only to be accomplished by great exertion, and working two or three hours later than usual.

Two days after this singular occurrence, I received an invitation to sup with the parties and their friends at the house where the unfortunate business originated,— no less a person than the host himself being the messenger. Now I really had no desire to receive an ovation for doing a simple act of duty; and therefore at first declined, saying that there was no call for a 'demonstration' under the circumstances: and that I was amply satisfied with having observed the divine precept of doing unto others as I would be done by. However the old man was too much in earnest to be put off; nothing would satisfy him but my promise to attend. So, after listening to his arguments couched in that style so peculiar to the Irish, I finally gave in.

The important evening arrived: and with some degree of reluctance I doffed my leather apron, and prepared to dress for the occasion; but ere I had well completed my toilette, the landlord accompanied by my young friend the breeches-maker was despatched to fetch me to the banquet, as the company anxiously waited my presence. The place of meeting was but a few doors off, and on our arrival, my two companions preceded me into the room; the old man announcing my name as we entered, whilst the entire company rose to welcome me as the guest in whose honor the festival had been got up.

Never did I experience a more hearty and enthusiastic welcome; the warm demonstrations of feeling that ensued quite overpowered me; and for some minutes my embarassment deprived me of the power of speech. On partially regaining my composure, I stammered out my thanks for this kind reception, and begged my entertainers would not overrate my little services, in proclaiming such trifles to the world. I had never before been in company with so many of the better sort of Irish: the majority were individuals holding respectable positions; such as clerks, warehousemen, small tradesmen, and so forth.

Whilst we sat talking before supper, a grey-headed venerable-looking man entered the room; at whose appearance every one rose, and bowed reverentially as the new comer raised his hands in the act of benediction. After a few words of kindly greeting, the old man took his seat; all standing till he had done so. I soon discovered that the priest (as I at once perceived him to be) was Father Devereux, one of the principal Catholic clergy in the metropolis, who had been mainly instrumental in raising the funds and had otherwise taken great interest in the erection of the large Catholic chapel then building in Moorfields.

Shortly after his arrival, supper was served; and the company being seated, 'his reverence' asked a blessing on the good things the Deity had bestowed upon his creatures. The covers being removed, the demolistion of the viands now began in earnest; and thanks to sharp knives and sharper appetites, they soon disappeared. The cloth being then removed, bowls of punch were introduced; when loyal and national toasts were given by the reverend chairman, and heartily responded to by the company. Some excellent songs were sung; especially those native to the emerald isle; and one young man in particular gave several of Moore's melodies in exquisite taste. I have never heard an Englishman sing Irish songs with such genuine feeling, which however, is not surprising.

The good Father took leave of the company at an early hour; and on on bidding me good night, passed a high eulogium on, what he was pleased to term, the noble and disinterested part I had played before the magistrate. Upon his departure, a gentlemanlike old man with white hair was called upon to preside for the remainder of the evening. The new chairman, I understood, was managing clerk to a solicitor's firm in the city; the company addressed him as 'Mr. Walsh' and appeared to pay great deference to him, as to a man of superior attainments: and he certainly seemed to be a shrewd and intelligent person. His style of speaking was fluent and to the purpose; his manner and self-command well calculated to inspire respect.

Under these favourable auspices, the evening glided into morning; toasts were given; healths were drank; the glasses rattled on the board; and, as the potent liquor began to operate upon the brain, the true Hibernian blood rose up to fever-heat. A confusion of tongues prevailed,—all talkers and no hearers,—the chairman who had endured the disorder for some time with praiseworthy patience, at length rose to vacate his seat; but prior to his doing so, I begged to thank the company for the handsome treatment I had received at their hands; and when in conclusion I was about to bid them good night, I was surrounded and retained against all remonstrance: though certainly in good nature carried to the admired extreme. Having been sparing in my cups, I thought it best to humour their folly till a fair opportunity offered for escape.

Shortly after, the host made his appearance; and in his winning and peculiar brogue, tipped with a little bit of genuine blarney, prevailed upon 'the most respectable men in the city,' as he was pleased to call them, to be 'after moving.' Then, just as some of them actually began to move, this true son of Erin invited the 'darling boys' below to take a dram of rale Irish whiskey, at the bar, *out of his own bottle;* saying, 'the devil a bether drop ever came across the wather'. They now began gradually to draw off by threes and fours; so I took my hat, and making an abrupt exit by the back-door, soon reached my own quarters. Indeed, as the week was drawing to a close, it was necessary that I should make the best use of my remaining time, in order to complete the work I had in hand by Saturday night.

At the end of the week I repaired to our usual place of meeting to spend the evening, and entering the little parlour, commenced playing at draughts with an old gentleman named Mitchell, who kept an eating-house in Golden-lane, and was certainly one of the best players I ever sat down with. No other persons dropping in, we played a series of games; and time passed on until the clock struck ten, which was the old man's hour for retiring.

I then sat smoking a solitary pipe and looking at the papers, when my young friend whom I have spoken of before, came in, having just left work. According to custom we took a dram of whiskey; and getting into conversation, my companion informed me that a meeting had been called in the club-room upstairs for the purpose of establishing a 'boot club;' to which, if I thought proper, it had been agreed that I should be appointed the maker. As we still sat talking the landlord came in rubbing his hands, and in his usual way of speaking said: 'Indeed, gentlemin, yeer company's requisted just above, will yees be afther obleegin meeself and the rest of us?' Without further ceremony we ascended the stairs; and on going into the room I perceived Mr. Walsh sitting at the head of the table, with a book before him and a pile of silver beside it.

After a short time he rose to communicate to me the wishes of the meeting. It had been proposed, he said, and resolved upon by the gentlemen present to establish a 'boot-club;' the business of which they would be glad if I would undertake, at my own list of prices. The number of members already down and paid, was one hundred and one; but as there's luck in odd numbers, he had no doubt they would increase and prosper. He felt the more confident, because all were known to each other, and not a man amongst them but was in a responsible position: so that there was no fear of having any defaulters. Although the style of work was heavier than I was in the habit of making, there were many in 'the trade' who would be glad to earn the money, to whom I could give it, and pay myself for cutting and fitting.

I therefore at once accepted their generous offer, and submitted a scale of prices, which was approved. This part of the business being concluded, slips of paper were put into a hat according with the number of subscribers: upon two of which was written the word PRIZE; and whoever drew one of these had the privilege of having the first pair of boots for which the money had been subscribed. Thus the business proceeded: until every member was supplied with goods to the amount of his money paid into the hands of the treasurer. Having arranged all minor details, we wound up with an excellent supper to the entire satisfaction of all parties.

I believe, that if well treated, there is not a more

generous people on earth than the Irish. Some few days after the party above chronicled, I received an invitation to dine with the priests appointed to officiate at the new chapel, together with a numerous body of the subscribers. This entertainment was given at a house in Long-alley, Moorfields, kept by an Irishman: where, on my arrival, every room in the lower part of the premises was crowded with company all dressed for the occasion.

In about half-an-hour it was announced that dinner was quite ready: whereupon having taken our seats, father Devereux made his appearance, attended by several others of the priesthood, who were received by the company with the usual demonstrations of respect. The waiters now placed the various dishes on the table; and an excellent spread it was, served up in a style that might have satisfied the pampered appetite of an alderman. After ample justice had been done to the good things the cloth was removed: and Father Devereux then addressed the company upon the occasion which had brought them together. 'They were assembled,' his reverence observed, 'to celebrate the erection of a building for public worship in the heart of the first city in the world: and he felt perfect confidence in the result of their endeavours to restore Catholicism to this highly-favoured land.'

In the course of his speech the reverend gentleman called upon the Father of mankind to turn the hearts of the people towards the only true religion: at the same time intimating that all without the pale of the church of Rome were naturally booked for a doubtful, if not hopelessly unpleasant future. Knowing that the speaker had been trained up to believe in the doctrines he promulgated, I had no right to question his sincerity: albeit his conclusions appeared, to my imperfect sense, somewhat strange and irrational. Having concluded his address which was well delivered, the Father resumed his seat amid the plaudits of his highly gratified audience. The business of the evening then proceeded in the most orderly manner possible; some good speeches were delivered; hilarity reigned free from excess; and (independently of what I considered religious prejudices) the evening passed off without alloy. As the principal actors in the scene began to draw off, I also retired, and reached my garret as the clock struck twelve.

On the very next evening, at the same place, I dropped in upon a room full of company, mostly strangers; but there were amongst them three or four shoemakers, who were three parts intoxicated. These men were the most brutal in their manners and expressions that ever came under my notice. One of these fellows in the most savage manner, swore 'by the holy mother' that nothing would give him so much pleasure as ripping up the entrails of a Protestant. This disgusting language, I discovered, was provoked by the preference shewn to *me* by their countrymen, in regard to the boot-club; it was fortunate they did not know me by sight, or even suspected my presence: for I never appeared abroad in the garb of a member of the craft. So far secure, I prudently beat a retreat, and left the savage bigots to revel in their drunken fury.

CHAPTER XII.

A DISTRESSING INCIDENT—DOG-FIGHTING—'JACKO MAKAKKO'—A VISIT TO THE 'CROWN AND ANCHOR' BOOTH AT STEPNEY—ENCOUNTER WITH A 'BARGEE.'

ABOUT this time a most unhappy circumstance occurred in Murphy's family. He had an only daughter, to whom he had given an excellent education; having kept her at boarding-school till she was quite a woman. Thus although the father and mother were rough, homely people, the daughter presented a striking contrast; her manners and appearance being refined and lady-like. It was very soon evident that she did not feel at home under the parental roof; nor could the fact well have been otherwise; for to serve in the bar of a public-house in a low neighbourhood, must have been inevitably disgusting to a female educated as she had been. However as it was understood that old Murphy was tolerably warm, several suitors for the young lady's hand presented themselves; and amongst the number, one of gentlemanly exterior and address. This candidate succeeded in pleasing both daughter and parents; so after a short courtship, the old people gave their formal consent, and the wedding took place.

On the evening before the ceremony, I went into the bar-parlour to congratulate the bride upon her approaching nuptials, when she very politely handed me a glass of wine; in which I drank to her long life and happiness, and hoped that disappointment might never pale her cheek. As she thanked me for my good wishes, I perceived one little tear steal from the corner of her eye; but what it foreboded, was beyond my power of divination. The morning came, the carriages drove up, the postilions and horses were decorated with virgin favours; and as the bridal-party emerged from the house, all seemed joyous and happy. But alas!—shortly after the marriage, it was discovered that the man who had wedded this unsuspecting girl, was a bankrupt; and worse than that, a fellow of the most depraved and dissolute habits. The thought of his daughter's prospects thus crushed in the bud, preyed upon the father's mind, and bowed his spirits to the earth. He became quite unfit for business; and his wife's nerves had received so severe a shock from this unexpected calamity, that she too was completely prostrate.

Under these circumstances poor Murphy resolved to dispose of his business, and retire; which was effected without difficulty, as they were doing an excellent trade. Within a few days the new occupants took possession; and the old couple withdrew to spin out the remainder of their days in private. When I called to bid them good bye, the mother sat listlessly by the fire, whilst the daughter stood on one side pale and ghastly, with her large black eyes fixed and motionless: a study for a sculptor. The good-natured old man shook me by the hand, but he was evidently lost in grief.

I knew that words would be of little avail; and therefore simply expressed my sorrow for their present unhappy state, bidding them confide in that power which alone can heal a broken spirit. As I approached the unhappy girl, she started from her reverie; and bursting into a flood of tears, dropped her head upon my shoulder, and sobbed aloud. We had been on very friendly terms from her first coming home; and in leisure moments she would amuse herself by teaching me a few words of French or Italian, and laughingly called me her pupil, with as little reserve as if I had been her brother. She was indeed an open-hearted good-natured girl; and it grieved me sorely to see her thus blighted by such heartless villany.

The scene became too painful to bear; I took a hurried leave; and thus ended my acquaintance with this kind-hearted Irish family. Not many weeks after their leaving, I heard that both the old people had died broken-hearted. Some three years later, I met the daughter in widow's costume, who told me of her husband's death, in a fit of *delirium tremens;* and added that from her father, she had inherited a handsome provision for life. After some few minutes conversation, we parted; nor have I ever seen her since. Moreover the people who took the public-house brought with them a fresh connexion. I never entered the place again; and, as most of the old customers betook themselves to some more distant resort, I lost all my Irish acquaintance, as briefly as we had come together; but ere quitting this part of my narrative, I beg to state that I never experienced greater kindness than at their hands.

I have already described myself as fond of seeing life

in all its varied forms. I visited every place of public entertainment to which I could gain admission, between Temple-bar and Whitechapel; dog-fighting, badger-baiting, rat-catching, wrestling, sparring, private theatricals, and almost every known species of amusement came in for a share of my patronage. Of all the savage scenes I ever witnessed, there is no exhibition so disgustingly brutal as setting dogs to worry each other to death. There is no limit to the ruffianism and savage propensities of the gentlemen connected with the canine 'fancy'; they resort to the most horrible brutalities to gratify an insane passion for cruelty.

I have heard of a monster who made a bet that his favourite bulldog would pin a bull, after he had *cut off its fore-feet!* The dismemberment took place; and the animal being set on actually accomplished the disgusting feat, to the huge gratification of his unfeeling master and the semi-devils who witnessed the barbarous experiment. I should add, that, by way of a climax to this refined amusement,—the human fiend cut the poor dog's throat; which however may be regarded as the most merciful part of the business.

About this time, a novel combatant appeared in the ring. This was a savage animal of the monkey-tribe, whose fighting propensities had been discovered almost by accident. A dog being chained up in the place where the ape was kept, the latter broke loose and killed the dog (a well-bred terrier) in a few minutes. Such an incident as this roused the attention of the owner, who shortly after offered to fight his monkey against any dog of equal weight. Here was something new indeed; the entire fancy was up in arms at this fresh source of excitement. A match was soon made with a very excellent dog of the bull-terrier breed, and the betting was all in favour of the dog; but had its owner been in possession of the full capabilities of the monkey, he might have pocketed a hat-full of money. The day having arrived for this extraordinary event to come off, the company mustered thick and fast; and long before the usual time of commencing operations, the pit was crowded with eager spectators,—all waiting with intense anxiety to catch a glimpse of the now celebrated 'Jacko Makakko,' as he had been named.

At the hour announced, the animals were placed in the circle by their respective owners. The dog, as soon as let loose, went in at a run upon master Jacko; who quick as thought jumped up and avoided the onslaught. Again the dog turned to seize his antagonist; but ere he had time to get round, the monkey was upon his back, and leaning over his shoulder caught him by the throat, holding fast by his fore-claws round the dog's neck. The ape then twisted his body round: and, thrusting his hinder legs under the belly of his unhappy opponent, began ripping him open with his hind claws. In a few seconds the dog's entrails were trailing on the floor, the monkey still holding on by his throat: and after a few ineffectual struggles, the poor mutilated creature dropped dead in the circle. The spectators stood aghast at this sudden and unexpected termination of the contest: while the blubber-headed fool who owned the dog stood blaring like a bull.

Some of these gentlemen who possessed dogs of excellent quality were not quite satisfied with the brute bearing off the palm, and therefore matched their dogs against him; but he despatched them one after another with equal facility, to the consternation of the entire fancy. The animal, naturally savage, grew worse by degrees: so that it would devour hot coals, burning tobacco, or anything that was thrown to it. At length it seized a child, for which act the beast was tried, condemned, and executed. Thus ended the life of the celebrated Jacko.

One fine summer's evening, I took it into my head to go to Stepney fair, a place I had never before visited. The company, generally, was of a low description. While looking about me and observing the various scenes around, I came to 'Alger's Crown and Anchor tavern,' an immense dancing booth lit up by glass chandeliers and variegated lamps. The band had just struck up a very popular dance, and the crowd flocked thither thick and fast; but those who entered appeared for the most part well-dressed young people of the working class: so being particularly fond of dancing, I paid a shilling for admission and went in with the rest. There could not have been less than five hundred persons present in the place at the time, all dancing in different sets to the same music; the immense area was divided into compartments by ropes running across at equal distances and down the centre: thus each set was kept from interfering with, or running against the other.

Before the next dance commenced I selected a partner with little difficulty, as ceremony was not much studied amongst the motley visitors that crowded this monster ball room. At the conclusion of the dance, I presented my amiable partner a glass of lemonade and a biscuit; and from this time we became friends and continued partners during the remainder of the night,—until the sun began to shine brightly over head, and the last dance was announced by the master of the ceremonies.

Feeling somewhat tired and heated with my exertions, I went to the drinking department to get some refreshment, and seated myself on the end of a form opposite a table where sat six men having the appearance of 'bargees.' One among them, better dressed than the others whom I took to be their captain, challenged me to toss for a bottle of stout; which I declined, telling him I was going to have a bottle to myself. To this he replied—'Don't be a cur!' 'As to that,' I said, 'it matters not; if it will be any accommodation to you, I'll toss you with pleasure.' I did so, losing; and the liquor was brought, for which I paid: but no sooner was the bottle put upon the table, than my opponent seized it and divided the contents amongst his companions, giving me none. Disgusted at this scurvy trick, I however simply observed that I thought the true English fashion on such occasions was to drink together.

Hereupon they all burst out laughing at my simplicity; but treating their low knavery with contempt, I requested the waiter to bring me a bottle to the opposite table; which he had no sooner done, than the young woman with whom I had been dancing came to request me to lead off the concluding dance. I had only taken one small glass of the stout, when she came to summon me; and hastening to oblige her, left the bottle upon the table, telling the man in attendance that I would return at the end of the dance and finish it.

Having arrived at the bottom, I led my partner to a seat; and went out with the intention of taking her a glass and drinking the remainder; but on my arrival, I was informed that the six gentlemen opposite had appropriated my stout, and also a pipe which I had filled with the intention of smoking. Hearing this, I proceeded to tax the offending party with their unhandsome conduct; but was instantly assailed with the most opprobrious and disgusting epithets, was ridiculed as a dandy, and was promised, if I didn't speedily 'hook it,' to have a thoroughfare made through me.

This last threat emanated from the fellow who was smoking my pipe—which, having made nearly red-hot, he now applied to the back of my hand. I said quietly: 'Don't do that again, there's a good fellow.'—'I shall,' he said, 'if you don't take it away.' I as before quietly replied: 'You had better not.' However, in spite of the gentle warning, he burned my hand a second time: when I told him, it was evident that he was but a cowardly scoundrel. The words were no sooner out of my mouth, than his fist came bang upon it, cutting a slit through my lower lip against my teeth. I then requested him to keep his seat till I had finished my engagement with the young woman with whom I was dancing. He did so; probably judging from the apparent disparity between us, that there was little fear of my keeping the appointment.

The bargee was at least thirteen stone and stood near six feet, whereas I was under ten stone, and not over five-feet-eight. However I was in rare condition, being all muscle and bone; and at the time, one of the quickest creatures to be found in the shape of man. As soon as the dance was over, I addressed several of the young men who had been dancing; and having informed them how I had been treated, requested they would go out and see fair play; to which they at once consented.

This settled, I, in company with about half-a-dozen of my new acquaintance waited upon the bargee fraternity, to say that I was quite ready; and expected satisfaction for the insult, as well as for the blow that I had received. I believe the fellow who had struck me thought it a good joke: for he laughed and sneered in the most contemptuous way imaginable; but on seeing matters begin to assume a serious aspect, he jumped up in a great rage, blustering and bullying, along with his five companions, all of them 'big uns:' especially the captain, who, when stripped, was one of the largest men across the chest I have ever seen.

The captain volunteered to second his companion: and before we came to the scratch, or any ring was formed, offered twenty pounds to five,—and to stake the money: but there were no takers. Many of the people cried out—'Don't fight, young man! You are overmatched.' I could not help smiling at their fears: well knowing, as I had often proved, that 'knowledge is power.' Before we commenced, I addressed the people and told them how I had been served; and having great odds to fight against, I begged of them to give me room and not press upon me if I came near them. The fact is, I well knew that I must 'draw' my man in order to bring him down to my own weight.

All being at length arranged, we walked to the scratch, shook hands, and threw ourselves into attitude, when I saw at once that my antagonist was not well up in the art. I intended he should make play; and a feint, which I tried to draw him on, had the desired effect. He attempted to put in his left; this I stopped, and returned the compliment with a tremendous blow over his right eye, which made him stagger, and shake his head, as if he didn't understand exactly how he got it. In the next round I repeated the dose, which made my bargee wince sadly; he now came rushing in (exactly what I wished for), and as I retreated, my left kept busily at work, making sad havoc of his 'signboard.'

At the close of this round, the enemy looked like a man with *odd* cheeks, fat on one side and lean on the other: with one eye open and the other closed; I therefore having succeeded so well in ornamenting one side of his figurehead, now shifted my tactics, and fought right-handed: which seemed to puzzle him more than all; as he could not stop with his left. Thus we kept on, till both eyes were bunged up; and at last he came up hitting wildly. Knowing this to be the time, I stepped in for a rally and finished the job. After standing some time to be hit, he fell like a sack of sand quite blinded, and with his head carved in all directions.

At this crisis, there being a great many Jews present, they kept shouting out,—'Take him avay! Do you vant a corner's inkvest held in the fair? S'help ma cot, you'll be tried for manslaughter; vy, can't you see the little man will kill him!' This kind of chaff was going on all round the ring, until the annoyance became unbearable to my opponent's second; who feeling sadly chagrined at the result, and being irritated by the laughter of the people, rushed like a maniac upon my poor little second; and knocking him down, turned to attack me. But upon this the ring was broken, the people rushed to the rescue, and I being seized upon by

Y

some friendly individuals was carried back to the booth, where I washed and put on my clothes.

Meanwhile, the bargees, seating their friend on a form, sponged his face, and lanced the skin below his eyes; this done, the blood flowed freely, which reduced the swelling and let daylight into his optics. The first object that caught his sight was myself, standing before him without a scratch; the only blow that I received during the fight would not have made an indentation in a bladder of lard. Seeing me in such trim, whole and clean as if nothing had happened, he exclaimed,—'Are you the little man I've been fighting with?' I said, 'Yes, of course you remember me.' He replied somewhat significantly,—'I do: you're a good little man; will you have anything to drink?'

I told him that I should take some brandy, and pay for it myself, as I was already under great obligation to him for giving me the opportunity of chastising a blackguard. So after taking a glass, I made the best use of my legs and reached home about six o'clock; promising myself never again to mix in such company.

BARNWELL OLD CHURCH.

TOWN-HALL AND HOBSON'S CONDUIT.

PART IV.

I MARRY,—AND EXPERIENCE FURTHER VICISSITUDES IN LIFE: BUT, AS I HOPE, FINALLY COME TO A SAFE ANCHORAGE.

CHAPTER I.

I THINK OF 'SETTLING DOWN'—AND GO A-COURTING—EDMONTON FAIR—AN UNCIVIL DRIVER—MY INTENDED AND HER FAMILY—UNFORTUNATE CIRCUMSTANCES—A WEDDING-FEAST, AND NO WEDDING—THE EXERTIONS OF A YOUNG MARRIED COUPLE—THE OLD 'COBOURG' THEATRE—'LITTLE COLEY' AND 'LONG DICK'—I GIVE 'JACK HOLLOWAY' A LESSON.

I HAD now arrived at twenty-six years of age, and began to feel tired of the monotony of a single life;

whilst taking into consideration money spent on pleasures with which I began to be surfeited, I was fully satisfied that my present means would, with greater thrift, enable me to keep a wife. I therefore made up my mind to look out for a neat, modest, and industrious young woman, answering the description I had read in the *Economy of Human Life*. This little book (to which I have before referred as a favourite with me) is said to be a translation from the Chinese. How that may be, I know not: but of this I am certain, that the picture therein drawn is very beautiful, and also an excellent guide to young men desirous of entering upon the sober realities of life.

Something like chance seemed to favour my design. One fine sunny morning I rose to begin work; but tempted by the beauty of the day, and knowing that a fair was then being held at Edmonton, I resolved on making holiday. Having then dressed myself for the occasion, I started off full of health and spirits, and on passing by my mother's door, looked in with the intention of taking my sister with me, who chanced to be at home at the time.

I found her in the little parlour busily engaged on needlework, together with a companion,—whom I had often seen there before, but never could prevail upon to stay in my presence. As on all former occasions, so soon as I entered she left off work, and having rolled it up prepared to depart. I however apologized for intruding upon their privacy, and finally prevailed upon her to resume her work; which she did with a courtesy and good breeding that greatly took my fancy. After chatting some time, I proposed to take them and my mother (like John Gilpin's family) in a hackney-coach to Edmonton. After some little entreaty, they consented: and we all started for the fair.

Arrived at the scene of festivity, we strolled through the motley array of shows and stalls of various kinds ranged in order; while gongs, drums, and trumpets uttered their sounds. After pushing and squeezing through the dense crowd till fairly tired, we repaired to the 'Angel' inn, to get some refreshment and temporary repose. Towards the evening a sort of miscellaneous concert prevailed,—made up of fiddling, singing, and spouting, accompanied with a confusion of tongues to which that of Babel must have been a trifle.

There was one fellow who amused me exceedingly; besides a little conjuring, he gave an excellent imitation of the various 'calls' as performed by boatswains and their mates in the navy. I never heard anything more perfect; the whistle was so shrill and clear that it might have been heard a mile off: and this was achieved simply by a peculiar method of doubling or twisting his tongue. However, as the evening wore on, and unmistakeable symptoms of inebriety began to prevail, we made up our minds to retire. I had already spoken to a man who was waiting with a hackney-coach for hire: and after bargaining with him for ten shillings we started for town,—but had not proceeded far, when a woman with a child in her arms pleaded hard to be taken up. Pitying her situation I gave up my seat, and mounted the box with the driver.

The night was dark and chilly, and the poor horses quite done up; so that we crawled along at a pace something worse than a walk. It was therefore after a most tedious journey, that we reached the coach-stand opposite Shoreditch church about twelve o'clock. Upon dismounting, I tendered the money I had agreed to pay: but the fellow demanded two shillings more, and behaved in the most blackguard and insolent manner possible. To get rid of the nuisance, my mother slipped the money (as she thought unperceived) into his hand: but I saw it, and demanded instant restitution; which coachee refused in terms not fit for ears polite, and moreover threatened to perform a most degrading operation upon my person.

Thinking this was my cue to fight, I stepped up, and delivered a smashing hit through his guard followed by several more in rapid succession, which made my adversary's head play at nut-cracking against the window shutters. My mother and sister, knowing it would be useless to interfere, walked away; while friend Jehu bawled out lustily for the watch; and in a few seconds up came three or four guardians of the night, with their eyes barely open. They made a clumsy attempt to secure me; I slipped through their fingers and bolted, my heels doing as good service as my hands had done before. Then turning down the next street, I reached the back premises of my mother's dwelling; and climbing a high paling, was snug in-doors before the party came up; and so, after enjoying a hearty laugh over this last adventure, we retired to rest.

Such was the commencement of my courtship; rather a rough one, I must confess. However, as it was undeniable that the coachman had behaved exceedingly ill, the after incidents passed over smoothly. The next evening I made overtures to my new acquaintance, and being accepted, accompanied her home, where I was introduced to her father and the family. I soon found myself on good terms with the entire circle. The governor was an exceedingly good-natured man; and as we coincided in sentiment and feeling, our friendship continued unbroken. He was as fine a man as my eyes ever beheld, and gifted with talents of the highest order, so that in his own trade (that of a watchmaker) his equal was not living; this I learned from men reputed to be themselves first-hands, such as finishers and examiners employed by Brockbank, Barraud, McCabe and other first-rate manufacturers in the metropolis.

But, most unfortunately for himself and family, my intended father-in-law had been some years afflicted with an ulcerated leg, which ended in an affection of the spine; through which, despite all the skill of several eminent practitioners, he ultimately lost the use of his hands. This misfortune drove the family to great straits; as for three years the old man lay in this helpless state, during which time my betrothed and her sister worked early and late to support the household. This heavy affliction, together with constant confinement, sorely affected my future wife's health, and eventually brought on a low and nervous debility. It was indeed a sad thing to see good people so bowed down by necessity and distress; still, with care and good management, they continued to keep a roof over their heads, although at the expense of much suffering and privation.

At length it pleased the great Disposer of events to release the poor afflicted father from his earthly thraldom. When the day appointed for the funeral arrived, his brothers attended (all in excellent suits of mourning), two of whom were in good circumstances and without children. I naturally thought that they would each take one of the boys, and at least help them to a trade; but no: they left the poor widow to buffet with the world as best she might. This heartless proceeding roused my indignation; I felt ashamed that such libels on our common nature should exist. However, as action has ever been my motto under all circumstances, I proposed to take the elder boy and teach him bootmaking; which was certainly better than nothing: though a poor business as compared with the beautiful trade in which his father had been first, in the very first line.

Having now formed ourselves into a small republic, we prepared to battle with the waves of adversity: and in a few months managed to get the younger boy apprenticed to a boot-closer, who worked for the same shop as myself, MACLAREN's of Cornhill; but his mistress was an ill-tempered woman, so that the poor fellow had a miserable time of it. Desirous of holding sacred my promise to the father on his death-bed, to do the best I could for his family, I at this period taxed my energies to their utmost power. I worked constantly with my watch hanging before me, doing every part of my work to time; by which system I accomplished wonders; frequently doing two days' work in sixteen hours, a pair of boots being considered one good day's work.

On one occasion, I made two pairs of boots between five A.M. and eight P.M., and within that space went from the city to the new river to bathe; a performance held at the time to be unprecedented in the trade. I also began to purchase some articles of furniture in order to commence housekeeping, and gradually scraped together a few chairs and tables with other things indispensably necessary. The ordinary term of mourning having now expired, we agreed to get married; and the banns were published at St. Luke's church. On the day named for the wedding to take place, preparation was made for the entertainment of our friends; but as I wished to have the ceremony performed with as little ostentation as possible, we were accompanied to the church only by my wife's uncle and my sister, who were to act respectively as father and bridesmaid.

On our arrival, I was informed by the clerk that we were too late; as an alteration had taken place in the Marriage Act, according to which we were a week behind time. This was a sorry dilemma! There was no way left but to have the banns republished, and to come again within the prescribed time. But how were we to satisfy the guests who had been invited to the wedding-feast?

Ever ready at invention, I proposed that we should return as if the ceremony had taken place: and, to give an appearance of reality, placed the wedding-ring upon the finger of my intended,—at the same time requesting our small church-party to take no notice of the disappointment, but to conduct themselves as though nothing out of the way had occurred. We consequently accepted the congratulations of the assembled company, and suffered the untoward fact to pass unsuspected.

The day was spent in feasting and merriment, which I took every possible pains to keep up; and as my powers of mimicry were of no common order, succeeded in diverting our friends from anything like a suspicion of the little trick we had played off upon them.

Nor indeed, until all the guests had taken their departure, did we inform the old lady of our disappointment, and retired to our separate apartments as usual. Nothing further was said; but at the expiration of the time provided by the Act, we again repaired to church with our father and bridesmaid, and were this time joined together for better or worse.

As I was ever light-hearted and full of jollity and fun, it was my constant practice to feast my wife with prospects bright and beautiful, far beyond the hope of realization. If this practice served no other purpose, it at least gave us cause for mirth. One morning while I was waiting for a leg,[1] I busied myself in stretching some old boot-fronts for the purpose of cutting out a pair of 'uppers' for my own wear; but upon applying the pattern, found it impracticable without piecing. My wife seeing me puzzled, laughed at the notion of making shoes out of such apparently worthless materials; but whilst joining in the laugh, I promised her that from such humble means should originate a splendid carriage, which I was to present her with on some future birthday. This sally, she at the time of course set down as so much nonsense, dreaming not that such a vision could ever be realized.

Thus we kept working on,—she nimbly plying her needle, I hammering on the lapstone,—and by degrees completed our stock of necessaries for domestic purposes without running into debt; for I always had a great aversion to borrowing. There was however one very

---

[1] From the 'closer's,'—which is properly a distinct business. Hence the obvious advantage of my wife's services (presently to be mentioned) in that line.

essential article that was still wanting, namely a chest of drawers; and as we needed so many things at the beginning, this was a difficulty not easily surmounted. But necessity is the mother of invention: and my wife's ingenuity supplied the want by sewing together some sheets of thick brown paper, which made a famous *ex tempore* wardrobe, the depository of our Sunday clothing.

As I felt anxious to improve my circumstances and to make my wife satisfied with her position, I made the best use of my time: frequently working sixteen hours out of the twenty-four; whilst my partner, besides attending to her domestic duties, earned from two shillings to half-a-crown a day. Thus, by the help of great perseverance and care, we possessed ourselves of sufficient household goods for present use; but, as we scarcely ever went out for a holiday except on Sunday, I soon missed my accustomed exercise, and therefore proposed to myself henceforth to strike work at eight o'clock two or three nights in the week, and indulge in half-an-hour's 'set-to.' So much sedentary labour ill agreed with me; and, in truth, I began to find that I was intended by nature for employment of a more active kind. But no immediate change could be effected; I must wait till an opportunity presented itself.

In the course of a short time my employer offered me the situation of 'clicker,' which was preferable in point of comfort, although I could earn more money on the 'seat.' I therefore accepted the post and entered upon its duties: but had not been long in my new situation, ere I perceived that my employer's son grew jealous in consequence of the kindness shewn to me by his father. The young man soon evinced his disposition through the medium of petty annoyances, which I did not feel inclined to brook: and matters gradually progressed to such extremity, that I requested the old gentleman to allow me to return to the seat,—upon some excuse which I devised,—to avoid sowing dissension betwixt father and son.

On Saturday night, at my usual time of leaving, I went into the counting-house for my wages, which the old gentleman paid me almost without speaking; I could see clearly that he had a shrewd guess at the cause of my leaving. After receiving my money, I told him that I had fitted the lasts and tied together the legs and stuff for a pair of boots ordered by an old customer, for whom I had been in the habit of making ever since I first worked for the shop, and asked if I should take them home to begin the week with? He gave the required permission; whereupon I took up the materials and departed.

Monday morning came: I fitted my stuff, tacked on my inner soles, and then proceeded to look up my kit and get all in readiness for work. After dinner, the weather being fine, I proposed to my wife to take a walk and make an afternoon's holiday,—a rare thing with us, as already observed, since our marriage. Calling on some of my wife's relations, it was proposed by the females to visit the Coburg theatre in the evening; whilst myself and the men agreed on repairing to a house kept by one of the family where we could play at skittles, a game very beneficial to persons of sedentary occupations.

I had promised to follow the women at half-price, in

order to see them safe home; and therefore left my party about eight o'clock, and proceeded to the theatre. Upon entering the pit, where I had appointed to meet my charges, I perceived a fellow just before me striking a young woman on the bonnet, and in vulgar terms desiring her to hold her head aside. Indignant at his cowardice, I requested him to conduct himself properly; instead of which, he repeated the dastardly act, when the young woman herself turning round to expostulate, I perceived that it was my sister, who seeing me, at once said,—"I'm glad you're come! This man has been striking me repeatedly on the head, and not very gently." Happening to know the money-taker, I went out; and having stated the case to him, the ruffian was presently ejected by an officer in attendance.

The house was densely crowded; they were playing at the time a piece that was very popular, called *The Old Oak Chest*, to witness which thousands crowded nightly. The principal actors were Bengough, Bradley, Blanchard, Davidge, H. Kemble, &c. &c. The performances over, we took some refreshment, and wending our way homewards unmolested, were about to part company at the corner of Golden-lane, Old-street. But at this moment a notorious character called 'little Coley' (who fought the 'Islington cow-boy') came up: and forthwith began using most bestial language. I instantly requested the women to walk on; and turning round, asked the brute what he meant by such conduct. This interrogatory of course procured me a second dose of the original sample, followed up by a threat of ' putting my head in chancery.'

Somewhat annoyed hereat, I begged my wordy foe

to exemplify the process of which he talked; and no sooner was the invitation given, than he came up in fighting attitude. But before he was aware of it, I shot out my left hand, and catching him a stinging hit on the eye, sent him down; when, just at the nick of time, up came the watchman; and I gave my man in charge for an assault and making use of obscene language. As we were taking him to the watchhouse, one of his pals came to the rescue; but the guardian of the night, being a much stronger man than most of his fraternity, held his prisoner in safe bondage; whilst I seized Mr. 'Long Dick,' as he was generally called. When we appeared before the officer of the night, he recognised them both as old offenders; I therefore preferred the charge, giving my name and address, and promising to appear at Worship-street next morning.

Resolved, as far as in my power, to check such abominable nuisances, I repaired to the court at the time named, being accompanied by a witness in the person of an elderly female who had been present at the fray. The prisoners being placed in the dock, I was called upon to give evidence against the dirty-minded knaves, whose looks were sufficient to condemn them. When asked what they had to say to the charge, Mr. Coley said that I struck him, and drew the magistrate's attention to an eye which was black as its owner's name: and his companion urged that I had nearly strangled him. The magistrate, however, observed that they were rightly served, and sentenced them both to the treadmill for a month.

Some five or six weeks after this occurrence, I went, at the request of Ned Neal, to a set-to at a benefit got up for a poor fellow well known to the boxing fraternity, (and also a brother craft of mine) who had long been suffering under a severe illness. I considered it therefore my duty to render him such services as lay in my power. When I entered the room, there was a tolerable muster of celebrities. On the right hand, near the door, sat several of the notorious dog-priggers, including 'king Hobdel' and his brother-in-law Jack Holloway, a fighting cove, together with Mr. Coley and his friend 'Long Dick.' In passing by, I heard the latter say in a whisper,—'That's him, Jack,—that's the thief that sent us to the mill.'

In the course of the evening, Mr. Holloway came over, and asked me if I would set-to; intending no doubt to pay me off for the little act of attention I had rendered to his friends Coley and Dick. I answered that I had no objection, if he would play light; to which condition he very blandly acceded.

As soon as the parties then engaged had finished, we tucked up our shirt-sleeves and put on the gloves. On toeing the scratch, we shook hands as usual; but as I was in the act of bringing back my right leg for the purpose of putting myself into an attitude of defence, Mr. H. stealing a march upon me hit out with all his force,—his right hand encountering my ribs. I had just time to draw in my body, and partially evade the force of the intended compliment; though it reached me in sufficient strength to make me cough audibly, in spite of all efforts to the contrary.

Disgusted with this piece of treachery, and bent on revenge, I now shook my left-hand glove clear of the wadding, thus leaving nothing to cover the back knuckles but the leather. My opponent commenced with an attempt to deliver a crushing hit with his left upon my frontispiece; but I stopped it, and returned a blow upon his nasal organ, which levelled the bridge, and made him reel like a drunken man. Following up the advantage, I administered several severe hits in rapid succession before he had time to recover his wits; until, his friends perceiving that he bled copiously, one of them rushed towards him, and taking off the gloves, exclaimed,—'S'help me, Jack, it's no go!' This was the work of a minute; and from that day forward I traversed courts and alleys unmolested.

Some weeks after, while passing by the Bank on my way to Cornhill, I met the redoubtable Jack leading a French poodle white as snow. I purposely accosted him, and jocularly enquired if he felt any ill effects from 'that crack' he got on the nose. But the fellow with a serious face declared that he had never since been able to sleep with his mouth shut: adding,—that he mistook me for 'a cove what played at cherrystones,' (that is, a simpleton who plays with little boys on the pavement) and was never so taken in, in his life.

CHAPTER II.

SERIOUS ILLNESS OF MY BROTHER—WE BRING HIM HOME FROM MARGATE—POOR 'TOM'—I RESOLVE ON SETTLING IN CAMBRIDGE—MY DIFFICULTIES—A FRIEND IN NEED—MY OLD EMPLOYER—I ENGAGE WITH HIS SON—ADVENTURE WITH A DROWNING MAN—MY DIFFERENCE WITH 'THE MARQUIS'.

I HAD now been married about two years: during which time I had heard but little of my brother, save that he was rather ailing than otherwise. One morning, as we sat at work, the postman brought a letter enclosing a one-pound bank-note, with a request that I would immediately start for Margate; where my brother had ruptured a blood-vessel on the lungs, and was not expected to live. I instantly prepared for the journey: and taking my mother with me, arrived at Margate about five P.M. We were met upon the jetty by my brother's wife, and several persons from Cambridge. She was a woman of majestic figure, with an air and bearing expressive of great haughtiness; yet when the facial muscles were relaxed, her countenance wore a singularly sweet smile. The contrast between the two expressions was the strangest I ever witnessed.

Arrived at their lodgings on the Marine Parade, I was ushered into an apartment on the ground-floor, having bow-windows that looked out upon the open sea. Some little time elapsed ere my brother was prepared for the meeting. I was then shewn into his room, and on approaching the bedside was truly shocked at the change which those fine features had undergone. All our boyish love rushed back upon my heart, and my feelings were overcharged beyond the power of utterance. Taking his hand, which had been like my own a powerful one, I shuddered at the touch; for it was now as the hand of a skeleton.

Consumption had done its destined work; the temples were hollow, the bright orbs had lost their lustre, the cheeks were sunken, the fine aquiline nose had become attenuated, and the entire frame was reduced to skin and bone. Here was a total wreck of the creature I had idolized from my childhood; yet, sadly reduced as he was, poor Bill bore his seemingly approaching end with manly fortitude.

In about a fortnight his physician and surgeon, who were very attentive to the case, gave their sanction to his removal. It was greatly desired that he should reach home alive; but the coach journey from London to Cambridge was much to be feared, as the motion of the vehicle might bring on a paroxysm of the disease; the consequences whereof would be immediately fatal. However, after a pleasant run up the Thames, we reached my dwelling in a hackney-coach; where my wife soon prepared some refreshments, of which the sufferer partook, and appeared well pleased to see us so comfortably circumstanced.

Even in this last stage of existence, my poor brother still was lively and amusing. During his short stay, we ran over the varied scenes and difficulties we had encountered from our boyhood. Being now in good circumstances, with a business returning profits to the amount of four hundred a-year, he advised me to leave London, and establish myself at Cambridge, where his credit might render me good service. I did not however, at the moment, make up my mind to this proceeding; for I had an instinctive aversion to leaning upon any one for support.

Before my brother and his wife took their departure, the former expressed a wish to take with him an extraordinary large cat which we possessed, one of the finest of its species. My wife not liking to refuse, poor 'Tom' was with some difficulty secured in a basket, and packed off with their luggage to the 'Green Dragon' in Bishopsgate-street, whither we also repaired to meet the coach, and see our relatives fairly started on their homeward journey.

About three weeks from this time, after mature consideration, we decided upon migrating to Cambridge. I therefore made arrangements for the removal of our furniture by waggon; and leaving my wife to look after our little property, proceeded in advance to our destination, in order to secure a home before her arrival. Having reached my journey's end, I went direct to my brother's house in the main thoroughfare of the town, and on approaching the door, I perceived through the muslin curtain two female figures, whom I presently found to be my brother's wife and her sister; two of the finest looking women in the county, standing about five feet ten and formed in just proportion.

They were farmer's daughters, and had been accustomed to equestrian exercise from their girlhood: which no doubt gave them that almost masculine freedom of body and limb, which they possessed in an extraordinary degree. On advancing to pay my respects, I was greeted by the sisters in terms of hearty welcome: and upon enquiry, learned that my brother was much better, and had driven out to witness a trotting-match against time, by a mare belonging to our stammering friend Bob Laxton. This affair must yet be remembered by many; it came off on the Milton-road.

In about half-an-hour Bill returned, and was not surprised at seeing me; indeed I had already written to him to enquire about a cottage in an airy situation and at a low rent, as my finances were by no means flourishing; for all our savings had been devoted to buy furniture, and the thousand and one things necessary to housekeeping. The usual salutation over, we retired to a back-room where tea was prepared: after partaking of which, pipes and tobacco were introduced; and as we sat smoking and talking, my brother recalled to my memory numerous funny incidents of former days.

All on a sudden, I heard the mewing of a cat up the chimney: when—not having before thought of poor 'Tom', and now enquiring after him—I was informed, that as soon as they opened the basket, he bolted up the chimney and had never been seen since. Upon putting my ear to the aperture, I heard the same faint cry repeated; and thinking I knew the voice, called out 'Tom, Tom, Tom!' when down rolled something upon my head, blinding me with soot. As soon as able, I looked down: and there, sure enough, lay the poor beast, black as a sweep, and starved to a skeleton, with not sufficient strength left to crawl.

After a little time, he recovered sufficiently to raise his head; and turning his eyes towards me, cried in most piteous tones. I requested the servant to bring me a little milk in a saucer, and held it to his mouth; he lapped only about a spoonful, then stretched himself at full length, and after resting a while, by degrees revived. From this time puss gradually recovered, and becoming reconciled to his new home, grew to be one of the finest cats ever beheld; but he turned out such an incorrigible thief, that it was eventually deemed necessary to put him to death for the many depredations he had committed against the law.

My visit here passed pleasantly enough, my sister-in-law being particularly gracious. I had been at Cambridge a fortnight, when I received a letter from my wife, informing me that the furniture had been sent off by one of Swann's waggons; and that she had booked herself to come on the morrow by the old Union coach. The next morning I went down to the waggon-yard in Hobson's-street, where I had often been when a boy with cart-loads of meat for delivery to Cork our salesman in Leadenhall. On going into the counting-house to enquire about the expected goods, I saw the same clerk, Mr. Mordecai, that used to be there when I was a little boy at home; and asking if he had any packages from London in the name of 'Brown', he replied, yes, but they were not yet unloaded. I then enquired if he could tell me the amount of the carriage; and in a minute he presented the bill, which I paid, retaining in my purse the last 'splendid shilling'.

In the evening I went to meet the coach at its usual time of arrival, feeling assured that my wife would be weary and faint after a tedious journey of eight or nine hours on the road. I waited some time ere the creeping vehicle entered the Blue Boar yard, and the passengers alighted; amongst whom was my wife, worn out apparently by the slow torture she had endured. She had no luggage beyond what we could easily carry in our hands; but before leaving the yard, I parted with my last shilling to the coachman, old Mr. Pryor, whom I have often joked about it since. This was, in truth, beginning the world penniless.

When we arrived at my brother's dwelling, an excellent repast was already prepared for their expected visitor. Thus far everything proceeded very smoothly; in a day or two we got matters arranged, and took possession of our little cottage: and now came the grand struggle. Our money was all gone—not a 'brown' in our possession, save the name we bore; and that of little value in a place where we were perfect strangers. Thus driven to my wits' end, I turned over the miscellaneous articles of our accumulated store; and finding a stove for which we had no use, sold it for ten shillings. With this sum we procured a few necessary articles, such as coals, bread, butter, tea, sugar, &c.

The next thing was to look out for something in the shape of work: for dependence is, in my estimation, the worst kind of slavery; and to this I could not bow in any form, however speciously it might be presented. During my short stay at Margate, I had become acquainted with a respectable and intelligent man who used frequently to visit my brother; he resided in the same street at Cambridge, and one morning as I was passing by, asked me what I intended doing. I told him I really could not say; it was the long vacation time, a most inopportune season, and I saw no prospect of doing anything till October,—for not only were the Colleges empty, but the principal inhabitants were also absent.

This, my friend observed, was unfortunate. 'However,' he continued, 'you are here, and must live, by hook or by crook. Just by way of a beginning now, suppose you make me a pair of top-boots and a pair of Wellingtons.' Here I was in a fix, for I had no money to buy the materials; but feeling the force of the truism, that 'necessity owns no law', I told him exactly how I was circumstanced, and offered to place the little plate that I possessed in his hands as security, if he would advance the amount required. 'Oh, nonsense!' he replied, 'how much do you want?' I named two pounds, which sum he at once threw on the table; and thus supplied, took my new customer's measure, and went joyfully to purchase the stuff.

When I had paid for the materials and grindery[1] necessary for the accomplishment of the work, I had eight shillings left; which I took home and gave to my wife, as she was always banker. As the Wellingtons could be soonest got ready for making the bottoms, I cut them out first, and set my wife to closing the legs, who was now tolerably expert at this process; though she had not been many months at the craft, and the work greatly differed from that to which she had been

[1] The materials used in the manufacture of boots and shoes, such as wax, bristles, hemp, pegs, &c.

accustomed, namely stitching on muslin. She merited great praise for her perseverance and determination in overcoming obstacles almost insurmountable; but the bent position in which she was compelled to sit, was for a long time the cause of incessant pain across the loins, not to speak of the punishment inflicted by the threads cutting into her fingers. But even under these trying circumstances, I would cheer her by picturing brighter scenes in store.

By Friday evening I had completed the order, and having dressed myself neatly, (for, as in London, I never went out in the clothes in which I worked) took the boots home to the customer: who expressed himself well pleased, and paid me the balance, which was one pound fourteen shillings. This sum I carried home to my female shopmate, feeling assured that she stood in need of it.

On the Monday morning, as we had nothing particular to do, I took my wife for a walk, with the intention of shewing her the Colleges and such parts of the town as she had not yet seen; she had also expressed a wish to see my native village,—which I intended to gratify. As we passed down St. John's-street, nearly opposite the College gateway stood my former barber-master. Upon catching sight of me, the wretch crossed over and offered his hand; but I declined the honor, and reminded him of the scurvy trick he had played me. 'A pretty fellow to shake hands with!' I observed; and walked on, leaving him with a silly grin upon his countenance.

I afterwards learned that he had been discommuned[1]

---

[1] Tradesmen or others who offend against the University statutes, are said to be *discommuned*; the effect is to prevent any undergraduate from dealing with the offender, under severe pains and penalties.

for some dirty trick; and that his son had succeeded to the business, which was certainly the first in the place. After I left him he had come to London, and applied to the clicker's society for a man; but no one would engage with him in consequence of his unhandsome conduct towards myself: for I had taken care to give *him* a character, although he had refused *me* one. He was however informed by the Secretary, that there was a man in the workhouse, who had lost his character and situation in consequence of getting drunk, and not being able to account for forty pounds the property of his employer.

Driven to this last shift, my old employer had to put up with 'Hobson's choice'—though not so bad a choice after all: for there was not a more talented man in the trade; and had he not been addicted to drunkenness and other disreputable practices, he would have been a valuable acquisition to any establishment. This unfortunate man was the means of raising a splendid business from the foundation laid by myself a few years before; and my pseudo-craftsman the barber might have realised his proudest hopes, had he been wise enough to conduct himself with common decency.

Our small means were now husbanded with great care, as we had yet two months of vacation before us. The money I had taken for the boots served to sustain us for three weeks, at the expiration of which we were completely aground. The succeeding week we lived almost on bread and water; only, morning and afternoon, instead of tea and coffee we had each a little milk-and-water. For myself it did not so much matter; but I could not bear to see my wife suffer such bitter privations, and there was no immediate prospect of a change for the better. On the ensuing Monday morning, after taking our milk-and-water and a small piece of bread, (for we had but little in the cupboard), I proposed to go round to the different shops and try to get work: in which it was barely possible that I might succeed, as there wanted but little more than a month to the commencement of term. So I started off to try my fortune but with little hope of success. My brother all this time was ill, and confined to his bed: and my pride or self-respect, or whatever name you like to call it by, would not allow me to make known my unhappy circumstances to his wife. I could see that she was proud, and had a mortal aversion to laying myself under obligations in that quarter, or even giving her the satisfaction of exulting over our poverty. Having, however, to pass the house on my way, I enquired after my brother's health, and then bade my lady good morning.

Immediately afterwards, while looking at some books in a shop window, I was accosted by the son of my former master the barber: who asked me why I did not call to see him, observing that I had grown proud. I told him, he knew well there was no such nonsense about me; and that I should be only too happy to make him a few pairs of boots if he had any to spare. He jokingly replied that he had got more makers than orders, but he wanted a clicker, as the old man who had been there ever since I left was getting quite useless; therefore, if I thought proper, I might take the situation.

I reminded him that his father had treated me very ill, and that I did not desire a repetition of such favours.

As to that,—his father, he admitted, was a great rogue, and had behaved quite as ill to himself. I therefore thinking it just possible that the son might be a better man than his father, accepted his offer, and went with him back to the shop. On entering the place, I saw the wretched man of whom I have often before spoken, as having been taken from the workhouse. He had been apprised beforehand that some one was coming to take his place: he still being retained to superintend the ladies' department of the business. Upon handing over the books, tears started from his eyes.

On looking over the order-book, I perceived that several pairs of Oxonians stood first on the list to be put in hand. I therefore selected a suitable skin and cut them out at once. When dinner time arrived, I said to my new employer: 'I suppose you will not object to my giving these to my wife, as she is an excellent closer.' 'Certainly not,' said he, 'do just as you please.' So putting half-a-dozen pairs in my handkerchief, I proceeded to carry them home. I had not got far from the shop, when I met my old schoolfellow, of whom I have made honourable mention in connection with my former visit to Cambridge. I told him how I was situated, and asked him to lend me ten shillings till Saturday night. With all the frankness of a generous soul, he took out a sovereign, and putting it into my hand said: 'Pay it back at your convenience.' Heartily thanking him, I entered the nearest butcher's shop and purchased some chops, which I wrapped in paper and took home.

My wife sat crying over some needlework. 'Come, cheer up,' said I, 'there are better things in store for us: never mind these little misfortunes.' She answered:

'I could not help crying, I thought you had made away with yourself.' 'Oh, nonsense!' I replied, 'have greater confidence in that power that watches over all things.' 'Oh, yes!' she said, 'I know: but when you left the house tears were in your eyes, a thing I never witnessed before.' 'True,' I said, 'but never mind,—there's an old saying, when things are at the worst there must be a change.' And with this I emptied out the contents of my handkerchief on the hearth-rug, and related my morning's adventure. She soon dried her tears and began to prepare our meal. Whilst the chops were cooking, I went out for a loaf and a pint of ale: and with these we made a dinner,—a luxury that had become a stranger to us. My hour of absence was by this time nearly up, so handing my wife fifteen shillings of the change out of the sovereign, I returned to the shop; and began to trench out legs and uppers, and cut up butts in readiness for October. Then in the evening my new employer invited me into his private room to play at draughts, and during our play introduced a bottle of port: of which however I drank but sparingly, as I had scarcely tasted wine since I was on board ship.

About half-past nine I proceeded homewards; and found my wife had laid the cloth for supper, which consisted of bread-and-cheese and ale. We now again began to feel somewhat comfortable; and on casting my eye around, I perceived she had nearly completed closing two pairs of Oxonians, the wages for which were two shillings. This seemed the turning point of our fortunes: the old feeling came over me, and my fertile imagination conjured up such scenes as made my wife fancy I was a little cracked. But there was not much the matter: it has ever been my custom to sink minor difficulties by revelling in prosperity yet to come.

Thus we went on till Saturday night arrived, when my wife came with her bill, which I looked over, comparing the numbers with the order-book; and when I had signed it, she went into the counting-house to get paid. When the clock struck nine, I requested the cleaner-up and the apprentice to close the shop, and went directly home. Here my wife was busy looking over the provisions she had purchased with her earnings. She had laid in a stock of bread, butter, tea, sugar, and various other articles for the ensuing week's consumption; and, to use her own words, 'never did money seem to go so far.' After supper, I went to seek my friend, and to return the sovereign I had borrowed. I found him, as I expected, smoking his pipe at the then celebrated 'Red Bull,' whither all the stage-coachmen and heavy swells at that time resorted. Alas, what revolutions take place! It is now transmogrified into a cold meat shop, in front; whilst the back premises are converted into the printing-office whence these sheets issue. I now repaid my friend, smoked a pipe, and then returned home well pleased with my week's work.

On Monday evening, having little or nothing to do, I strolled up to the Old ladder to bathe; when, just as I was ready to jump in, I perceived a young man struggling and floundering in the middle of the stream, head downwards! There chanced to be nobody nigh, except a couple of bakers at a little distance on the bank; I afterwards learned that their names were Farrington and Lander. I called to them to come and assist to save the drowning man; and myself instantly jumped in. Upon reaching the party, I caught hold of the back of his arm; but by a sudden effort, he sprung round, and seizing my body pinioned my left arm to my side. I did not lose my presence of mind; but struck my man under the ear to make him relax his hold. This had the desired effect; for when we reached the bottom, a depth of ten or twelve feet, I managed to disengage myself from his grasp: and shoving him over my head followed him up. He was now nearly exhausted: so on coming to the surface, I took hold of his left arm just under the shoulder and swam with him towards the bank, where the two bakers kneeling down each took an arm and drew him on land. I then swam to the ladder, and got out not at all desirous of another such encounter. After holding the man up some time, and letting the water run from him, he came to: but still looked more dead than alive. Upon inquiry, I was informed that he was Dr. Okes's groom.

As I was quite a stranger in the town, it was not known at the time who saved the drowning man's life. But some twenty years after, I happened to be at the 'Crown' in Jesus-lane, when a person present mentioned the circumstance: and one of the two bakers who lent their aid was there also. 'Ah,' said he, 'I remember it well enough; but who the man was that went in after him, I never knew; whoever he was, he had a rare struggle for his life.' I then related the particulars of the circumstance, which he said were perfectly correct: but that he was dreadfully frightened at the time: and as I was undressed, he did not know me when he saw me again. This was the most perilous adventure I was ever engaged in.

October had now arrived, and business commenced in earnest. Tramps, as usual, came down from London; these generally consist of men of the most irregular habits, and the greatest drunkards in the trade,—but for the most part are excellent workmen. Orders came in thick and fast: so that I had great difficulty in getting them executed to time, as there is no dependence whatever to be put in drunken men. I had given out a pair of boots to a notorious fuddler called 'the Marquis'; they were for a fellow-commoner of Downing College, and were to be delivered as early as possible. But day after day passed away, and no boots arriving, I becoming somewhat impatient, sent the apprentice to see what state they were in. On his return, I learned that the inner soles were tacked on to the lasts, and the stuff fitted; which would amount to about half-an-hour's work. Vexed at such delay and consequent disappointment to our customer, I desired the lad to fetch away the legs and stuff; as by this time the gentleman had called, and angrily countermanded the order. Still however thinking to save the credit of the house, I went home, and sitting up all night, completed the boots, so as to have them treed-up by nine o'clock the next morning. Being very desirous of getting over the difficulty, I took them home myself, and apologised for the delay; but it was all fruitless. I had the mortification of bringing the boots back, and losing an excellent customer, which to me was a source of great annoyance.

That same evening, the dirty sot who occasioned this trouble, had the audacity to come into the shop for more work; which I refused, and requested him to go about his business. Finding he had got into different hands to what he had been accustomed to, he next challenged me to fight: at which my half-witted employer seemed delighted. By this time, a number of persons had congregated before the shop, and amongst them, one whom I had fought with when a boy: who seeing the annoyance to which I was subjected, called out—'Master John, you don't put up with that nonsense, do you?' As there seemed no other way of getting rid of the nuisance, but by accepting his challenge, I stepped into the Crescent; and on my giving him 'one for his nob,' down he went, at the same time splitting his dilapidated inexpressibles across the seat; after which he gathered his rags together, and walked off for good. I was informed by the fellow's shopmate, that he substituted an old great-coat for trousers, by shoving his legs through the sleeves and binding the skirts round his body; and in this guise, went on tramp to Northampton. This anecdote reminds me to mention, that the poor devil whom I had superseded, still clung to his degrading habit of intemperance, despite my advice, and every other means used to prevent him; several times I paid his public-house scores to prevent unpleasant consequences, but all was utterly useless; he had become a slave to the despotic fiend, Drunkenness, and so continued to his death.

CHAPTER III.

I REBEL AGAINST INJUSTICE, AND SET UP MY STANDARD AT FORT ST. GEORGE—MY BROTHER'S DEATH—THE BOWLING-GREEN THEATRE—MY FIRST APPEARANCE ON THE BARNWELL STAGE—A CHANGE FOR THE WORSE—THE GARRICK CLUB—MY 'ACCEPTED' ADDRESS—UNIVERSITY DRAMATIC CLUB—THE THEATRE IN JESUS LANE—CAMBRIDGE THEATRICAL ANECDOTES.

I HAD been two winters in my situation; during which time I had done my best to advance the interest and respectability of the firm. It was in the course of the third long vacation—that withering time to tradesmen and College servants—that I made a most important discovery. Having an order for several pairs of dress shoes and pumps, I went to the leather-seller who served the shop, and desired to see some dog-skins; as there is no leather so suitable for such purposes. But instead of the article enquired for, I was shewn some calf-skins that had been spoiled in flaying,—a thing that frequently occurs if the butcher is not an expert knifeman. The skins (long enough to cover a donkey) were skived[1] down to the

---

[1] So reduced in thickness, that the substance of the leather was completely perished.

grain; being so reduced as to be literally worthless. I of course objected to using stuff entirely unfit for the purpose for which I wanted it; and so went my way. But I had no sooner entered our shop, than a man following upon my heels threw the skins on the floor. Indignant at this proceeding, I was ordering them to be forthwith removed, when my poor drunken shopmate soon enlightened my understanding; and acquainted me that our employer was entirely at the disposal of the tyrant leather-seller.

This was a state of things by no means in accordance with my notions of business; and I at once determined not to subscribe to such a rotten system. The sequel is soon related. On the return of our helpless governor, I was given to understand that his tyrant creditor must be obeyed. 'Well then,' said I, 'here's one who will not use his knife to rob the public at king Log's dictum.' So taking my kit, I straightway departed; and thus ended my connexion with a man who ought to have made a fortune; instead of which he became one of the most abject things in life.

Being now tolerably well known in the town, and in some degree respected, I soon picked up a few orders: and having a little cash in hand, managed to get a living. Many of the College servants rendered me good service by recommending me to their masters, and selecting such as paid their own bills; and I am happy to state, that by such custom I never lost a shilling.

About this time also I became acquainted with a man who brewed very good beer, and held several public-houses. Amongst them was the 'Fort St. George,' which had formerly been the residence of the river

Conservators' man who looked after the tolls and attended to the locks. This place was proposed to me as being a most advantageous position. It certainly was a pleasant summer residence; being situated on the open common, or rather on a small island, with the river at the back and the sluice pens in front. It required but little persuasion to induce me to embrace a kind of life for which I was tolerably well suited. Having agreed upon terms and the tenure of holding, I proceeded to furnish the place; providing pots and glasses, together with the numerous things necessary for public business. As 'new brooms sweep clean,' I became a general favourite; and all my numerous qualifications being called into play, had the effect of bringing round me an excellent connexion. Frequently on a fine day, we have taken from ten to twelve pounds; which in a small house standing alone on a common, was considered extraordinary.

I had not been more than three months in my new situation, when it became evident that my brother's dissolution was nigh at hand. One Sunday morning our old stuttering companion from Leadenhall made his appearance, and expressed a wish to see Bill once more and take a last farewell. They had been friends from boyhood, having been apprenticed to the same trade at the same time; they had travelled the road of life together, and seemed to entertain a brotherly love for each other. Repairing to my brother's house, we there met with three or four old friends who had also called to pay him their last tribute of respect. Presently we were all invited upstairs: and on entering his room, there lay poor Bill a living skeleton, who (strange to say) had lingered on for nine years in a hopeless state of consumption. But no sooner had we entered, than the lamps of life were lighted up; and the same winning smile played about his mouth, as when he was in the vigour of manhood. As his London comrade gazed on the wasted form, he could not contain his grief; and the melancholy scene equally affected the entire group ranged round the bed of their fast declining friend; until their stifled emotions burst forth in sobs and tears. 'Nature will be obeyed';—every one was drowned in sorrow, save only the object of all this deep solicitude. His latest words in life were those of hope; he was leaving a mere probationary state, feeling perfect confidence in the arrangements of the Omnipotent, and in humble submission to his Maker's will. Fearing to tax unnecessarily his exhausted powers, we now all in turn took his hand, each invoked a blessing upon his departing soul, and gently left the chamber.

After lingering on for a few days, he felt his end approaching, and we were summoned to witness his last moments. On our arrival, his spirit was still quick, but its frail tenement could hold out no longer. Propped up by pillows, my poor brother, after a few brief words, calmly bade every one 'good bye,'—then, leaning back upon his wife's and the nurse's arms, with a gentle sigh 'shuffled off this mortal coil,' and entered that state 'from whose bourn no traveller returns.'

William Brown expired 15th June, 1831, and his remains were interred in St. Giles's churchyard, in a brick-vault made for the occasion. He was so generally respected and beloved, that I never heard him spoken of but with pleasurable feelings.

But to return to business: thus matters went on for twelve months, nothing remarkable occurring. I may as well here state, that along with the house, I took (amongst other articles) a large bagatelle-table. At this game I played till I became an adept; and when not busy, used to practise billiard strokes: that is, such as could be accomplished on such a table.

During my short occupancy of this place, a strolling manager came to the town: and as he was unable to get permission to perform in public, I allowed him to put up his theatre on our bowling-green: and contrived, by soliciting my friends, to ensure him very good business. To aid his short company, and to render the performances more attractive, I played myself: a novelty which brought cash to the treasury, and made the little manager quite happy; nor did I lose by the speculation, as the audience were all customers to the bar. Not long after this the regular theatrical season commenced; and nothing would satisfy my particular supporters, but my appearance on the boards of the theatre in my native village, Barnwell. Being tolerably well up in Shakspeare, I consented to their desire; and my friends having communicated with the manager, I was introduced to that important personage; when, after delivering Othello's address to the Senators by way of sample, a night was fixed for my first appearance before a regular Cambridge audience. Knowing the importance of playing so arduous a part before an educated assembly, I took all possible pains to make myself thoroughly master of the business: the more so, as my attempt was deemed presumptuous by the critics.

The morning for rehearsal arrived, and I repaired to

the theatre, where in a short time the entire company assembled: and upon the prompter taking his seat we commenced business. This is an ordeal of no very agreeable nature: as the actors, if they are ever such sticks (and many of them are the veriest snobs imaginable), look down with immeasurable contempt upon all amateur performances. The conceit and puppyism of some of these gents are laughably vexatious. But, to return to the business, we proceeded on to the end, when the prompter complimented me by saying—'I have never met with anyone more perfect in the part.'

The bills were posted as usual in every part of the town: "Shakspeare's tragedy of *Othello*,—the part of 'Othello' by a gentlemen of Cambridge"; and this being something novel, the house filled to overflowing. At the appointed hour, all being ready, the play began. When my turn came, I made my *entré:* and was received by my friends with shouts of applause. The tumult having subsided we went to work. In delivering my first speech, which consists only of one sentence, I experienced a slight tremour, and my lips quivered. For I now felt the responsibility of the undertaking; and was aware also that I had laid myself open to a charge of vanity in attempting a task to which I was unequal. However, I was now fairly in for it; and nothing remained but to screw up my courage, and at all events do my best. Scene after scene passed on, the audience evincing unmistakeable proofs of contentment by uniform attention and well-timed applause. Thus we proceeded, warming as we went along: until, as the curtain fell on the conclusion of the play, one general and spontaneous burst reverberated through the house.

Thus, despite the envy and malice of some few little minds, my triumph was complete: that is, as far as under the circumstances it could be so. For all are well aware that it requires both great talents and immense practice to grapple with the mighty genius of our great dramatist.

At the expiration of a twelvemonth, the house which I occupied was offered to the highest bidder. The competition ran high in consequence of the business I had been doing: and the lot was knocked down to a rival brewer, who outbid every other competitor. This was a source of great annoyance to my old landlord. He begged me not to remain a tenant under the new man: and at the same time promised to put me into another house in the town. Like a good-natured simpleton, I complied: although repeatedly solicited by the other party to remain. This was one of the most grievous things that could have happened; we had to break up a comfortable home, and begin the world again. We were, moreover, worse off than before, having laid out all the money we possessed in buying furniture, and such things as were indispensable in a public business. This property was disposed of to a broker for less than a third of its original cost.

After waiting twelve months for the fulfilment of my friend the brewer's promise, I discovered that he was a great knave,—who had three times before cheated his creditors, and now again declared himself insolvent. I therefore hired a small shop, and opened in the boot trade: but having only scant means and little credit, I felt cramped at the beginning. Thus, by the time I had provided sufficient goods to make a show, my money ran short. Just at this crisis I fell in with a cunning knave, as mean and 'ignorant as dirt' in everything except making 'ewes and rams' of his gold. This fellow offered to lend me fifty pounds at *ten* per cent interest: an offer which necessity compelled me to accept. I was to have the use of this money as long as I could pay the interest; or, at least, until I could 'turn myself' in the way of trade.

About this period the Cambridge Garrick Club was formed, and I was invited to join it: which (thinking it might be in some respects to my advantage) I accordingly did, and played the leading business until the club reached the zenith of its fame. The society then numbered amongst its members the principal actors and dramatic writers of the time, namely, Macready, C. Kemble, Sheridan Knowles, Douglas Jerrold, &c. &c. On a certain occasion it was thought advisable to present an address to the patrons of the club and of the Drama generally: and as this was open to competition amongst the members at large, I thought I would try my hand with the rest. My attempts resulted in the following: which, being preferred to the other essays sent in, was delivered to the audience by myself.

ADDRESS TO THE PATRONS OF THE DRAMA.

> ONCE more we've met, to try our mimic powers,
> And give to scenic art our leisure hours;
> To woo with eager zeal the comic muse,
> Though bigots rant and hypocrites abuse;
> Do you, kind patrons, lend a favouring ear,
> If you approve, then disapprove who dare!

If smiles from you our humble efforts crown,
We fear no rigid critic's caustic frown.
What though no second Garrick treads our stage,
To seize your feelings or to mend the age;
Hope boldly cheers us on to plead our cause,
And strive from you to merit just applause;
Should you discover in our little band
The germ of genius—grant a fost'ring hand,—
Perchance the flower, when opening to the gale,
May to your soul its sweetest scent exhale—
Repay your kindness and reward your care:
For sons of Genius ever grateful were.
We kindly thank you for all favours past,
And hope such favours may for ever last.
With brim-full hearts we thank the ladies most,
Man's social friend, his partner, and his boast;
The brightest ornament of life below,
The nearest heavenly beings earth can shew;
Ah! formed alike to tread each path of life,
The tender mother, and the faithful wife,
The watchful daughter, by her father's side,
The gentle sister, and th' adoring bride!—
Bankrupt to woman, man can ne'er repay
The countless debt he owes her—EVERY way;
And yet he dares to hope—when all is due,
Another debt to add—a smile from you!
For English actors, and for English plays,
We ask your aid in these new-fangled days;
When nought but gewgaw trumpery is seen,
And dancing dolls and jugglers crowd the scene,
And foreign catgut-scraping knaves are fed,
Whilst British worth and talent pine for bread.
See classic Knowles in sorrow leave the land,
Compell'd to go at folly's base command;
That child of nature, skilled in ancient lore,
Disgusted flies, to seek some kindlier shore.
Go, exiled Bard, thou friend to virtue, go,
May peace thy gentle spirit ever know,

May choicest blessings on thee still attend,
And well earn'd laurels crown the Drama's friend,
In praise of thee my humble muse could dwell,
But time forbids,—so once for all—farewell!

I now, with reverence due, approach his name,
Who charmed the world with works of endless fame,—
Immortal SHAKSPEARE! to thy shade we bow,
And at thy sacred shrine we take the vow;
Thou great explorer of the human mind,
The noblest, brightest painter of mankind,
While mem'ry holds her seat, thy name shall stand,
The pride and glory of thy native land:
Revered by every nation on the earth,
Mankind shall bless the hour that gave thee birth:
For thou wast born, if rightly understood,
By Heaven's decree, for universal good,—
The wondrous powers of thy master mind
Were inexhaustible and unconfin'd.
Neglected now, to England's lasting shame,
With many more who still stand high in Fame;
Great Massinger, and Otway, who have run
Their famed career round Shakspeare's golden sun:
Bright satellites that shewed the centre orb,
Whose dazzling light must every sense absorb.
Shall man degen'rate, and himself disgrace
By changing things like these for vile grimace?—
I trust not so, and hope the poet's lyre
May fill each languid heart with nobler fire;
And in that hope we thank you,—and retire.

The Undergraduates of the University had also raised a theatrical club, and built a theatre in Jesus-lane, which was fitted up completely in all respects. Shortly after this house first opened, the party who had the management of the place requested me to assist him in getting up the *Merchant of Venice*, and I played 'Shylock' there accordingly. But for this heinous offence, my name was erased from the books of the Garrick Club. That body had been weak enough to insert a clause in their rules prohibiting the members from playing with any other party, on pain of expulsion. I would not submit to, what I deemed, such puerile tyranny; and was immediately visited with the penalties of my disobedience. The more flattering result to myself was, that I in consequence became acquainted with some University gentlemen of high standing and unquestionable talent. With them I played 'Brutus' in *Julius Cæsar;* and otherwise aided in bringing out their pieces, the business being generally private and select.

When the regular company returned for the season to the theatre royal, Barnwell, I was requested to play for an Undergraduates' bespeak; and on this occasion selected Cumberland's play of the *Jew;* in which I enacted 'Sheva' the principal part. For this performance I received much approbation and cordial thanks. Dr. Thackeray[1] also came down to my house to compliment me upon my success; declaring that he had seen Banister and Elliston in the part, but neither of them played it so well as myself. He also gave me an order for dress shoes; and promised to recommend me to his friends.

I append to this chapter some local stage reminiscences of this period. They are strictly matter of fact, and may perhaps amuse my readers.

[1] An eminent local physician.

THEATRICAL ANECDOTES.

CAMBRIDGE was always strong in the dramatic line, but never more so, than at the period under notice. I have already made mention of the Garrick and University clubs; but there was a third society called the 'Shakspeare,' to which nobody in particular belonged; its ostensible 'head and front' being the same party, whom the University men had enabled to build the theatre,[1] then existing in Jesus-lane. This man's name was Andrew J. Tempany; he was not, I think, of Cambridge origin; but had come out of the Midland counties, and was by trade a paper-stainer. He did not lack talent, and had an off-hand 'devil-may-care' way of doing business, that made him rather popular with the Undergraduates of the day. The said Andrew was, in truth, equally reckless and improvident at home and abroad; he seemed to prefer a 'hand to mouth' state of existence; and his ordinary habits possibly engendered the quickness and fertility of resource, that I have sometimes witnessed in him.

T.'s favorite *rôle* was 'Pangloss' in the *Heir-at-Law*; and on a certain occasion when dressing for this part, (an operation which he had, as usual, deferred until the last moment,) the indispensable black silk stockings of the 'LL.D. and A.S.S.' were nowhere to be found. 'No time to lose,' quoth Andrew, 'too late to send anywhere; must paint *these!* Here, you sir, fetch that bucket here—take up the brush, and lay on!' But the black paint would not take kindly to the white

---

[1] The shell of this building is now occupied by Messrs. Death and Dyson as stabling. It contained two tiers of boxes, and a good pit; the stage was nearly forty feet in depth, and the proscenium was (out of some absurd rivalry) made slightly wider than that of the Barnwell theatre—a great drawback in point of convenience.

cotton 'continuations'. The case was obviously hopeless; 'Pangloss' would never have been fit to appear that night, but for the intervention of a master-stroke. Andrew's genius was however equal to the emergency. 'Take 'em off altogether', was his decision, 'and paint *me!*' Painted he was accordingly, from the knees downward; and, as his legs were ever and anon 'touched up' during the evening, I am not aware that this cool expedient ever became patent to the public. Perhaps, indeed, some of the ladies in front may have admired, as the old song hath it, 'the fineness of Mr. Snout's linen:' but let that pass.

This absurd anecdote recals others to my mind. Here is a story that partly concerns myself. Upon one occasion of the University club giving some performances, the part of 'Othello' was undertaken by a gentleman of Trinity College, whose patronymic certainly was *not* 'Browne,'—although his godfathers and god-mothers may possibly have bestowed that name upon him at his baptism. 'Browne,' however, he continued, amongst his intimates, to the end of the chapter,—with the variations of 'Brown with an *e* at the end', and 'Browne the aristocrat.' On the day succeeding the performance above specified, the following dialogue is *supposed* to have taken place in the streets of Cambridge:

Mr. P.[1]—Good morning, Mr. Brown! Of course, you went to see your namesake's 'Othello' last night?
John Brown.—I did, Sir.
Mr. P.—And what thought you of his performance?
John Brown.—Why, Sir, during the three first acts he put me in mind of a chimney-sweeper's apprentice; who, sneaking out at night without his master's leave, had got drunk, and was 'seedy' in the morning. And in the two last acts, Sir, he reminded me of the same chimney-sweeper's apprentice, *drunk again* at night!
Mr. P.—By all the gods, you've hit it off exactly! Ha! ha! Adieu!

[1] The actual compiler of the dialogue, and identical with the *corpse* of 'Julius Cæsar', to be presently introduced.

The truth is, my namesake experienced an attack of stage-fright, and had recourse to Dutch courage in the shape of *porter*. Long before the end of the play, his wits were so drenched in this not over-intellectual fluid, that the man's whole bearing was that of a May-day sweep far advanced in liquor. I remember well, that in the last scene where 'Othello' makes use of the words—'If that thou be'st a devil, I cannot kill thee!'—Mr. Browne, instead of stabbing 'Iago' according to the text, charged him head downwards like a wild buffalo, or a West-India 'nigger' butting at a hogshead. The audience positively screamed with laughter!

Mr. Browne did not hear the last of his 'ill-weaved ambition' for a long time; but he bore all good-naturedly, to do him justice. The evening that succeeded his first, and let us hope, last appearance in 'Othello', witnessed his triumphant success as 'Miss Lucretia Mac Tab', in the *Poor Gentleman*. His *forte* was Comedy; but, like some others, he only discovered his proper vocation by the grace of accident.

I have before alluded to my having sustained the part of 'Brutus' in Shakspeare's *Julius Cæsar*, which play was got up in a very complete manner, at the time to which I refer. Nevertheless, on the first night of performance, there occurred more than one incident of an obtrusively comic nature. I shall not easily forget 'Marc Antony's' oration, with altogether new readings and accompaniments. My friend Mr. P—— of Trinity did enact 'Cæsar', and, after being duly slain in the Senate-house, was carried upon a bier to the forum. The 'bier' was what, I believe, is called a 'hand-truck'; and, so far as appearances go, would have been admirably suited to the intended purpose. But, alas, the modern frame-work had been imperfectly draped; and the (scarcely Roman) legend, 'METCALFE AND Co.' offered fearful temptations to risibility. However, the audience behaved with much discretion, and an intelligent supernumerary contrived to mask the incongruous text. But unfortunately, matters did not end here. The truck was evidently not designed for the repose of any living man; and even 'dead Cæsar' found himself rather uncomfortable than otherwise; his neck resting on one iron bar, his heels upon another, and a third cutting into his spine, upon the least attempt to lie at ease. Under these favourable circumstances, 'Antony's' celebrated address commenced somewhat as follows:

Antony.—Friends, Romans, Countrymen—
Corpse.   *Oh, d——n it, oh!*
Antony.—*Why, what's the matter now?* Lend me your ears: *You, Jem,*[1]—*what is it?*
Corpse.   *This will never do!*
Antony.—I come to bury Cæsar, not to praise him. *Just look to Mr. P——d.*
Corpse.   *And look sharp!*
Antony.—The evil that men do, &c. &c.

Eventually, under their leader's instructions, the mob were brought to close round, so as to admit of 'Cæsar's' slightly shifting his position; and on the second night of performance, a better arrangement was secured. This incident serves to shew, how much depends on the 'property-man's' business being carefully executed.

Another funny circumstance which occurred the same evening, went nigh to making a burlesque of the well-known quarrel scene (in the fourth Act) between 'Brutus' and 'Cassius'. Mr. A—— of Caius College, played the trifling part of 'Titinius'. He was a tall fellow, with a naturally comic cast of features; but on the present occasion, his countenance wore an irresistibly ludicrous aspect, by reason of his helmet being shipped back-part foremost. Probably ignorant of stage rules, his interest in the scene had caused him to take up a position at the wings, right in view of the audience: whose attention was soon diverted by the remarkable appear-

[1] The individual who played 'first mob,'—a very noted character still living.

ance he presented. The culprit seemed wholly unaware that the laughter which ensued was of his own provoking, and some little delay occurred, ere he could be seduced from his post; indeed he made a wild demonstration, as if intending to cross the stage, which was happily checked in time. But as it was, we had hard work to bring our audience back again to the 'Tent near Sardis.' Poor A. (as good-natured a man as ever lived) was extremely sorry, when he came to understand the nature of his mistake.

There lived in a neighbouring county about this time, a gentleman of good family and estate, who was an amateur actor of some local note. He had played a good deal with the provincial company that made a regular circuit of the country towns in that district. The opulent squire's patronage, as a matter of course, brought grist to the manager's mill; and I need hardly add, that Mr. S——'s theatrical bark sailed over halcyon seas. The gentleman, however, was quite free from self-conceit, and by degrees suspected that his talents were perhaps not being subjected to a *bonâ-fide* test. Under these circumstances, he addressed an University friend at Cambridge, expressing his desire to play 'Hamlet' to an audience, which, as being entirely strange, might be deemed impartial. The party to whom this application was made, referred the matter to me; and we very shortly informed Mr. S. that he need only name his day, when he would find all duly arranged.

The Jesus-lane theatre was accordingly engaged for the date eventually fixed. Mr. S. brought over from Huntingdon the manager, his wife, and a lady of their company; by whom the parts of 'Laertes,' 'Queen,' and 'Ophelia' were to be respectively filled. The University friend already mentioned was bespoken for 'Horatio', whilst I myself volunteered for the 'Ghost', and, betwixt Town and Gown, contrived to make up a very creditable cast of characters. The evening of performance arrived, and everything was in readiness. The hero of the occasion had expressed a particular desire that his audience should *not* be too 'select'; a wish that was very faithfully carried out. The curtain rose at the appointed hour; and the best part of the tragedy was walked through in a very respectable manner; at all events, without any sort of hitch or hindrance. The house was in an amiable mood; and the audience chose to evince their playful disposition by taking every occasion to bestow unlimited applause upon 'Horatio' and my 'Ghost'-ship: the latter proceeding being clean against stage etiquette.

In the meantime 'Hamlet' was getting on swimmingly. The Prince shewed a good figure, was well-dressed, and had studied his part with evident care; but of *acting* it, he really seemed to have very little notion. His performance amounted to no more than tolerably well enunciated declamation. In the third act, certain references as to 'going in', and questions regarding the 'time of commencing work,' began to circulate audibly. But at this critical juncture, the celebrated 'To be, or not to be' intervened; and the actor delivered the soliloquy in a style so much superior to any of his former essays, that the audience now apparently made up their minds to hear him out. And perhaps they would have done so without pronouncing any verdict, but for an accidental circumstance.

In the last scene of the fifth act, 'the poisoned cup' (a vessel holding about two quarts) had been placed on table brim-full of strong ale; and, although certain modest quenchers indulged in by the Court of Denmark had considerably reduced its contents, there remained at least a pint and a-half unconsumed, at the period when 'Hamlet's' faithful friend swears to share his fate:

Horatio.—I'm more an antique Roman than a Dane,
        Here's yet some liquor left! (*attempts to drink.*)
Hamlet.   As thou'rt a man,
    Give me the cup; let go!

Horatio.   *Take care, take care!*
                  There's deuced nigh a quart—
Hamlet.   By heaven, I'll have it.
Horatio.—Throw it behind you, then!

But 'Hamlet', not understanding the force of this last stage direction, did the very contrary; and a foaming tide of ale rolled its way down the boards towards the orchestra. 'Hallo! —— old boy,' cried a lady from a neighbouring village, addressing 'Horatio' by his own name: 'you were'nt given to throwing away good liquor in that fashion!' It needed only this spark to fire the tinder. The curtain was judiciously dropped on the Prince of Denmark's dying agonies, amid yells of laughter, cat-calls, shouts of *Encore!* and all sorts of ironical applause. Mr. S—— probably went home a wiser man than he came.

I had nothing to do with the rest of the evening's entertainments, on the occasion to which the foregoing reminiscence attaches. These were left to the discretion of a gentleman who had played 'First Grave-digger' (waistcoats[1] and all) in the tragedy: the same individual, in fact, of whom honorable mention has been hereinbefore made, as leader of the mob in *Julius Cæsar*. The sun of 'Hamlet' had scarce set, ere an amusing interlude was extemporised by this worthy. Mr. Jem ——, already dressed as the hero of a popular farce called the *Unfinished Gentleman*,[2] forthwith made his appearance in front of the drop-scene, and discoursed somewhat as follows:

"Ladies and Gentlemen,

"We beg your permission to substitute the *Unfinished Gentleman*, for *Raising the Wind* advertised in the bills of this

---

[1] This well-known bit of buffoonery has held its ground for many years, and must rest on some very ancient tradition. I believe it is still tolerated.

[2] An *Adelphi* 'roarer and screamer' of the broadest description. All I can now remember of it is, that the principal personage describes himself to have begun life, as the 'hind-legs of a *h*elephant.'

date. We were some days since apprised that a *gentleman* from London, who was expected to play 'Fainwould', could not possibly be in attendance; and we subsequently relied on the services of a *person* who has often before played the part, and who undertook it with apparent good-will. That individual has most treacherously failed us at the eleventh hour, [*great excitement—Where is he?—pitch him over!—hooray!—hear, hear!—name, name!*] and now sits amongst you, for the better enjoyment of his fancied triumph! [*Awful uproar—Who is it?*] Far be it from me, Ladies and Gentlemen, to suggest anything of a personal nature; *only, as Mr. T—— is conveniently located in the centre of the Pit there*, he may perhaps think it worth while to explain his extraordinary conduct. Ladies and Gentlemen, we shall not detain you many minutes."

With this, the ingenious apologist abruptly retired, leaving poor T—— to extricate himself as best he might: who had some difficulty in satisfying the audience of his not being in fault. The truth is, that T——, being a member of the Garrick Club, had good-naturedly consented to play 'Fainwould' on the emergency represented—not supposing that such a case came within the rule of that society, to which I have before referred. However, on the eve of the performance, he got due notice, that if he played he would be expelled, as I had been previously; and, not coveting this alternative, Mr. T—— withdrew his promise. Thus the attack so publicly made, albeit very laughable, was rather hard. But the wily orator (the 'Unfinished' One) had gained three points, all of some importance in his estimation; for,—

1st. He had, by implication, had a slap at the Garrick Club.

2nd. And a good dig at a rival low comedian, his natural enemy.

3rd. He had (and this was genuine business), while poor T—— was engaged in defending himself, secured all the indulgence in point of time that could possibly be required behind scenes.

I won't attempt to analyse the proceeding in reference to strict morality. For verily, the children of this world are wiser in their generation than the children of light!

Some of the scenes painted for the Jesus Lane Theatre, by old Northhouse of Lincoln and other professional artists, were perfect pictures. But the gem of gems was the 'Dark Passage' got up expressly for Lord Byron's *Werner*. It embraced a perspective shewn through four distinct 'drops.' I well recollect the surprise and gratification expressed, on seeing this unique performance, by that sterling comic actor old Tilbury, on an occasion of his being professionally engaged at Cambridge in company with Miss Wyndham,—the talented Miss W. of that day.

Many recollections connected with these days float on my memory: but having kept no journal, I am unable to recal the details of each story. The foregoing are, however, veritable 'Gleanings' from the Cambridge boards in bye-gone days.

CHAPTER IV.

I AM BEGGARED AGAIN BY AN ACT OF ROBBERY—THE FRIENDLY HOST, AND THE HONEST USURER—STANZAS—A MERRY CHRISTMAS—THE 'ODD FELLOWS'—MY HONOURABLE DISCHARGE UNDER THE INSOLVENT ACT—I ACCEPT AN ENGAGEMENT—THE DIVIDED INHERITANCE—SIX WEEKS OF SLAVERY.

ALL now seemed to go smoothly; but Dame Fortune had not yet done with me. I had been making an unusual number of first-rate boots, the greatest amount of orders I had executed within the same time since I began business; and being naturally desirous of exhibiting my handicraft to the public, I kept a number in the window for show. On going one morning to open shop, (for we lived in a small house some distance off) I applied the key: but found it would not turn. I then twisted the handle, and the door flew open: when to my surprise and horror, I perceived that the place had been cleared of everything; even the boot-trees were gone, and nothing remained save a pair of pump-uppers which hung high up on a nail. This blow fairly prostrated me. After taking down the shutters, I returned to breakfast, in such a state as to be scarcely conscious of what was passing around me. My wife was blowing the fire: but as I had returned sooner than usual, asked what was the matter, as 'she had never before seen me look so bewildered.' I replied, 'Nothing;' and sat down hardly believing in the reality of what I had seen. Again she put the question; when I informed her that the shop had been robbed of all it contained. Scarcely realising my words, she exclaimed—'What did you say?' I repeated the statement,—'Some thieves have cleared out the shop; it's as empty as when I took it: they have left nothing!' Then as if stunned, my wife too sat down in despair.

Presently springing from my seat, I exclaimed in the bitterness of my heart—'Why does fate so cruelly pursue me? What wrong have I committed—whom have I injured, that I should be thus persecuted?' Something here seemed to whisper—'Patience!' But had I not been patient? Overcome by my feelings, I walked back to take a look at the desolate scene, and found there a concourse of people; some looking serious, others laughing and joking. One hoary-headed man, as great a knave as ever disgraced a mother, said loud enough to reach my ear—'He's been robbing himself.' This speech was delivered in a strong Norfolk accent. Some, who entertained a higher opinion of me, offered to get up a subscription to assist me over my difficulty; but this aid I declined accepting.

There was one spectator, whom I must ever remember—the landlord of the 'George' inn, next house but one to my miserable shop. He expressed great sorrow for my loss; and sympathising with me in my misfortune, invited me to his annual dinner, at which (he observed) there would be present about forty of the most respectable tradesmen in the town: and he had no doubt of being able to prevail upon each of them to give me an order for a pair of boots. Indeed, by way of starting the matter, he undertook to give the first order himself. Depending upon his promise, I concluded that the profit to be derived from his own order would defray the expense attending the dinner. On the morrow I appeared at the appointed time. There was to be sure a goodly company, and the dinner was served up in excellent style: the wine went round, and all seemed gay and jolly; whilst for myself, I wore as good a seeming as I could put on.

During the time of dessert, the waiter came round to collect the money, which was thirteen-and-sixpence a-head. Mine host had given me to understand that I should not be called upon to pay; but that with me was out of the question. Time however wore on, and my friend's more positive promise slipped away with it; about twenty-two years have passed, but the 'order' has not yet arrived. I never was so speciously victimized in the course of all my travels. At a subsequent period, I learned that this worthy publican used to secrete great-coats and umbrellas belonging to the passengers who came by coach. He had a room appropriated to this purpose, which the servants about the place called 'the condemned hole'; but despite his cunning, he died in poverty, despised by all who knew him.

As misfortunes never come singly, mine now followed one another fast. Immediately after the robbery of my shop, the only party with whom I had credit went smash: holding at the time my acceptance for a hundred pounds, payable at two months. Just at this opportune moment, my cormorant blood-sucking money-lender pounces down upon me, simply alleging that he 'heard there was a screw loose, and meant to be first in at the death.' Indignant at this gratuitous insult, I at once put my books into the hand of a lawyer, for the purpose of getting money to satisfy my unreasonable creditor. Enough was collected to pay the principal, together with *seven* per cent interest; which appeased his ravenous maw at the time. Not that the wretch was satisfied—far from it; indeed, I have no doubt that to this day he considers himself the injured party, notwithstanding my surrender of all that I then possessed. However, as far as retributive justice goes, fortune and his own subsequent misconduct have amply avenged me of this sordid usurer. I might, if so disposed, relate instances of heartless self-seeking and cruel persecution, which would exhibit the same individual's character in a still more odious light than his base usage of myself. But although the party to whom I refer might be fairly regarded as without the pale of civilisation, I refrain from pursuing this subject; lest I should appear to be violating the principle laid down in my original prospectus to these memoirs.

Thus driven into a corner and held at bay, I had no alternative but to take the benefit of the Insolvent Act. On the Sunday before Christmas-day, as I sat doing the turnspit and brooding over my unhappy fate, I felt inclined to commit my thoughts to paper: and they are faithfully, if not altogether elegantly, recorded in the following stanzas :—

In life's gay morn a thoughtless boy,
    I started forth with glee,
And dreamed that pleasures ne'er could cloy:
    For so it seemed to me!

All nature teemed with beauties then,
    To my weak sense 'twas so;
Alas! there's nought I see or ken
    In this sad world, but woe.

The rich man proudly lifts his head
    Above his poorer neighbour;
And frowns upon the humble shed,
    The lowly home of labour.

And treats him with indignant scorn,
    As humbly passing by;
Which makes him wish he'd ne'er been born,
    Whilst tears start from his eye.

Th' Almighty Father of mankind
    Did no such diff'rence make:
Then man to man should be more kind,
    If only for His sake.

Ye rich and great in time take heed,
    And soothe the sons of woe;
Rememb'ring your great Maker's creed,
    Which all of you should know.

The good man on his death-bed smiles,
    And leaves the world in peace;
Well knowing here end all his toils,
    That there his joys increase.

When God shall call him to account,
 He'll answer without fear;
And to the great Tribunal mount,
 Saying, 'Lord, Thy servant's here!'

And if the Almighty Judge approve,
 He joins the heavenly choir;
And sings the songs of praise and love,
 And strikes the tuneful lyre.

In endless bliss he dwells on high,
 Beside his Master's throne;
Where nought but what is pure comes nigh,
 Where sin is never known.

Then live in fear of God on earth,
 Your duty do to man;
So lived your Saviour from His birth;
 All must approve the plan!

On Christmas-eve, in melancholy mood, we left our comfortable dwelling and took refuge in an old tumble-down cottage on the outskirts of the town. Our furniture consisted of half-a-dozen chairs, a table, and a stump-bedstead. The weather had set-in intensely cold, and the thick and murky appearance of the atmosphere made us shiver as we entered our dreary abode. With sorrowful hearts we retired to rest; a strong north wind was howling in the chimney and whistled about the crazy doors and casements; and when, on awaking in the morning, I cast a sorrowful look around this scene of destitution, my heart sank within me. At the foot of the bed lay a heap of snow which had been driven through the dilapidated casement; the miserably fitted doors and windows chattered as if in mockery of our woe; and the naked appearance of the neglected chamber inspired me with feelings of horror. Never was Christmas-day ushered in more inauspiciously; all nature seemed to be in mourning, and everything looked cold and desolate. On peeping abroad, I found that the snow had blocked up the doorway: nor could we emerge from our wretched hovel until some kind-hearted people dug us out.

To describe my feelings under these trying circumstances would be utterly impossible. Within a week I was arrested and conveyed to prison. Here I was compelled to herd with divers loose characters: whose open boastings as to how they had cheated their creditors, made me feel heartily ashamed of the company into which I had thus been unfortunately thrown. Desirous to avoid, as much as possible, the contaminating influence of such pests, I confined myself within the narrow limits of my cell, an arched kennel, eight feet by six, having a small window with iron bars placed cross-wise. In a few days some kind friends came to visit me, with a deputation from an Odd Fellows' lodge, to which I belonged. After a few words of condolence, they handed me over three pounds, twelve shillings, and a *farthing*, which had been collected in the lodge on the previous evening. The uninitiated may be curious to know why the seemingly inconsequential farthing was given; and for their enlightenment I beg to state, that everything of this nature is done in accordance with the *title* of the Order,—the farthing having been thus added to make the amount *odd*.

Several of the brotherhood also gave me orders for boots: which I managed to get up by sending a written order to the leather-cutter for materials and grindery. When I had cut out the legs, my wife took them home with her to close; while I fitted my stuff, made my threads, and rounded and holed my inner-soles. By this time she had stabbed on the counters, whipped on the side-linings, and closed up the seams: so that I could now set to work to make the bottoms; thus we worked into each other's hands without loss of time. The prison authorities observing my industrious habits lent me every encouragement; the governor and turn-keys gave me orders both for themselves and their wives: considering it a favour to get a pair of boots of my handicraft. I was kept in gaol six weeks: during which time I lived well, and saved sufficient to pay for a suit of clothes.

On my going before the Court for examination, not a creditor appeared to oppose my discharge. My landlord came forward to speak on my behalf, telling the judge that I had acted most honourably: having left my furniture to be disposed of for the benefit of my creditors. After putting a few questions, the judge signified my discharge: observing that I was fairly entitled to the benefit of the Act, which was designed more especially for the relief of honest, but unfortunate, debtors. I thereupon made my bow, and retired.

During my residence in the county prison, I received from a manager in the north of England the offer of an engagement to lead the business of the company. This led to a formal agreement: and, it being settled for me to open in the part of 'Sheva,' in the *Jew*, I prepared for a start,—packing up such stage properties and dresses as I possessed. Amongst the members of the University Dramatic Club, were two who had always treated me like a brother. I could not leave Cambridge without bidding them good-bye: and on the evening prior to my departure, sought their respective lodgings for the purpose. One I found: but the other was gone out, as his landlady said, to a party. Determined however to see him, I went again next morning at seven o'clock, and found him in bed; but although it was broad day, a rushlight still burned in a candlestick placed in the wash-hand basin. With some difficulty I awoke my man to a state of consciousness; when, on becoming aware of my presence, he rubbed his eyes, and pointing to two piles of clothes and two little heaps of money, said: 'There is all my worldly wealth; I have divided it into equal parts: take which you please.' My poverty and not my will consented to accept the generous offer. I hesitated: but my noble friend insisted upon my compliance with the arrangement. I therefore pocketed the money, tied up the clothes, and, after shaking hands, bade him farewell. This was one of the most disinterested acts of friendship I ever experienced.

Returning home I took breakfast, and got ready for my journey. In about an hour the coach stopped at my door. The weather was bitterly cold: and the snow fell so incessantly, as scarcely to hold up during seventy miles' travel. On arriving at my destination, the first thing that attracted my notice was a play-bill stuck upon the gate-post as we drove into the inn-yard. The pieces announced were *Pizzaro* and the *Pilot,* my name being starred for 'Pizzaro' and 'Long Tom Coffin'! Here was an infernal trick to serve a poor devil! Neither of the parts had I ever studied: my engagement was to open in 'Sheva,' a part I could have played as well as any actor in existence. The truth is, the manager was a drunken sot, who was merely conducting a bankrupt concern, so that I had no hope of redress. I must either play such business as he put into my hands, or return home *minus* my expenses. Having little or no cash I submitted to the former alternative, and worked through six dreary weeks in one of the most inclement seasons ever known.

My study was unceasing; for frequently have I had *two* parts given to me at a rehearsal in the morning, to play at night! All this annoyance arose out of some blunder committed by our incapable head in making his engagements. However, I was resolved to have the six weeks' salary, and make him stand accountable to the public. Towards the conclusion of our term of agreement I was so worn out, that, to keep myself awake, I used to walk in the fields to study: the snow being at the time ancle-deep. This occurred in that long winter, during which, in some parts of the country, the cattle died for want of food; the ground being covered with snow, almost to the end of May. The people were disheartened: and the business of the theatre was most wretched. We, on one occasion, played *Macbeth* to nineteen shillings: and at another time, when *The Will* was to be performed, the curtain drew up to an audience which consisted of three little girls peeping over the orchestra. Having worked through six weeks of such hardship as few ever endured, I packed up my wardrobe and returned home. I reached Cambridge about midnight, nearly frozen, whither I had ridden outside the mail: the distance, as before observed, being seventy miles.

CHAPTER V.

I RESOLVE ON TRYING THE LONDON STAGE—I DELIGHT THE 'PEOPLES' IN SHEVA, AT THE PAVILION—'GOVERNOR DAVIDGE' AT THE SURREY—OTHELLO AT A DISCOUNT—A TRANS-PONTINE ROW—VIRGINIUS AND HIS DAUGHTER—'ONE FOR HIS NOB'—I RETURN TO CAMBRIDGE—TRY BILLIARDS—MY SLATE TABLE—TOM EGAN'S STROKE—I BEGIN TO GO A-HEAD ONCE MORE.

ON the morrow I consulted my University friends as to the best course to take. They advised me to go at once to London,—giving me letters of recommendation, and critical remarks on my performances, cut from the public journals. Thinking it better to begin low in the world, I waited upon Farrell at the 'Pavilion,' and exhibited my credentials; after looking over which he agreed to give me an opening on that day week, in 'Sheva.' I selected this part, because it had not been played by any actor for some years; and as all parties engaged in the piece would have a fresh study, it could not be put on the stage perfect in less than the time named.

The evening of the performance arrived, and I repaired to the theatre. As it took but little time to dress, I was soon ready; having nothing but my wig and beard, gabardine, and shoes to adjust. This done, I took a peep at the house which was crowded to suffocation; the audience being composed for the most part of the 'peoples.' Upon making my *entré* I was received with a round of applause; to which I responded by waving my hat sideways to the audience, without interfering with the action of the scene. This seemed to please them mightily, as they called out to each other—'Tat's pishness, s'help me got!' Thus all went on bravely to the end: much to the delight and satisfaction of the well-disposed Israelites, who at the conclusion of the piece, insisted on my appearance before the curtain. Never was a *debût* more gratifying or successful.

The play was announced for repetition on the Thursday night following, amid the shouts and 'bravos!' of the 'peoples.' On the appointed night the boxes presented a galaxy of wealth and beauty rarely congregated together. Diamonds and jewelry glistened on the polished brows of Jewish damsels, whose splendid costumes might have well become the queen of Sheba on her visit to witness the greatness and wisdom of Solomon. As scene succeeded scene, the excitement still increased,—the men applauding, the women waving their handkerchiefs; and on the fall of the curtain, I was again summoned to receive their universal congratulations. After the performance, I walked over to the public-house opposite, to get a glass of grog. The place was crowded with Jews, who were discussing the merits of the performance: many of them insisting that none but a Jew could have played the part so truthfully.

One fellow sang out at the top of his voice,—'S'help me got, Chreen's tone prown!' He referred to Green, then leading tragedian at the Pavilion. All this was very flattering at the time, and had I succumbed to the regulations of the management, I might have gained a permanent standing in the profession. But on being asked to play 'Virginius' on Saturday night, *as a second piece*, I refused; thinking it derogatory to the author, Sheridan Knowles, who belonged to the Garrick club when I was a member.

On the following morning I went down to the Surrey, and found 'governor Davidge' (as he was usually called) in the treasury; who, after looking over my letters of recommendation, promised me an opening in 'Rob Roy.' Sinclair was to have played 'Frank Osbaldiston', but here my evil genius pursued me. The piece was announced, and the day of performance arrived; when, to my unspeakable mortification, the great singer was unable to keep his engagement, in consequence of a severe cold, attended with strong symptoms of bronchitis. The season was now drawing towards its close; my little store of cash was nearly exhausted, and there was no alternative but to play for a benefit, which, as my only chance, I snatched at like a drowning man. The piece selected was *Othello*, in which I was underlined to enact the 'Moor.' The important night arrived, and I repaired to the theatre. The actors were getting ready; the house was crowded, and the gods aloft held most discordant revelry, evincing strong symptoms of their nectar having been unusually potent.

On my first entrance, followed by Cobham as 'Iago', the most horrid yell that ever assailed the senses burst upon my astonished ears like a clap of thunder. A regular storm prevailed, fights ensued in every part of the house, and confusion reigned supreme throughout the evening. I was afterwards informed, that Cobham and Booth, who had just returned from America, had packed the house for the purpose of 'damning' *me*—and damned knaves they were for their pains. But, although I was thus scurvily treated, they did not have it all their own way; for the impartial portion of the audience bundled the younger Cobham and his gang of parasites out of the gallery, and several of the blackguards got roughly handled in the pit. The most remarkable part in this Bedlamite scene was however enacted by a powerful young man in the boxes; who, seizing one of the yelping curs by the collar and breech, dropped him quietly into the pit, to the great delight of the audience and equal astonishment of the party so deported. This feat was hailed with the most deafening shouts and uproarious demonstrations that ever frighted the tragic Muse from her propriety.

Although I had to contend against the most discouraging circumstances that ever man experienced, I felt determined to go through my part, were it even in dumb-show. The general public will scarcely credit that this unfair trick has often been played off upon strangers making their first appearance on the London boards. At the conclusion of the performance, many persons connected with the theatre expressed their entire disgust at the conduct of the parties who had lent themselves to this degrading business. Before leaving the theatre, I was requested to play 'Virginius' for the box-keeper's benefit, who now holds a similar situation under my particular friends, Johnson and Nelson Lee of the City theatre.

On the night of performance I repaired to the scene of action: and having donned the toga, proceeded to essay one of the most noble and interesting characters in the entire range of the British Drama. I was this time received by the audience with great favour, as if they were determined to compensate me for the indignities I had previously suffered. The piece worked on smoothly, the attention of the people was riveted to the stage, and my frail bark appeared to be gliding over a glassy sea. On making my *exit* with 'Icilius', where we hurry off to meet the foe, I was honored with a hearty round of applause; and up to this point, all had gone well as heart could wish. When the cue was given for 'Virginius' to enter on his return from camp to rescue his daughter, (who during her father's absence, has been seized by Appius Claudius as his slave), the lady who played 'Virginia' rushed forward as usual, to throw herself into her parent's arms. In attempting this upon the present occasion, 'Virginia's' head came in contact with the nose of the unhappy 'Virginius'; whereby the latter was sent sprawling on his back, with the blood running in an ample stream from his damaged frontispiece. This accident occurred in consequence of my not having had a rehearsal with the lady, who, being the stage-manager's wife, took the unpardonable liberty of absenting herself from that important duty.

The smash was so terrible, that it was impossible to stop the bleeding. For nearly half-an-hour the greatest confusion prevailed; until at length the stage-manager went before the drop, and informed the house that it was impossible that I could proceed with the part, in consequence of the injury I had received. I was subsequently assured, that the beautiful 'Virginia' butted at me purposely, and with malice prepense. If she really did so, it was a most fiendish act. The lady is still living, although somewhat fallen into the vale of years. Should this record meet her eye, perhaps she will let me know whether it was accidentally or designedly done. To return to the scene; one of the theatrical hacks of the time read the remainder of the part, with a good deal of flourish, as if in exultation over a fallen foe. I could name all the parties connected with the Surrey at this period; but I choose rather to drop the curtain upon an invidious picture.

Although the plank upon which I had still floated was thus rudely swept from under me, I did not despair. I returned home, disappointed indeed; for I had hoped to make sufficient money to pay my creditors, whom I could not now bear to face. My first act was to make out a statement of the exact sums claimable by each person to whom I was indebted. I then went round to all: and renewed the obligations which had been cancelled by the Insolvent Act. When I informed them that my intention was to pay all in full, some laughed, others said 'Walker!' and one fellow, who paid court to the daughter of a last and boot-tree maker in Holborn, to whom I owed the immense sum of one guinea, upon my desiring him to tell his intended father-in-law that I would pay, sneeringly observed,—'Oh, ah, I dare say you will!' This I regarded as one of the most brutal insults I ever had to put up with. However, I *did* pay every creditor twenty shillings in the pound, though to accomplish it I worked night and day.

Being now my own man again, and having entered upon a speculation that paid, although slowly, I crept on by degrees. Possessing some knowledge of billiards, I bought an old wooden table, and taught the game among my fellow-townsmen, which was a source of considerable profit to me. Thus things went on for about two years, when I prevailed upon my landlord to build me a second billiard-room. This being done, I purchased another wooden table; but as slate was now beginning to supersede wood, the thought occurred to me that I would buy some slates in the rough, and make a bed for the table I had last purchased. I accordingly went to a merchant's yard, and bought four slabs of various size and unequal substance. I then commenced one of the most tedious and up-hill tasks that ever man attempted. I first chiselled down the surface as nearly as I could to a level face; and next sawed each slab to its proper size with a common hand-saw: a job that would break the heart of any lazy man.

Having proceeded thus far, I next secured a square piece of Yorkshire stone, and fixed it in a wood frame, with a long pole running across the top; this was the style of machine that we used to holy-stone decks with on board-ship. With the aid of this rude engine, I set two men to grind down the surface of the slate. This was accomplished by gathering a quantity of dirt from the road-side, and putting it into a sieve; whereby the soft portion is washed away, leaving the sharp gritty substance behind. This stuff when ground betwixt two hard surfaces will cut like small diamonds; but as slate is in its nature remarkably tough, the progress we made was slow in proportion. Whilst the two men drew the machine backwards and forwards, I fed the work by keeping up a constant supply of grit and water. Thus in about three weeks we so far prepared the slabs, as to be able to lay them on the frame of the billiard-table, in order to render the joinings perfect, and to justify the bed by a spirit-level.

As I was compelled to do this work at home, (having no other available place) it was a source of great annoyance to my wife; the slate slush running downstairs, and constantly inundating the lower part of the house. During the accomplishment of this arduous performance, I was constantly assailed by the impertinent remarks of passers-by; many of whom fancied that I had undertaken an impossibility, and had altogether overrated my capabilities. However the event solved all doubts. Having succeeded in levelling the bed and fitting the joints, I morticed the slate for the reception of the nuts: which, after their insertion, I secured by filling the interstices with molten lead. The bed was now perfect, and ready to receive the cushions; and these being screwed on to the aforesaid nuts, my task was completed. I sat down and viewed the result with triumphant satisfaction.

The room being got into proper order, and the table fixed ready for play, I determined (for the purpose of keeping my company select) to admit none but respectable tradesmen. When this was made known, the parties with whom I spent my money,—butchers, bakers, tinkers, and tailors,—all put down their names as subscribers; but none of them ever attended. The fact is, my landlord was going to the bad, and the beer was not fit to drink; consequently, I lost my customers, even to the last man.

Three dreary months had passed; Christmas arrived; and still, 'Sorrow drove my barrow.'

Things were now becoming desperate. I continued to hammer on the lapstone, in order to keep soul and body together; but my utmost exertions were insufficient to meet the expenses of the establishment. It seemed to be all up with me. Another solitary month passed away; it was a bitterly cold winter, and the snow fell in dense masses, darkening the atmosphere. Goaded by my feelings, and influenced by the gloom that surrounded me, I one afternoon jumped from my seat in a kind of frenzy, and seizing a sheet of paper, wrote in large text: 'BILLIARDS: A SLATE TABLE!'

I had now resolved to admit any one who might think proper to play. Within an hour from my exhibiting the above notice at my window, two members of the university, who were hurrying through the snow with their gowns thrown over their heads, chanced to notice the advertisement. 'Look here,' cried one—'Billiards: a slate table!' 'Oh,' replied his friend, 'come along; there's no billiards there.' On the following morning, a gentlemanly young man walked in, and requested to play a game at billiards. I acceded; and finding he was but an indifferent player, gave him five-and-twenty points (being half the game), playing only for the tables, as it has always been my rule never to bet. Thus I went on with my solitary customer, for three or four days.

It happened one evening, while we were playing as usual, that seven or eight young men rushed into the room: they were all Trinity men, and it required no conjurer to discern that they were the *élite* of their class. One noble-looking fellow (whom I remember with gratitude to this day) asked me if I had pool balls? I answered—'Yes, such as they are;' for they were small and by no means perfect. 'Never mind,' he said, 'we'll make shift till you can get better.' So I brought out what I had; and they commenced pool. I certainly felt ashamed to take the money for such wretched makeshifts; however, they played on without much complaining, till betwixt eleven and twelve o'clock; by which time I had earned half-a-guinea. I had not taken so much money, in the same time, for months.

My wife had retired to rest, being tired with her day's work, as we kept no servant. On getting up next morning, she saw the silver lying on the table, and exclaimed,—'Where did you get this money?'—knowing well that I had none the day before. Upon my explaining, she observed, that it would never do; unless we could get the sanction of the authorities. This I told her was my aim; and that I thought it might be accomplished. It appeared to me, that the best way would be to admit none but members of the university; and to put up rules prohibiting all gaming beyond the regular pool, which I fixed at as low a figure as was consistent with the circumstances of the case. I have an intense aversion to gambling: observation has taught me that it leads men to cureless ruin. Against this destructive vice I have ever cautioned all those who have come within my sphere of action, as being the most hideous monster that ever preyed upon the passions of frail humanity.

As time jogged on I became tolerably proficient in the 'noble game of billiards;' and as at the period to which I refer, most of the young men knew but little about it, I imparted my knowledge upon equitable terms: giving a fair amount of odds and playing for the tables only. I have already said, that I made it a rule not to bet: and this rule I never violated but in *one* instance,—which I shall in justice to myself narrate.

On a certain occasion, the celebrated Tom Egan had, by fine play, holed two balls at pool: and there being two others remaining to be put in, a question arose as to the odds about his holeing both. Being appealed to, I gave it as my opinion that the odds were twenty to one against it. The striker at once said he would accept the bet: but there being no takers, it was insisted that I ought to back my opinion not by the striker, but by the company, who began to insinuate that I had not delivered correct judgment. 'Very well,' said I,—'just to satisfy you, I will for once break a custom.' The bet was therefore made in sixpences. The striker proceeded in breathless silence; the first stroke was accomplished in beautiful style: the ball quivered on the edge, but dropped gently into the pocket. By a delicate touch of the side stroke, which required the nicest precision, he had brought his own ball into such a position as to render the second hazard barely possible. All were now anxiously awaiting the result; at length the ball came like a shot from the striker's cue, and catching the object ball on the very out-line, cut it two feet down the cushion into the corner pocket, amid the most tremendous cheering and hammering of cues upon the floor, that was ever heard in a billiard-room. In admiration of this marvellous performance, I paid down *twenty six-*

pences: in order that all parties present might bear it in remembrance.

I will endeavour to describe as accurately as I can, the position of the balls upon the table. Before the first stroke was made, the striker's ball rested near the middle spot on the balk-line; the first ball to be played on lying midway betwixt the balk-line and the right-hand middle pocket: so near to the cushion, that it was doubtful whether it could be put in with the point of the cue. This was clearly demonstrated by the fact of the ball actually touching the shoulder of the cushion as it fell into the pocket, but so delicately that, instead of altering its direction, it only trembled a second on the edge, and then dropped. The striker's ball now rested near the centre spot betwixt the middle pockets; the ball to be played on lay rather more than half-way down the left-hand lower cushion, almost touching it: so that, if the stroke were made, the striker's ball must of necessity glance off in the direction of the opposite corner pocket. The side-stroke essential to the object in view would inevitably have that effect, as a certain degree of strength must be employed to send the object ball down to the corner pocket. The losing hazard was thus more likely to be made than the winning; however, the player's aim was attained with a hair-breadth escape of losing his 'life.' I have recorded this incident for the purpose of recalling it to the memories of several gentlemen still living,—and also as likely to interest all parties having a knowledge of billiards.

I had by this time purchased a new table from Burroughes and Watts, and my condition began to improve. The authorities too had not interfered: as

I always allowed the officials free access to my premises, —treating them with marked respect. And now, having heretofore through life been ever harassed and hurried from scene to scene, I desired at length to pitch my tent and settle down in quiet. No fair means were left untried by me to win a character, and to establish myself in the just estimation of society. Thus matters progressed smoothly for two or three years. I had furnished my house in accordance with our desires from top to bottom. My tables, rooms, and appointments were acknowledged to be the best in the town: and the customers were of the very first order. Hundreds of the best gentlemen players, now scattered over the earth's surface, are 'graduates' (as I may say) of my establishment; and I can aver with honest pride, that all of them will bear testimony to its character for truthfulness and impartiality.

CHAPTER VI.

FRESH DIFFICULTIES—A DREADFULLY ZEALOUS OFFICIAL—MY APPEARANCE BEFORE THE 'HEADS,' WHO DECIDE IN MY FAVOUR—FROM WHICH EVENT, MY STEADY TURN OF FORTUNE APPEARS TO DATE—'THAT' CARRIAGE IS BOUGHT—I DO A BIT OF GOOD SAMARITAN, AND GET MY REWARD—SOWING GOLD.

THE fourth winter of my then happy state arrived: and with it came 'a frost, a killing frost.' It happened that a man who had just been appointed one of the junior officers to the governing body, took it into his head to put down billiards as a game prohibited by the statutes of the University. Being apprised of this, I now, with all deference, make a candid avowal of the plan I adopted to frustrate his intended operations for my destruction. I had certain bells of fairy dimensions hung in the darkest corners of the rooms, which could be put in motion by a person stationed for the purpose. I then planted a man at each end of the entrance leading to my premises: who was supplied with a dog-whistle, and had strict orders, whenever the expected visitor appeared in sight, to sound a loud and shrill call. This easily reached the ear of the person stationed at the bell-pull; the alarm was given, and the players bolted through a window which closed after them with a secret spring. At the same moment the gas was turned off at the main: so that when the hostile functionary entered, the place was in total darkness, and still as death. Being thus repeatedly foiled, my enemy grew desperate: and, as his open endeavours proved futile, resorted to stratagem by coming stealthily down upon one of my 'look-outs' in a dark passage. My fellow, though rather caught napping, at once blew his whistle: which so exasperated the zealous officer, that he struck the man with all his force,—a proceeding witnessed by two persons close at hand.

On the following day, a summons was served upon the reverend gentleman for this assault: and at the time appointed he appeared before the magistrates to answer to the charge. The result was that, after having taken the evidence of the witnesses, the bench adjudged the defendant to pay twenty shillings and costs. This miscarriage, instead of cooling his ardour, drove my persecutor frantic, and also made him reckless of consequences; for shortly afterwards, he so far committed himself as to take a man from his fireside in his shirt-sleeves to prison, because he refused to allow him to search his house. An action for damages ensued: in which the official was cast to the amount of something considerably above a hundred pounds,—a very natural consequence of his folly.

The authorities perceiving the discredit thrown upon their government by these ridiculous proceedings, now thought proper to call a council and investigate the conduct of the parties concerned. At the request of the Vice-chancellor, I attended upon the 'Heads' to render an account of my proceedings and answer to whatever charges might be brought against me. Here, instead of experiencing harshness and gross partiality, as I had been led to expect, I met with the most generous and disinterested treatment. Throughout my examination and defence, I was listened to with respectful attention; and every circumstance was weighed in the scales of justice. At the conclusion of this imposing scene, I was dismissed with the evident good will of this august assembly, amounting to a tacit licence for the future. Right well pleased I proceeded homewards; but as I had occasion to stop on the road, the senior-proctor had been at my house before me: who left word that he wished to speak with me, naming the time he should be at leisure.

At the appointed hour I waited upon Mr.———: and after being very cordially received, was invited to take a seat. We then entered into conversation upon the business of the afternoon, which had occupied the greater portion of three hours; after which, I gave him at his request a brief sketch of my antecedents, with which he seemed well pleased. Moreover, as I was about to take leave, he expressed himself in terms of admiration at my conduct before the court; saying that he could not suffer it to pass, 'without making his grateful acknowledgments to me for the noble and manly way in which I conducted my defence.'

Much gratified at the termination of this unpleasant business, I went directly home and conveyed the welcome intelligence to my wife: who received the information with feelings better to be imagined than described.

PLATE 1.

PLATE 2.

Being now free to pursue my business, I made divers alterations and improvements; and having a coach-house and stabling, I also bought horses and vehicles, which I let for hire. My stud consisted of eight as good cattle as any man could desire to cross, with saddles, bridles, and appointments all new. From this time my fortune seemed to change; it appeared as if the capricious dame was tired of persecuting me any further, and had left me to pursue my own course.

I rented additional premises, and enlarged my establishment: for by this time I was master of a little property; and my credit being firmly established after so many trials and struggles, I felt humbly thankful that perseverance was at length crowned with success.

About this period, being in London on business, I chanced to pass a coach-builder's establishment, bearing the name of 'Rubridge.' Knowing that my wife had an uncle and cousins of that name in the trade, I entered; and as I stood looking at a splendid clarence fresh from the workman's hand, the master came towards me. I asked him the price of the vehicle, which he named in *guineas*. 'Make it *pounds*,' said I, 'and it's mine; knock off the shillings, and here's a cheque for the amount!' 'Well,' he replied, 'as I want money, you shall have the carriage: where shall I send it to?' I handed over my card, whereon he observed that he had a cousin of that name residing at Cambridge: her husband was a boot-maker. 'Did I know him?' 'Not quite so well as I ought', was my answer, 'for it's rather difficult to know one's self!' This speech bringing us to an understanding, I was introduced to his wife and family: and after taking some refreshment and writing a cheque for the amount agreed upon, I took my departure and prepared for home.

On the following afternoon, as I was walking in front of our house (the entrance to which is at some distance from the public street), porters belonging to the railway station came down with my new purchase. Hereupon the neighbours flocked around; and as the master of one of the colleges kept his carriage and horses near my house, they concluded that the Doctor was 'coming out strong.' My wife and nieces were also attracted to the door, just as the men were enquiring if a person of my name lived thereabouts. 'All right,' said I, and asked their business. They at once informed me that the carriage they had brought was to my address: and taking a piece of paper from one of the lamps, handed it over for my perusal. Whilst I was looking at the direction, my wife enquired whose carriage it was? To which I replied: 'You've but an indifferent memory; this is the equipage that I promised you some fifteen years ago, when I was cutting up some old boot-fronts to translate into a pair of shoes for my own feet.'

My next job was to order a set of harness, having already purchased a horse for the occasion. Thus in a few days my turn-out was complete, and a smart affair it was; in proof of which, I may state that a coachmaker offered me ten pounds for my bargain. Besides this clarence, I had a phaeton and two gigs; which, together with my billiards, helped to realise a tolerably profitable business.

About this time my mother became unfit to look after her little shop, being sorely afflicted with rheumatism. I therefore arranged to allow her an annuity, and such other helps as I could afford. Thus we crept on by degrees, adding every now and then to our previous stock; and never keeping more cats than would catch mice. My wife and her mother, who lived with us, did more work than could be expected from two servants, although the old woman was nearly seventy. It appeared as if dame Fortune was determined to try what effect prosperity would have upon the nature that adversity could not subdue. Wealth in abundance was showered upon me; to make use of my wife's words, it was like 'being pelted with money.' Still we pursued a steady course, bearing in mind that 'it is just possible for a man to bite off his own nose'; and thus my store so increased, that I had about £500. lying idle just at this time.

One morning as I passed by Trinity-gates, a man whom I had known for some time, stood in the public way making bitter lamentations. Upon enquiry, I found that he had lost his situation, that of carpenter to the college. Knowing he had a large family, and feeling sorry for the man, I proposed that he should build me a house without contract or agreement: so that he should have free scope for his powers, and an opportunity of recommending himself to the public. Before the workmen dug out the foundation, I gave him a check for £100, and other sums as he progressed with the work; but never was there such a gratuitous victim of misplaced confidence. I was not only plundered of my cash, but laughed at for being a fool; and eventually arrived at the same conclusion as the Cottenham jury, (in the case of a man tried for the murder of his wife), whose foreman in returning the verdict said: 'They were unanimously of opinion as it sarved her right; for she were such a tarnation bad 'un, as no man could live with.'

Before the building was properly finished, the man died: and one of his foolish or knavish executors brought an action against me to recover £43; but, to make all they could by the job, I was sued for £999, being the entire amount booked for work done on my account during three years. And the plaintiff was one of my so-styled 'friends.' How true to nature was our immortal Shakspeare, when he said that 'knavery's plain face is never seen till used.' Nor less true are the following beautiful lines of Oliver Goldsmith:

> "And what is friendship but a name,
> A charm that lulls to sleep;
> A shade that follows wealth or fame,
> And leaves the wretch to weep."

About this time, the Cantabs, in honor of our noble and virtuous Queen's accession to the throne, attempted to establish what were designated 'Coronation Races.' Now in my estimation, racing is a harmless sport indeed. I am aware that some weighty authorities differ with me in opinion; but let that pass,—there is a great deal in the impressions made upon the clay when soft. I at all events patronized and subscribed to this popular amusement, and entered a pony to run. It thus occurred, that on the day before the sport was to come off, I repaired to the course for the purpose of giving my pony a gallop over. Just as I was in full swing, I suddenly felt something tap my foot; again and again the tap was repeated, and on looking down I caught a glimpse of something yellow shooting off my boot. All of a sudden it flashed across my mind, that I had upwards of fifty sovereigns in a silk purse in my pocket; so pulling up at once, I ascertained that the contents of the purse had escaped through a hole, the money being regularly sown in the grass as the pony took his strides. In an instant I dismounted; and following the track, found the sovereigns lying at equal distances, and gradually recovered all of them.

As I pocketed the last coin, up came some stablemen, who fancied that I must have fallen from my horse, as they had seen me galloping a few seconds before. They were, as I say, just in time to see me pick up the last piece. After explaining what had happened, and giving them a gallon of ale for bringing up my pony, I again mounted: and ere returning home, went direct to deposit my cash in the bank, after the narrow escape of passing from me and my heirs for ever.

After the railway had been extended to Cambridge about two years, the fares were raised to what the Cambridge folk considered exorbitant demands, both for passengers and luggage, but more particularly for small parcels. As we sat one evening at the 'Woolpack' inn, talking over these matters, some one hinted that a four-horse coach might pay, if it could be set a-going on a scheme of £5. shares: and it was considered that £1000. capital was necessary to working out such a scheme. In short, we resolved to raise the needful by subscription, each subscriber to take one share only. This was done in order to enlist as many influential persons as possible, and so all the better enable us to organize our plan; for we should thus have two hundred persons interested in the success of the undertaking.

On the following morning, just by way of experiment, I made out a list to start with; and, in company with another of the projectors, proceeded to canvass the town. To the astonishment of all parties, we succeeded beyond our utmost hopes; every body seemed to fall in with our views, and the list soon began to look handsome.

As the design now bore the stamp of reality, and all concerned seemed sanguine of its success, it was resolved that mine host of the 'Woolpack' and myself should go up the road towards London, and solicit the co-operation of the principal inhabitants on the line. Being well got-up for the occasion, and having a good horse and trap, we started on our mission, and pulled up at every house where appearances warranted our expectations. By some we were received with smiles of welcome: a coach being the thing of all others they desired to look upon again. It fell to my lot to play the spokesman, and as I had a tolerable yarn ready spun, it only required 'paying-out'; for really believing the speculation to be a good one, I went to work with great confidence. Having met with tolerable success, we put up at Royston (where it was market-day), and dined at the farmers' table. Here, over our wine, we propounded our plan of action, and exhibited the list of subscribers with the view of inducing as many as possible to join us. The business of the day over, we returned to render an account of our proceedings to the committee.

All now appeared to go swimmingly; the day was fixed for commencing our enterprise; the public was on the tiptoe of expectation, and the youngsters all in anxious anticipation of once more hearing the sound of the bugle, with the accompaniment of wheels rattling over the long silent stones. Nothing remained but to make proper arrangements for a start; the management of which devolved upon my coadjutor the host, who, being a retired knight of the whip, was considered the most competent to conduct this business to a successful issue. He and I next set off for London, in order to secure stabling along the road, and to fix the coach's destination; which was ultimately agreed upon to be the 'One Bell', Holborn. Our manager having completed his arrangements, the eventful morning arrived. The glittering turn-out was brought round to the front of the inn, where passengers and luggage made a most business-like show. The coachman, in his smartest professional array, stood whip in hand ready to mount the box; whilst a crowd of admiring spectators, all wishing success to the undertaking, waited in anxious expectation of once more beholding a 'four-in-hand' dash through the streets. The passengers being seated, coachee gathered up the ribbons, and off she went in gallant style, amid the shouts of the populace; the spirit-stirring bugle playing 'Oh dear, what can the matter be!' &c.

The sensation created by the resuscitation of a real stage-coach and four live horses was of so novel and exhilarating a nature, that our coachman and guard were enthusiastically greeted along the road, at every town and village, and even upon their *entré* into London. On its return journey, the coach came in loaded like a waggon; and the inhabitants throughout the line of country travelled, were everywhere abroad to hail the passing vehicle. In Cambridge too there were scores who ran themselves out of breath, in order to witness the arrival and unloading of the popular craft; nay, so eager was the crowd, that the porters had scarcely room for their operations. The street before the inn was often quite blocked up by a dense mass of anxious and admiring spectators; and the entire population appeared to feel interested in the success of the undertaking. This was a tolerable source of profit to our manager, who moreover reaped a pretty good harvest in other respects, as he was allowed the money for booking and delivery of all parcels, great and small: which must have amounted in the course of six months to something worth having.

Notwithstanding such apparent prosperity, the company's receipts were not commensurate with the expenses. Yet we were informed by all parties that the coach loaded well along the road. It consequently appeared certain that we had got into the hands of a regular set of Philistines. Those well acquainted with coaching matters, cried 'shame!' and pronounced the whole gang to be most unconscionable knaves,—who, not satisfied with three wheels out of four, must needs take half the spokes of the other wheel also. Thus things proceeded on for some time: the books shewing clearly that we were rapidly going to the bad; whilst, among the honest gentlemen concerned in driving and conducting, it seemed to be a regular scramble, and the devil take the hindmost!

A committee meeting was at last called to investigate the business, and to adopt measures for checking this wholesale robbery. It was now resolved that such members of the committee as could spare time should accompany the coach on its journey to and from London, and exert themselves to stay the system of plunder that had been so unblushingly carried on. Feeling indignant at the knavery by which we were surrounded, and being in some degree responsible to the subscribers and the public, I volunteered to take the first turn. Having entered in a pocket-book the number of passengers and their destinations, I took an inside seat and noted the distance of each fare on the journey, keeping a regular account of the monies received; and I believe, if this plan had been adhered to, that the cash sunk might have been saved, and the coach kept running. But 'what is everybody's business is nobody's;' and so it turned out in this instance. We had no sooner pulled up at the 'One Bell,' than on alighting I was surrounded by gaping creditors of a small description. One man came up (saying, he was told I was the proprietor), and complained bitterly that the coachman refused to pay him for washing the coach; another that he had got a little bill for repairing the pole, which the driver had the misfortune to break by running foul of a heavily laden van; a third had put in a square of the best glass which had been broken nobody could tell how; a fourth had repaired the hinges of the boot, the door of which being by some means left open had been carried away by a passing omnibus. Another and another followed: and I directed them all to wait on me in the coffee-room in a quarter of hour, when I would inspect their several claims.

True to the appointment, the entire bevy assembled and presented their demands, which I entered in my book; promising to lay them before the committee on my return. Satisfied with this acknowledgment of their several accounts, the complainants then withdrew. On reaching home I made my report to the committee, and advised that the course begun should be persevered in as the only means of preventing this wholesale 'shouldering,' as it was termed; which, in more explicit language, means plunder. However, as no one of our own body appeared to have any great feeling of devotion to the business, it was merely resolved that a person should be specially appointed to attend to the passengers and to take charge of the receipts, with a view of ensuring the amount justly earned by our venture. Consequently, upon this determination, a poor fellow of honest character, who had been porter to one of the old coaches, was installed in the office; and, being in rather sorry plight at the time, I rigged him out from my own wardrobe, besides purchasing for him a new rough over-coat: so that he might appear comfortable to his new situation. Thus equipped, our agent started on his journey, and returned tolerably sober: but after a while they brought him home turtle-fashion, strapped down flat on his back to the top of the coach. Upon being taxed with the impropriety of his conduct, the offender alleged that he must have been drugged: as he had taken but one half-pint of porter. However, it was difficult to arrive at anything like a correct conclusion. Drunkards are ever fertile in excuses, and, even when scarcely able to articulate, will swear they have had nothing to drink: making the most profane asseverations in support of their innocence.

The result of all this was that some of our shareholders took fright, and withdrew from the concern when it was proposed to call up the remaining £3. per share; £2. only having as yet been paid. Many also of our best men became disgusted, and almost indifferent:

but a few stuck together, and determined on prosecuting the affair to a conclusion. By degrees, however, things went still worse; all parties concerned disregarded the orders of the committee; while the manager and coachmen (the only persons profitably interested) took to doing just as they liked. It had been settled by the committee that the coach should start from the 'Woolpack,' proceed straight down Sidney-street, turn up St. John's-street, and stop at the 'Blue Boar' in Trinity-street to take up passengers; from thence proceeding by King's-parade and Trumpington-street on to the London-road: and on the return journey the same route was to be strictly observed.

But our manager (to suit his own purposes) hesitated not to set all law and order at defiance. He therefore met the coach at the town's-end, mounted the box (taking the reins from *our* coachman), and instead of driving in accordance with the directions given, turned short round St. Mary's church, and down Market-street, direct to his own house. Upon being made aware of this proceeding, I took the earliest opportunity, in company with another member of the committee, of being on the spot in order to prevent a recurrence of this open violation of all rule. We stationed ourselves at the corner of St. Mary's, with a view to hinder the coach from taking that turn, and called to the driver to keep straight on; expecting of course that he would do so. Instead of which, the off-leader was pulled so suddenly upon me that I was within a hair's breadth of being run over,—and by a fellow who had no more business with the reins or horses than the man in the moon. Expostulation only elicited from the same party coarse threats and the foulest abuse. His principal object in perpetrating this outrage, was the conveyance of passengers direct to his own house, against the intentions of the committee; for, as already noted, he was amply paid by the receipts for booking and delivery of parcels. Such was the grateful return made to me for being instrumental in getting the coach to start from this man's house, upon the grounds that, as the scheme was first mooted there, it would be only fair to give him the benefit.

The foregoing was not a solitary case of delinquency in the same quarter. It will scarcely be credited that on one occasion, if not oftener, through his neglect our coach was seized by the officers in London for the duty, which it was his business as manager to defray. There was however no possibility of stopping under six months, as contracts had been entered into for that time; and the result was that we, who had subscribed to what was undeniably a good and just cause, were plundered of something like £800. over and above the coach's earnings. It was nevertheless believed by good judges that, under proper management, our enterprise could have been worked out satisfactorily; but where insatiable greed ·usurped the reins of government, what more or less could be expected?

'Why then the devil give him good of it!'

CHAPTER VII.

'I SHALL LICK YOU!'—THUNDER AND LIGHTNING—PUTTING ON THE SCREW—I BECOME A TOWN COUNCILLOR—MY ROBE OF OFFICE—A FEW HINTS UPON BREWING.

ON the commencement of term business began, and customers flocked in. It happened one evening as we sat at tea, that a young gentleman who had been playing a short time before and had managed to tear the cloth, came to the door: and called out very impatiently, and without ceremony,—'Where's this table we're to have?' My niece quietly observed—'That is the gentleman who tore the cloth.' Hearing this, I told him very civilly that he ought not to have gone away without mentioning the accident,—as we then could have set to work, and put the table into playing order. 'Oh,' said he, very cavalierly and with the assumed *hauteur* of a full-blown 'Verdant-green,'—'don't be impertinent, or I shall lick you!' Almost distrusting my ears I exclaimed, 'WHAT!'—and he repeated his equally silly and vulgar threat.

'Upon my word, young man,' I replied, 'it strikes me forcibly that you'll fall.'

'What do you mean by *fall?*'

'Why, I think you'll go down.'

'What do you mean by *go down?*'

Incensed at this display of puppyism, I explained as follows:—'I'll knock you down, and jump your ribs in! Do you understand *that?*' With this I hastily rose, and putting aside my cup and saucer, prepared to chastise this unbearable insolence. But on the first evidence of my purpose, this rare specimen of birth and breeding made his *exit* like a threatened cur.

Having finished my tea, I went into the public-room and related the foregoing incident to the company there assembled; which was composed of as fine-spirited young men as ever walked the earth. These now agreed to give my friend, on the following morning, a taste of what they called 'THUNDER' and 'LIGHTNING.' Their plan being laid over-night, early on the morrow they knocked him up; saying that it was a particular Saint's day, and that unless he attended chapel he would lose his term. Being a newly imported freshman, and as aforesaid rather green withal, the victim took the bait and turned out for morning prayers. At the conclusion of the service, it was generally agreed to take a constitution walk at the backs of the Colleges. The unsuspecting simpleton was now led on, until, having reached a convenient distance, they commenced operations by asking him: 'What he meant by threatening to lick a man sitting by his own fireside?' This interrogatory was followed by a bonnetter which smashed the deal trencher-top of his freshman's cap, accompanied by a shove forward which brought him in contact with a strong fellow, by whom he was quickly sent back upon those behind. Thus did they hustle him backwards and forwards in handsome style, till at last the culprit effected a bolt. The game having thus broke cover, off started the hunters in pursuit, and kept up the chase till they ran him to earth.

In the evening, as the party were relating the tale to their friends, and enjoying a hearty laugh over the fun, I was informed that the gentleman who had torn the cloth the day before, desired to speak with me. On entering the room where he was, I bowed and asked his pleasure, just as if we had never met. His dejected appearance made me feel sorry for him, and vexed with myself for having been the means of his humiliation. The poor fellow, with tears ready to start from his eyes, asked what he had to pay for tearing the cloth. I told him that the usual charge in all public places was a guinea; but as he did not appear to be much acquainted with such matters, I would merely charge for taking off the cloth and repairing it; asking nothing for the deterioration, or loss of play. The charge would thus be half the usual amount, namely ten shillings. This sum he paid down, and expressed a hope that we should be friends again. I told him that as far as my feelings were concerned we never were otherwise; for upon reflection, I could not refrain from laughing at the remembrance of a scene so truly ludicrous.

Somewhat more at ease, the gentleman now asked if he could go into the public-room. I replied, 'Certainly,' and offered to usher him in, as he had never been there. As we entered the room, the entire company greeted the new comer with a deafening shout of welcome; every one in turn shaking him by the hand with a force enough to disjoint every bone in his frame; all of which he bore with admirable resignation. During this scene of noise and fun, a quaint and very satirical young man drew with chalk upon the door a full-length portrait of the subject of their mirth. It was an unmistakeable likeness, even to an incipient moustache which the subject had just began to cultivate. Immediately above the head the artist inscribed the word 'Adonis': and over that, 'The Easy Shaving Shop—2d. each.' As the company tired of more boisterous amusement, this cartoon attracted their attention, and owing to its wonderful fidelity, had such a peculiar and instantaneous effect, that all were convulsed; even the original joined heartily in the laugh against himself, whilst the boy who was marking grinned and jumped about like a monkey in hysterics. This lesson was 'worth a city's ransom' to Mr. Green; for he turned out one of the most amiable young men of that period, and was so esteemed during his sojourn at the university. I verily believe in the efficacy of a sound first dressing.

As time rolled on my means increased: and it was evident that I had become a mark for envy's poisoned arrows. My landlord (to whom I had always acted most honorably, and something more than that), was induced by circumstances and influences which he could not resist, to raise my rent: the sum now demanded being nearly three times the original amount. Rather than yield to such grasping iniquity, I resolved to leave: hinting at the same time that I had been offered premises in every way more suitable, at a smaller figure. This seemed to stagger his resolution: for he dropped one third of his covetous demand; and as I had laid out something very considerable in alterations, I acquiesced in the modified imposition, rather than knock down all I had so laboriously erected.

Another year passed away: and another turn was given to the screw of the vice in which my poor landlord was fixed. At last they squeezed him flat as a pancake; and all his houses except mine were advertised for sale. Within a few days, he called and offered to sell me the estate by private contract: the price named being £800. This was a hundred more than the property (in its then state) was worth; however, I ultimately agreed to his demand in consideration of my business: which was indeed very good,—as it needs must have been, seeing that I began without a shilling. Having made such arrangements as secured the premises to myself, I again set about building and making extensive improvements, —which proved a source of great attraction. Thus I worked on, until by degrees I found myself master of the largest establishment of the kind in the provinces, and second only to one in London.

Having always been consistent in the performance of my public duties, I was held in some estimation by my fellow-townsmen: and on a vacancy occurring in the town council, was solicited to become a candidate. This honor I would have declined, upon the ground that such positions were better suited to men of independent means. However, my objections were overruled, and I consented to stand: but at the time distinctly told my friends that I would not cross my threshold to solicit a vote; had a dukedom been the prize, I would not have begged for it. I know there are men who will not believe this; but let me remind such, that these things depend on self-culture and individual organization. It is simple folly where an individual presumes upon his own judgment as an universal standard; but each has a right to interpret his own feelings, and act in honest accordance with his own principles: leaving to others the same freedom that he claims for himself.

At the close of the poll I was elected one of the guardians of the rights, privileges, and interests of my native town: but without taking any active part in the contest. Some of my female neighbours now enquired whether I intended to wear a gown? I fancied that the duties of the office could be as well performed without: *they* however, thinking otherwise, set on foot a subscription for the purpose of presenting me with one. The money was raised: and a first-rate robe-maker being employed, in the course of two or three days a splendid silk gown trimmed with sable was sent home with the subscribers' compliments. Thus auspiciously commenced my career as a member of the local government. My first appearance in the council chamber was also marked by demonstrations indicative of a friendly feeling; and I may safely say for myself, that I never betrayed the confidence reposed in me. But these memoirs are designed for a record of private life, not as an official chronicle. I will not therefore pursue a topic, that might seduce me into trespassing upon the slippery ground of local politics.

Ever since I had purchased the premises, I brewed my own ale, and prided myself upon its quality: to ensure the excellence of which, neither pains nor expence were grudged. That nothing might be wanting,

I ordered twenty new barrels of best English oak: and employed a brewer said to be one of the best in the country. For some time we went on exceedingly well, and our beer was acknowledged to be as good as any in the town; which it deserved to be, as nothing was used in brewing it but the very best malt and hops. However, 'as the course of true love never did run smooth,' so it turned out with me and my brewer, who by-and-by grew negligent and spoiled the materials.

Annoyed and disappointed at the loss thus incurred, it struck me that, by consulting some proper authority, I might possess myself of knowledge requisite for my purpose; and as I happened to have in my possession an elaborate work on fermentation, I determined to make myself master of this mysterious art. Noting the principles laid down for my guidance, I essayed to execute my design: and by strictly following out each rule, produced as good a brewing of beer as ever man tasted; nor have I lost a single pint since I first commenced.

For the information of those who may feel desirous of brewing their own ale, I will here set down a receipt, with all needful instructions. Proportion of ingredients requisite for brewing a barrel of ale:—malt, three bushels; hops, three pounds; sugar (just boiled up), three pounds; the average cost will be about thirty shillings. Every person intending to brew for himself must be careful to see the malt measured and ground: as it is just possible there might be a mistake both in quality and quantity. The tubs and vessels must be perfectly sweet and clean, as any defect of this nature would mar the whole brewing. The mash-tub should be particularly attended to; and a wisp of clean straw or hay is to be put over the bottom of the vessel in the inside, to prevent the malt running off with the liquor. The malt being emptied into the mash-tub and the water brought to boil, dash the boiling water in the copper with cold water sufficient to stop the boiling, and leave it just hot enough to slightly scald the finger. Brewers use a thermometer: the first mash being usually taken at 180°, and the second at 190°; but in the absence of a thermometer, the foregoing rule will be found sufficient with a little practice: always remembering to draw off the second mash somewhat hotter than the first. The water being thus brought to a proper temperature, ladle it out of the copper over the malt, till the latter becomes thoroughly wet; mashing it well to prevent the malt from clotting. If the water is poured on too hot, it 'sets' the malt; and when that happens, it can only be recovered by adding cold water. Cover up the mash-tub close, in order to compress the steam and prevent the liquor from evaporating. In small quantities this should be carefully regarded.

Let the wort stand two hours and a-half, or three hours, after mashing; then let the liquor run off into a vessel prepared to receive it. If at first it runs thick and discoloured, draw off one or two pails-full; and pour it back again into the mash-tub, till it runs clear. In summer, put a few hops into the vessel which receives the liquor from the mash-tub; this will prevent it turning sour. Let the second mash run as before, and let the liquor stand an hour and a-half; then run it off: but never let the malt stand dry. Keep ladling fresh liquor over it till the quantity of wort to be obtained is extracted; always allowing for waste in the boiling. The first wort must be boiled an hour and a-half together with the hops: and the latter strained away, in order to be boiled with the second wort. In hot weather one-third more hops may be used to prevent the beer from turning sour.

After the wort has boiled an hour, run it off into your coolers. In summer it should be quite cold before it is set to work; in winter it should be kept till a slight degree of warmth is perceptible by the finger. When properly cold, set it to work by adding yeast in proportion to the quantity. If considerable, and if wanted to work quickly, add from one gallon to two. Let it work till it comes to a good deep head; then throw in a handful of salt. The liquor is now fit for barrelling. Fill the barrels full; and keep filling them up till they have done working. Let them stand three or four days before you hop them down; then knock down the bungs, making them perfectly air-tight. In about six or eight weeks, the beer will be fit to draw. I have pursued this system for ten years, and have never met with a failure.

CHAPTER VIII.

SOME DETAILS OF MY ESTABLISHMENT—RE-APPEARANCE OF AN OLD FRIEND—HIS ACCOUNT OF HIMSELF—I BEGIN TO FEEL MYSELF TOLERABLY COMFORTABLE—MY MOTHER IS BROUGHT TO END HER DAYS IN OUR FAMILY CIRCLE—PRACTICAL SUGGESTIONS AND ANECDOTES CONNECTED WITH THE GAME OF BILLIARDS—A RARE CHANCE AT CRIBBAGE.

As it became patent to the world that I had done exceedingly well, what I had long anticipated now occurred: namely, that others began to start in the same line. To counteract the effect of this, I laid out some hundreds: being determined if possible to keep my standing. The outlay was not misjudged; and, thanks to staunch patrons and my own careful habits, I am still able to live: and have been fortunate in keeping always the best set of players.

My establishment consists of two public-rooms for pool and billiards, together with seven private billiard-rooms, and a racket-court furnished with the best appurtenances. These places of business are detached from the house: which is just large enough for my family, consisting of myself and wife, her mother, who is in her eighty-third year, three nieces, a nephew, and servant-girl. Besides these, I employ a racquet-maker, charwomen, and laundress. My best public-room was built from a design of my own. It is thirty feet long by twenty broad, and fifteen feet in height; having four skylights of the best plate-glass, so arranged that the rays of light cross in the centre of the table, precluding all possibility of a shade being thrown along the cushions.

This room has a fireplace at each end, with chandeliers of three lights each placed in a direct line with the middle pockets on either side, and four revolving lights over the centre of the table. Thus the light and heat are equally distributed, and an uniform degree of temperature maintained. By means of this arrangement the cushions are always true: the india-rubber being equably affected all round. There is a large mirror over each mantelpiece, and a long seat extends on one side nearly the length of the room, being divided into compartments, having elbows with backs and seats stuffed and covered with horsehair. This is raised from the floor for the convenience of those looking at the play. On the opposite side are fixed the marking-board, cue-rack, and rules. The marking-board is by Burroughes and Watts, and is as yet the most complete that has been manufactured. It has two revolving rollers for marking billiards, with five faces: each face numbering twenty, so as to mark up to a hundred. On either hand is a pool marking-board for seven balls, making a complete board of fourteen; in the centre is fixed a slate, exhibiting six columns for the use of the six days in the week: and underneath is the pool-till, with a glass front divided into compartments, so that it can be seen whether the money is in or not. In the centre under the slate, is a drawer fitted with lock and key to hold the balls. This is rather an elaborate and expensive piece of furniture.

At one end of the room above the mirror hangs a clock: and directly opposite, on a bracket, stands the bust of my favourite Shakspeare. Opposite each other on either side are statues of Venus and the 'Greek Slave.' The floor is covered with cocoa-nut matting, which completes the interior picture of my best public room. The legs of the table (which weighs twenty-one hundred-weight) stand upon dwarf walls running the entire length of the building; the apartment has thirteen ventilators; the walls are fourteen inches thick, and the foundation is concrete. In the erection of this building I played the important parts of architect, clerk of the works, and common bricklayer.

During the summer of the Great Exhibition year (1851), as I was one day walking round my premises to see what repairs were necessary, one of the buttery-men belonging to St. John's, whom I had known ever since my return to Cambridge, came down in great haste to inform me that Mr. T. B. S—— had come to take his master's degree, and was anxiously enquiring after me. This was no other than my 'very noble and esteemed' good friend, who shared his wardrobe and money with me when I took leave of him some fifteen years before. Delighted beyond measure at the prospect of again meeting him in life, I hastened to the college: and on enquiry was informed that he had gone to breakfast with the tutor. In returning I stopped to speak with my neighbour, Mrs. Scott, wife of the college cook,—when, as we were still in converse, a man wearing a master-of-arts gown entered the front gate, about a hundred yards distant from us. I asked Mrs. S. who he was. She did not know: but a second glance led me to exclaim—'Whoever the *man* may be, those are T. B. S——'s *legs* he's making use of!'—'Oh dear, no,' she observed, 'he's gone to breakfast with Mr. —— the tutor.'—'Well,' I rejoined, 'if so, perhaps he has lent this man his legs for the day: at least I can swear to the walk.'

At this moment the tutor passed by, and as he met the individual in dispute they shook hands and walked towards us; but at some few yards' distance a third party stopped the tutor for a minute or two: while my friend (for it was himself) walked slowly on. Assured of his identity, I advanced: and taking off my hat, saluted him with 'Good morning!' He stared: and with a rigid countenance uttered the words, 'I don't know you.' Feeling more than I could express, I exclaimed in an unmistakeable tone: 'What!'—when he held out his hand, saying: 'I know you now!' Our greeting over, he enquired where I lived: saying, that within half-an-hour he would be with me.

I was desirous, as may be supposed, of having a long talk with him; and, some time ere the half-hour had expired, was standing on the doorstep waiting his arrival. Just as Trinity clock struck, the expected visitor hove in sight: and was evidently seeking for the large brass door-plate, to which I had directed his attention. Presently he looked a-head, and I raised my arm to signal that he was right; for my friend is near-sighted and could not distinguish objects at fifty yards' distance. As

I stepped forward to meet him, it is impossible to describe the joyous feelings that possessed me. A mixture of confused thoughts rushed across my brain in rapid succession, leaving no more palpable trace on the memory than a flash of lightning. I have little acquaintance with studied forms of politeness: but, as far as a hearty welcome may atone for lack of ceremony, I trust I was not wanting in my duty on this happy occasion.

Having entered the house and seated ourselves quietly, I proposed that each should go through the history of his adventures from the time of our parting; conceding to my guest as a matter of courtesy, the choice as to which should begin. He, however, unhesitatingly agreed to commence with his own recital. But by way of prologue, I in the first place asked, what he would take in the shape of drink; at the same time stating the contents of my cellar, which comprised old and mild ales, port, sherry, claret, and champagne. My friend without more ado chose mild ale, saying, that for many years he had scarcely tasted any fit to drink. I therefore ordered a jug to be brought, and then gave him his cue to begin.

It was with no common interest that I now listened to the talented narrator's account of the trials and hardships he had encountered in the ungenial climate of Russia. Without friends, or even a smattering of the language of the country, he had to work his way amidst difficulties almost insurmountable. At length he became connected with an English family who had been living there many years; and, acquiring a tolerable knowledge of the Russ, managed to support himself by taking pupils, until he obtained an appointment in one of the minor educational establishments of the state. Thenceforward his career was prosperous; nor was it long ere he became professor of English Literature at the University of Tzarsko-selo near St. Petersburgh, a post in itself of no little dignity. But the professor has since enjoyed a position of still greater importance and emolument, as confidential tutor in the imperial household; and I believe that a second generation of the reigning family is now profiting by his instructions.

When my old friend had concluded his curious and amusing narrative, I in turn related many incidents, with which my readers have already been made acquainted; and then, after a tolerably long sitting, we rose to partake of some more substantial refreshment. During the professor's stay, which embraced only a few short days, the time passed pleasantly, but all too quickly. The hour having arrived for his departure, we separated perhaps never to meet again—such is the uncertainty of human affairs! He returned to his duties abroad; but a few days afterwards I received, 'with the author's kind regards', an excellent work bearing his name on the title-page; it was published by John Murray, and I believe had a good circulation. These things have more weight with me than all the gold that sordid misers worship.

Being now firmly established in my position, and enjoying the confidence of all who have honored me with their patronage, I cannot but think myself well rewarded for all the hardships I have endured from boyhood upwards. It was about this time, that in course of nature my mother's approaching dissolution began to be anticipated. She was now nearly eighty years of age, and had grown very feeble. My wife therefore proposed to go to London, where the old woman still lived: and, after selling off the furniture, bring her away to end her days with us, where she would be much better cared for,—there being in all no less than six females in our family. This plan was adopted, and the poor old creature seemed perfectly happy; amusing herself by doing anything that suited her little remaining strength. She had been a remarkably strong woman, but rheumatism had sadly pulled her down, and time had nearly done its work upon her frame. What a change since days that I could remember!

Even in this stage of existence my aged parent was lively and witty, and of an evening would laugh and talk, and sing old comical ditties to the girls in the kitchen. The little circle was composed of my wife, her mother, my old lady, and four young women, all nearly related to each other: so that they arranged and performed their household duties in accordance with the directions and under the superintendence of 'the governess.' How all these duties were executed, I must leave to the judgment of the thousands who have patronized the establishment.

About six weeks after my mother's arrival, as I was passing the kitchen-door to go into the cellar, I heard the poor old soul chanting a stave, the last she ever tried. The first line of the stanza that caught my ear ran thus: 'I fell in love with a bit of leather.' On hearing my foot-fall, she stopped short and said: 'Hush! here's the governor coming.' Reluctant to mar innocent mirth, I beat a retreat in order that they might enjoy their little performance undisturbed; for although the old girl could not sing quite so well as she used, she was still an excellent mimic, and could at will set the kitchen in a roar. This faculty I in some degree inherited from her; nor is it in my estimation the least among nature's gifts;—at least, I know, it has done me good service through life.

On the Monday after this little exhibition in the kitchen, I had occasion to go to London on business; and when I returned on Tuesday night, they informed me that my mother seemed in a strange and restless state of mind. So going into her bedroom, I asked if I should put on my great-coat and lie down on the carpet? At this she laughed heartily; telling me to go to bed, as there was nothing the matter with her. Knowing it was useless to thwart the old lady, I retired to my own room which was next to her's on the same landing: making up my mind to keep watch. About four o'clock I fell asleep, but had not been long in this state, when one of my nieces came to the door, and said that her grandmother was dying. Huddling on some clothes, I entered the room and found her quite warm, but dead. There was a childlike smile playing about the mouth, as palpable and pleasant as I had ever noticed in life.

As I mused over this solemn scene, and called to mind the incidents of the past, it seemed strange indeed how Providence should have willed that I alone was to be instrumental in fulfilling all the last sad duties to my parent; that I, the runaway, the scapegrace, should be the agent appointed to shield my mother in her days of helplessness, to close her eyes, and to lay her honored remains in their native earth. She was buried in the churchyard of the Holy Sepulchre, within fifty yards of where she died, and but a short distance from the place of her birth. As I turned from the spot at the conclusion of the last sad rites, I offered up a silent prayer to the throne of mercy for the peace of the departed soul: and marvelled whence should spring all the base and degrading passions of our nature,—since pride, envy, hatred, and the like must all find their level here.

As my arrangements were not quite to my mind, I now set about making everything complete as possible. I underdrained the entire premises in all available directions: and, to ensure a constant supply of water, put up tanks, one of which holds 140 gallons. Into this the rain-water is conveyed by gutters and pipes from every part of the surrounding buildings; a good smart rain will fill it in half-an-hour. To prevent any deficiency in the dry season, I also sunk a well in the kitchen, and put down a force or lift pump: by which means I can fill my tanks in twenty minutes, and send the water to every part of the premises by iron and lead piping. To the pump is attached a brass tap for the supply of the house: about a hundred feet from which, at the back of the Racquet-court, there is a copper fixed, and this too is filled by pipes led round the buildings.

During the nights from September to May, the billiard-table cushions, being stuffed with india-rubber, are much affected by the temperature, and in cold weather become hard as wood, rendering the tables wholly unfit for use. To obviate this difficulty, tin pipes are filled with boiling water from the copper above-mentioned, and applied to the face of each cushion; in about an hour the rubber yields to the heat, and the table is then in playing order. I have frequently heard gentlemen complain that their own tables were never fit to play upon; the reason is, their servants have perhaps never been accustomed to this sort of thing, and therefore do not know whether they have succeeded in getting the cushions into proper order or not. When a table has been long out of use, the best and readiest method of restoring the india-rubber to a proper state of flexibility is to take off the cushions, and lay them before a good fire, about a yard distant, so as not to scorch the cloth; but the person entrusted to perform this duty should be particularly careful. Any ordinary carpenter or cabinet-maker could take off the cushions and screw them on again in an hour: though perhaps it will be necessary to inform him, that he need not draw the tacks from the pockets, but merely take out the screws that secure the brasses or pocket-plates into the woodwork of the cushions. This done, raise the plates from the beds, and let the pockets drop down; when the cushions are screwed on, simply replace the pocket-plates and screw them tight, and the table will be ready for play. The whole business can be completed in two or three hours.

As I have passed a great portion of twenty years in a public billiard-room, I think myself fairly entitled to make a few general observations connected with the game. In the first place, the player should possess confidence and a perfect command of his temper: otherwise his entire nervous system will become affected, and a degree of tremulousness communicated to the balls, through the cue, from the striker's hand. The balls ever true to their formation will obey the touch; not only the striker's but the object ball will be in like manner affected, and more particularly so in side strokes. Thus the player's best efforts will be marred if he does not possess perfect command of his cue, which should be used with the delicacy and precision of a violin bow.

Nothing is more common than to hear players complain of the balls or the table being untrue; when a little reflection would bring them to a more just conclusion. It must be a sorry table indeed if the bed be untrue, as nothing can be more simple than the setting it level. The proper method is to get a joiner to shoot off two straight-edges, one twelve and the other six feet long. Let both faces of each piece of wood be smooth; as a spirit-level must be placed on the uppermost edge. To test the truth of the table, apply the longer piece from corner to corner each way, and down the centre, observing if the edge touches the bed throughout its entire length; next take the short one, and use it in the same manner from the corners to the middle pockets each way, and in every direction over the surface. By this process it will be ascertained whether the plane be generally true or not. In the next place, the spirit-level must be made use of for the purpose of fixing it *perfectly* true. This is done by applying the instrument in every direction; and wherever there appears the slightest incline, a couple of wedges reversed must be driven under the nearest leg, until the vacuum appears directly in the centre of the tube. This being carefully done in every part, the table is adjusted, and may be pronounced as perfect as human skill can make it.

As it is just possible that the person employed to make a straight-edge may be ignorant of the method to be adopted, I will here set it down. When the wood is planed off as level as possible the first time, lay it on a smooth plank, and rule a line along the edge. Then turn the wood over, and draw a line opposite the one already made; it will thus be ascertained how much the edge is out of direction: which must then be planed until a straight line can be drawn by it between the two former lines. This being accomplished, the straight-edge is perfect and fit for use.

Although the table can be made level as water, the balls cannot be made perfectly true, for two obvious reasons. The first and most important is, that it is not within the range of man's capabilities to make a perfect sphere; the second is, that the material of which the balls are made is not in every part of the same consistency, the ivory in its growth being more dense on one side than the other. Hence the many vexatious disappointments that occur, where a ball is played a dead strength down to the object on the lower spot. This more frequently happens at pool, when the striker is playing for safety. Just before the ball reaches its destination, being imperfectly weighted it loses its balance, and dies off gradually on one side: when, in passing over the smallest particle of chalk or any minute portion adhering to it from the point of the cue, the ball will turn from its course. I believe this may generally be attributed to the ball's travelling on the divisional line that marks the growth of the ivory. Another thing is certain, that the striker frequently gives his elbow a twist when in the act of making a stroke, and, instead of hitting the ball directly on its centre, touches it partially on the side. When this happens, it is almost sure to be fatal.

I once witnessed a marvellous performance at pool.

There were fifteen players, the majority of them having two or three lives; when a Mr. Lewis, of Caius college, came into the room, and on being asked by some one to take a ball, acceded and joined in the play. He was however entitled to only one life, the lowest number on the marking-board: that being the rule under the circumstances. I should presume, by his mode of proceeding, that this gentleman had never handled a cue before; for when it came to his turn to play, he hammered away in the most awkward manner possible, and several times missed the ball played on; but, as luck would have it, his ball always returned from the cushion, and striking the object ball saved his solitary life. Thus he kept on till all the balls were dead but one, and that one reduced to the last life. It was the owner of this ball's turn to play; and the hazard to be made being very easy, every one concluded that the striker had won the whole pool. But here Mr. L——'s luck brought him through; for the striker missed, leaving him the recipient of the entire amount of the pool. This was the most extraordinary thing of the kind that ever came under my notice.

Another curious instance within my recollection, of the uncertainty of billiards, shews the folly of betting long odds. I was once looking on, when two excellent players were contending: the score of one had reached forty-eight, and his opponent stood at fourteen. They were playing 'fifty up': and the odds were St. Paul's to a pigsty. Two or three strokes were now played on either part before a score was made: when the player who was behind got a break, and finished the game in good style. But the most wonderful part of the business is, that in the course of the day a game was lost in exactly the same manner by the party who won in the first instance. These facts should suffice to deter persons from betting long odds. During my large experience of billiards, I have not seen a ten stroke made in the regular course of play more than three times. I will now take leave of this subject with a general caution: never play with strangers for money. There are scores of men who go about assuming the style and bearing of gentlemen, but are no better than 'skittle-sharps'; although I have known some who affected to hold their heads pretty high.

I recollect a very remarkable instance of sheer luck occurring at the game of cribbage, in which, as noticed in some earlier pages of these memoirs, I was once tolerably proficient. This case arose whilst I was playing with three others. We were playing five-card cribbage: and, it being my deal, our opponents wanted four of the game; whilst our peg stood within eight holes of home. The cards were played round without scoring a fifteen, sequence, or pair; and at the conclusion not one of the four held a hole. I then took up the crib, which contained the exact number required to win the game! This is, I should think, the most wonderful incident that ever happened at cribbage. Perhaps Professor Babbage could inform us how long, according to the law of chances, it will be before the like can again take place.

CHAPTER IX.

I BEGIN UPON THESE MEMOIRS—ANOTHER ANCIENT ALLY RETURNS IN GOOD SEASON—WITHERS'S POEMS—MY ADDRESS TO THE AUTHOR, AND OUR SUBSEQUENT MEETING—SIR JOHN PATTESON'S ARBITRATION BETWEEN TOWN AND GOWN.

HAVING put my house in order and covered every available piece of ground with bricks and mortar, I set to work in earnest upon these memoirs,—a desire for the completion of which had been expressed by many members of the University, as well as by my private friends. One morning as I sat pondering over my task, (for I had to write entirely from memory, never having kept a diary or even recorded a note,) I received a letter which, as the postman observed, wore a professional exterior, being directed in a singularly neat style. I turned over the envelope, to see if I could remember anything like the hand; but no, it was perfectly strange to me. On breaking open the seal however, I cast my eye upon the subscription, and recognised the ever-welcome name of my other University friend, of whom I had once only caught a transient glimpse since he left college, nearly twenty years before.

I will not attempt to tell how glad I was to see him on that occasion. He was even then much changed by some years' sojourn in a distant clime beneath a burning sun. His manly countenance was bronzed by the scorching rays that too frequently strike Europeans with certain death; but although his skin was changed to almost oriental darkness, I found no other change in him. He was still the same calm, dignified 'gentleman' as when I knew him: bringing to mind the best definition of the word I ever met with. It was given by a lady, and ran thus: "A gentleman is one who inherits the courage of man combined with the tenderness of woman." Such is my ever honored friend. I trust he entertains a higher opinion of me than to suppose me capable of descending to the meanness of flattery. I declare in simple truth, I would not stand self-convicted of that contemptible vice to gain an empire.

At that period my old friend was at home on leave: and passing hastily through Cambridge, if my memory serves me, he just snatched a hurried dinner with a relative then resident in the University; after which I joined them, and having taken a glass or two of wine together, we parted at the railway station. But to return to my letter: on scanning it over I was glad to learn that the writer purposed paying me a visit for a few days. He had now retired from the service, and was residing in London near Berkeley-square. I need not say that I was only too happy to make preparations for his arrival: and having been apprised that he would arrive on a certain day by the express train, proceeded in a clarence to meet him. After waiting on the platform some few minutes, the train drove into the station:

and on its stopping, I looked in all directions for the object of my search; but, alas! I could see nothing like him.

At length, however, a man of large dimensions came walking towards me: and as he approached I perceived (as in a former case already recorded) that the party was mounted on my friend's legs,[1] with whose unmistakable action I was well acquainted. But the general appearance of the stranger made me hesitate, for he looked like two individuals of my friend's calibre cast into one: and, to render the metamorphosis more complete, had a most luxuriant crop of whiskers and moustache. However, on seeing him smile, my doubts were at once removed: and I bade him welcome with as pleasurable feelings as ever throbbed in the heart of man. Having secured his luggage, we entered the vehicle, and drove to the street where he used to lodge when an undergraduate, somewhere about twenty years earlier. I had taken the precaution to secure him rooms in the old place, thinking he would feel himself more at home than in a strange house. The people that lived there in his time had left; but the house is occupied by a family named French, than whom there are not more respectable and industrious people in the University.

On the following day, as we sat in conversation, I introduced my MS., and at the request of my friend commenced reading these memoirs, so far as then existing. He listened with strict attention to the end: and when I had concluded, gave me his opinion in kind and flattering terms, advising me to prosecute my task

---

[1] Recognising the *legs*, a habit acquired on the stage.

to its completion. Since this time I have received at his hands every encouragement and assistance in making my work presentable to the public; and if my "strange eventful history" should prove generally acceptable, it will be mainly through his generous aid. From this period I proceeded steadily on with my work: having no particular object in view beyond the approval of my fellow-creatures.

One morning, while in conversation with our family doctor about various matters, painting and poetry crept in: when all of a sudden, he asked me if I had read Withers's *Poems*. Upon my saying that I had never heard of them, he offered to lend me a copy: at the same time informing me, that they were the production of a poor self-taught man in a country town called Fordham, about fourteen miles distant. Withers was a sort of half shoemaker, half agricultural labourer, and, having a large family, had suffered great privations: being once compelled to take shelter in the district union. After carefully reading through these simple but beautiful little poems, I could not but acknowledge that such an amount of self-culture deserved every assistance and encouragement. So feeling desirous of contributing my mite, I addressed the following lines to my humble brother of the gentle craft:

TO J. R. WITHERS, POET.

HAIL! brother of the gentle craft,
   I've read thy poems through:
And on my kindred nature graft
   Thine own so just and true.

My fate like thine was hard indeed,
   In boyhood quite alone;
I had no friend to help me speed,
   And ev'ry hope was gone.

Yet still I journeyed on life's road,
   Though oft o'erwhelmed with grief;
And when I found a brief abode,
   It brought my soul relief.

Some kindly hearts would heed my tale,
   And deem my story true;
But when I tried—again to fail—
   My sorrows came anew.

Hope buoyed me up as on I marched
   Along life's trodden road;
Anon with thirst and hunger parched,
   And stung by misery's piercing goad.

Yet still I tried and trusted on,
   In hope of better days;
And by degrees I worked along,
   And trod some brighter ways.

Twelve dreary months—just like yourself,
   In botching shoes I passed;
The canting knave who took the pelf,
   Soon took me off the *last!*[1]

And cast me loose upon the world,
   To do the best I could:
To sure destruction I was hurled:
   But out of bad sprang good.

---

[1] A term used by shoemakers when they take the *last* out of a boot or shoe upon its being completed.

FROM LIFE'S HARVEST.

My little soul aspiring rose,
   And urged me on to fame;
When to myself I did propose
   To win a noble name:

To be by means as yet unknown,
   Something above the rest;
And when I first could stand alone,
   I felt supremely blest.

I walked to London's mighty mart,
   A dragging dreary way;
No cash to pay for coach or cart,
   Small choice of go or stay.

Thus time passed on, and I increased
   In knowledge and in fame;
And in exertion never ceased,
   Till I had won the game.

When I arrived at manhood's prime,
   I say it not in boast—
None could excel me in the time,
   Of all the craftsmen host.

Now years roll on, and I've grown old,
   Yet still am hale and strong;
My spirit too is quick and bold
   To crush an act of wrong.

A hand I have, and mind to boot,
   To aid my fellow-man;
And if I'm spared to take the route,
   I'll see you if I can.

I have ventured to make a few emendations here: as the original copy went to post without correction.

Some few days afterwards a grand treat was given to the school-children of the town, in celebration of peace restored on the termination of that bloody and destructive war with Russia. It was indeed a general rejoicing of the entire population. The mayor and members of the corporation met in the Town-hall; where open carriages were in attendance to convey them in procession to Parker's-piece, the spot selected for the festival. The mayor having first delivered an address from his carriage on the Market-hill, we proceeded through the streets,— the different schools being formed in marching-order, attended by their masters and teachers, and followed by the inhabitants, with some additional thousands who came pouring in from the surrounding villages. The whole assemblage constituted one of the most imposing pageants ever witnessed in a provincial town.

As I was at the time a member of the municipal council, my duties detained me till the conclusion of the ceremonies. But on reaching home, I had the pleasure of seeing my shopmate Withers the poet, who had come over to participate in the gaieties of the day. After giving him a hearty welcome (not forgetting the rites of hospitality) we entered into conversation: and I soon perceived that my new acquaintance was far ahead of many who have had the advantages of superior teaching. He is a fine-looking man, very erect, having a lofty forehead and pleasing countenance, with an expression of childlike innocence. From this time Withers and I became friends; and shortly after I drove over, spent a pleasant day with him, and visited his friends;

being most hospitably entertained by a lady who had been the means of bringing his poems before the public. Here I was also shewn over the house and garden. It was a beautiful country residence, with a lawn sloping down to a running stream, upon whose surface slept a little boat which had the appearance of having been moored there for years.

The proprietor of this delightful dwelling was labouring under a severe rheumatic affliction, and was led into the room by a youthful attendant. He had been a remarkably fine man and a great sportsman; and in one room hung portraits of his favorite greyhounds, upon whose merits he expatiated with lively feelings. There was one splendid-looking animal, which, as he told me, had won him some hundreds. I saw too at this place the most beautiful collection of old china that ever came under my notice; which the lady informed me she had been many years in getting together. As the day was fast declining, I took leave of these kind-hearted people, well pleased with my visit to our humble poet.

The last business of importance, in which I was engaged whilst a member of the town council, was an amicable settlement of the hitherto interminably contested rights in dispute between the University and Town authorities. It was proposed, and eventually determined, that the matters at issue should be submitted to the judgment, and left to the decision of Sir John Patteson. No better qualified arbitrator could have been selected than Sir John: though, at the time, I held it a dangerous experiment to entrust the rights of either body to individual judgment. However, the Award was passed and accepted as a final measure;

indeed it was most desirable that the two corporations should arrive at some just and honorable conclusion.

Some time after this business had been adjusted, it was agreed betwixt the parties to present the learned judge, in consideration of his services, with a testimonial worthy the occasion; and an elegant candalabra was fixed upon as being most appropriate. The day having arrived for presentation, the mayor, aldermen, and councillors repaired in their robes to Trinity-lodge, the residence of the master of that college. On arriving at this splendid abode, we were ushered into a spacious and elegantly furnished apartment, where the representatives of the learned body were already assembled. After some preliminary arrangements, we ascended that fine old-fashioned staircase, on which stands a most beautiful clock, said to have belonged to the great Sir Isaac Newton; and thence entering the splendid room appropriated for the occasion, formed a circle facing the master and Sir John Patteson. On a table in the centre stood the testimonial to be presented; and on each side sat some elegantly-dressed ladies. Altogether it was one of the most beautiful scenes I ever witnessed. As several of the speeches were delivered in Latin, I lost no doubt the best part of the treat. However, as that was a misfortune and not a fault, I consoled myself under the circumstances as well as I could.

The business concluded, we took a cordial leave of the veteran arbiter; and having made our obeisance to the learned head of Trinity, returned to the Townhall: where we doffed our robes and separated, each man to pursue his business and desire; 'for every man hath business and desire, such as it is.'

CHAPTER X.

THE MANCHESTER EXHIBITION—MY TROUBLESOME, BUT SUCCESSFUL SEARCH AFTER A LONG LOST RELATIVE—THE ATLAS IRON WORKS, AND OTHER MANCHESTER MARVELS—MY MANŒUVRES AS CHIEF OF A FIRE-BRIGADE—GRANDEUR OF THE EXHIBITION—DEATH OF CHATTERTON—SONG OF THE MOON—RETURN TO LONDON—MY ILLNESS—I REACH HOME AGAIN—A SERIOUS ACCIDENT—CONCLUSION.

THERE is one passage well worth recording, which I must not exclude from these reminiscences; and that is, my visit to the Art-Treasures Exhibition at Manchester, in 1857.

Having received an invitation from a gentleman whom I ever held in the highest estimation, (Mr. C. P. Stewart, of the Atlas Iron Works), I started from King's Cross: and having secured a first-class ticket, proceeded in excellent company to my destination. On arriving at Manchester, I found myself in a second metropolis, of which the bustle and traffic seemed incessant. The omnibuses here seemed the most commodious and beautiful things of the kind I had ever beheld; they were drawn by three horses abreast, and carried (as I was informed by one of the drivers) fifty-five passengers. The thousands of people emerging from the different mills, with their wooden shoes clattering on the pavement, was a curious aud altogether novel spectacle.

The town being full of visitors at the time, I had great difficulty in procuring a lodging. Feeling tired after so long and tedious a journey, I entered a coffee-house, and requested to be served with a cup of coffee. But on asking if I could have a bed,—the young woman whom I addressed made answer in a rich Hibernian accent—'The divil a bit of a bed is there in all Manchesthur!' As I sat listlessly sipping my coffee, a gentlemanly-looking man entered: from whose conversation I discovered that he was brother to the mistress of the establishment. Upon my stating that I had travelled between two and three hundred miles, and would pay anything in reason for lodgings (which I should require for a week), he withdrew, but shortly returning informed me that his sister would make the best provision for me in her power. Accordingly I was soon shewn up to a bedroom, which bore unmistakeable evidence of having been occupied by a female: for upon opening a drawer to deposit my linen, I found it full of feminine garments. Scorning further curiosity, I closed the sacred repository, and laying my own things on the top covered them with a handkerchief; feeling convinced (as I afterwards learned was the fact) that the landlady had resigned her apartment for my accommodation.

The morrow being Sunday, I resolved to go on a strange voyage of discovery. I had been informed that my sister heretofore mentioned (and whom I had not seen for thirty years) was living either at Duckenfield or Ashton-under-Lyne. So taking the train, I proceeded to prosecute my apparently hopeless task of searching her out. This happened to be the time of Ashton wake, and many persons were going there to see their friends. In the same carriage with myself was a young man (with his wife and little girl), to whom I communicated my intended business. On our arrival at Ashton, he introduced me to his family circle, who were plain, homely sort of people; the old dame handed me a glass of home-brewed, and the company, about fourteen in number, treated me very courteously. After this, my fellow-traveller offered to accompany me to Duckenfield, about two miles distant, in quest of my long-lost sister. I had merely heard some years before that she was living in that part of the country.

Having reached the place, my indefatigable acquaintance went up one street and down another; inquiring of the people and knocking at different doors as we went along, to ascertain if the name I had possessed him of was known. It was 'Webb Bernard'; the surname was common, but the christian name was nowhere to be found. After toiling three or four hours beneath a burning sun, my friend (for he deserves the title) put me on the right scent, and returned to spend the short time that remained to him with his relations. At this juncture, a funeral procession emerged from a short street; the corpse being that of a pitman, who had been killed by an explosion or some such accident. It was a solemn scene; his young widow and two or three children followed, lamenting their sad bereavement in tones of genuine grief.

When the people had cleared away (for there must

have been three or four hundred of them) I approached a little woman with a child in her arms, whose name I had been informed was the same as that I had been enquiring for. Having apologised for the liberty, I asked if her name was 'Bernard'; to which she replied in the affirmative. I then put the question—did she know 'Webb Bernard?'—'Oh, yes!' she said, he's my John's (meaning her husband's) uncle.' Without making known my business, I asked where the party was to be found; and was told that I should be sure to hear of him at Mr. Goldthorp's, Ashton-under-Lyne. Thanking my informant, I now retraced my steps, and hastened to the place to which I had been directed. Just as I reached the door two little boys came out, of whom I enquired if they knew a person named 'Bernard'; they did not, but referred me to the landlord of a public-house close by, which I at once entered, and enquired of the host if he knew a person in the cabinet line, of the before-mentioned name? But after vainly trying to collect his scattered thoughts, he too uttered that sickening 'No', which I had heard more than a hundred times during my tedious day's search.

At length it struck me that the person sought might (as now and then happens) be better known by his christian than by his surname. I therefore again asked, if he knew any one named 'Webb'? 'To be sure', he replied, 'Old Webb? I have known him for years, and worked in the same shop with him; and if you want a hand, I can assure you he's a first-rate workman; but the trade here has been dreadfully slack for a long time.' I hereupon stated that I had come from London; and being commissioned to deliver a message to his shopmate should be glad to speak with him. The publican immediately volunteered to fetch Mr. Webb; and in about a quarter-of-an-hour he arrived. I then introduced myself as the bearer of a Mr. and Mrs. Lambeth's kind regards to himself and family, also that they were desirous of hearing from them; and as the day was fast declining, I requested to be introduced to his wife,—telling him that I was specially charged with a message to her from Mrs. Lambeth, whom she had known from childhood, when residing in the next house to my mother's. Assenting to my wish, 'Old Webb' now conducted me to his home,—where he presented to me a poor attenuated creature, the mere shadow of that plump and rosy looking girl whom I had remembered in happier times. She was so altered I should not have known her; neither did she know me, any more than if we had never met. She still retained the style and stamp of respectability, although it was evident that poverty's iron grasp had fallen heavily on her shattered frame; her speech too had undergone a considerable change, evinced in a strong northern accent: which rendered the metamorphosis more complete. During our conversation, my sister asked me if I knew her brother John? I replied, 'that I had seen him, but could hardly say I knew him.' Seeing her so poor in health, I dared not make myself known; dreading the possible effects of a sudden shock. But on rising to leave, I promised to call again before leaving Manchester.

It was now almost time for the train to start; so, accompanied by the husband, I took my way to the station, where (having yet a quarter-of-an-hour to the good) I proposed a glass of brandy-and-water ere we parted. Indeed, I felt rather in need of a little stimulus after my tiresome day's pilgrimage under one of the hottest suns ever known in this climate. As we sat drinking our liquor, I handed over my card, saying that I was desired to deliver it to him. 'Why', said he, 'this is my wife's brother's name!' and then glanced alternately at me and the card, in a state of apparent bewilderment. As the train had now arrived, I made myself known: and putting a half-sovereign into my companion's hand, requested he would not inform his wife who I was till the morrow. I told him also that I would call again on Thursday, and at the same time gave my address in Manchester. On arriving at my lodgings I took some refreshment, having had nothing to eat since breakfast, and after a pipe and a glass of grog retired to bed pretty well fatigued.

The next morning, as I was sitting at breakfast, Katey our Hibernian waitress announced that a lady below desired to speak with me. On going downstairs I found my poor sister, whom I at once invited up: and as I had broiled ham and eggs just served, we breakfasted together: after which she returned by the omnibus to Ashton. Having seen my sister off, I next prepared to visit my friend at the Atlas Iron-Works. Here I met with a hearty reception, and was shown over the immense workshops, in which were employed 1500 men, in various branches, on the construction of locomotive engines. In one compartment were fifty furnaces, where the disciples of Vulcan hammered at the glowing iron, the heat seeming enough to melt their solid flesh. In another part of the building they were planing and boring steel, with as much ease as a carpenter would operate on a deal board: and I saw bars of iron cut in two, with as little effort as is used in severing a yard of butter.[1] When I had gone entirely through this truly wonderful establishment, my friend furnished me with letters of introduction to the different mills and warehouses; and never before had I seen such truly gigantic works. In one mill alone were employed 2000 hands, and I was informed that the area of its different floors was seven acres.

Having spent an entire day in these marvellous and most interesting hives of industry, I returned to my lodgings, and prepared to meet my friend Stewart at the 'Queen's hotel', where I was engaged to dine with him. The 'Queen's' is a splendid building, and everything appeared to be in first-rate style; the number of beds they made up is immense—I think my informant said 300. Dinner over, we took a cab and drove round the suburbs; after which we pulled up at Roberts's rooms, and played at billiards till the clock indicated it was time to retire.

On reaching my temporary abode, I took a candle and went directly to bed: but had barely put out the light and turned-in, when some one knocked at the room-door; and on my asking what was the matter, the landlady's voice informed me that a servant-girl had set fire to the bedroom overhead. In an instant I slipped on my trousers, and first desired every door and window to be closed; then rushing up-stairs, I drew forth the

---

[1] Butter is sold in the Cambridge market-place in lengths or *yards*. This seems so extraordinary to persons residing at a distance, that it sometimes provokes disbelief. In some of the counties, a frequent term of banter is used in these words—'Go to Cambridge where they sell butter by the *yard*.'

girl, whose night-clothes were in flames. These I seized at the part not yet burned: and, twisting them as one wrings out a dish-cloth, succeeded in saving her from further injury; which effected, I thrust her into the next room, and securing the doors retreated downstairs: for the smoke had nearly overpowered me. By this time the house was in the utmost confusion; the lodgers were running about half-naked, and evincing such terror as I have seldom witnessed. I entreated them to be calm, and to furnish themselves with all the water they could get in such vessels as were at hand. Being thus prepared, I marched up again at the head of my fire-brigade; giving orders that, as soon as I opened the door, each person should discharge upon the flames his supply of the liquid element, and then retreat immediately; for the room was now completely filled with smoke, so that it was impossible to stand against it. Then shutting the door, I threw myself on my face, and called to the people to 'bear a hand' with a second charge: which being well directed, the flames were subdued.

Not a moment was now to be lost, as the house was rapidly filling with smoke; so, seeing the landlady on the stairs, I asked her if there was not a window or skylight in the attic that could be readily opened. In a moment she flew to the spot, and succeeded just in time to escape being suffocated; indeed, it was with some difficulty that I managed to take her below. The front door was now opened: and, the smoke rushing up through the attic window, in a few minutes the house was tolerably clear. To make assurance doubly sure, I requested wet sheets to be clapped against the burning wood: and this done bade all retire to their beds, telling them that I would keep watch; which I did, until satisfied that all was perfectly safe, when I turned-in myself.

Amongst the lodgers was a German; who, as soon as the alarm was given, coolly dressed himself, put on his great-coat and hat, drew his portmanteau to the landing, and stood ready for a bolt. Of all the cowardly knaves I ever came across, this fellow was about the very worst. Feeling indignant at his unmanly conduct, I asked him where he came from: and when in answer he drawled out 'Ber-lin,' I replied: 'The sooner you go back to Ber-lin the better—and don't forget to keep there!' When we met at breakfast, he got a pretty good roasting: and Katey assailed him with some smart sallies of Irish wit. However, in the course of the day he packed up his kit and sneaked off. Whether he went to Berlin, or elsewhere, it matters little. For my own part, I received in hearty thanks ample remuneration for the service I had rendered on the occasion. The mistress of the establishment expressed her gratitude not unmixed with a leaven of superstition; for she insisted that Providence had directed my steps thither, for the express purpose of saving her from the dreadful calamity she had so narrowly escaped. Having put myself in order, I mounted a 'bus and started for the Exhibition.

To attempt a description of the beautiful and wondrous works of art brought from every available quarter, and here concentrated in one grand display of human genius, would indeed be futile. In my weak judgment the scene was lofty and sublime to an extent far beyond the limited comprehension of ordinary minds.

All, however, seemed lost in amazement, as they revelled in the matchless scene presented to their bewildered gaze. I was chiefly struck by one pictorial gem, which appeared to attract the attention also of thousands. Its subject was the death of 'the marvellous boy' Chatterton. What a beautiful halo the artist had thrown around this scene of poverty and despair! There lay stretched upon a poor couch, in a miserable garret, the corpse of him who fell a victim to his own mighty intellect. Around were scattered fragments of his works, the last evidence of his maddened existence; the light seemed to steal softly into the chamber, as if it would throw a veil over the melancholy scene; it appeared like subdued moonlight gleaming through a silvery cloud upon the pallid face of the self-sacrifed, ill-fated youth. With sorrowful feelings I turned away; but still the subject occupied my thoughts, until the picture became fairly stamped upon my mind: and there it is likely to remain, 'while memory holds her seat.' After feasting almost to satiety upon the splendid banquet that had been prepared to delight the senses, I retired: and taking a seat beside the driver of the 'bus, enquired what number of passengers he carried? His reply was, 'fifty-five': and he had been thirteen times that day to the Exhibition, carrying each time his full complement to and fro,—except once, and then he was only one passenger short. Having reached my hotel, I sought my private room, where feeling in a sombre mood and deeply impressed with what I had witnessed, I wrote the following stanzas:

SONG OF THE MOON.

I'm queen of the night, in my silvery light,
   Where millions of orbs around me play:
I'm queen of the night, and my silvery light
   Shall cheer the traveller's lonely way.

O'er temple, palace, and cottage I glide,
   Watching o'er all thro' the weary night;
And sailing along in my queenly pride,
   There's none to dispute my sovereign right.

I watch o'er the cradled and sleeping child,
   That smiles in its dreams and laughs aloud:
And the care-worn mother, placid and mild,
   When daily toil has her spirit bowed.

Young lovers I light through the copse and glade,
   And mark their vows of eternal truth:
Full many a young maiden's heart betrayed
   I've witnessed—by many a heartless youth.

The sea-boy I view on his tottering height,
   Who rocks and sleeps thro' the midnight watch:
As I gladden the heaving waves with light,
   That gleams through the sails the breezes catch.

I peep into the felon's darksome cell,
   And see him writhe in agony there;
Where nought but vice and misery dwell,
   By remorse attended and black despair.

On the good man's death-bed I shed my ray,
   And watch his spirit prepared to fly:
Who fears not the last, the dreadful day,
   But hails with pleasure his hour to die.

> I'm queen of the night, in my silvery light,
> Where millions of orbs around me play:
> I'm queen of the night, and my silvery light
> Shall cheer the traveller's lonely way.

In the evening I again dined at the Queen's hotel with my friend of the Atlas Iron Works: and only regretted that we were compelled to break up a pleasant sitting at an early hour; for Mr. S. had the superintendence of men at work both night and day. This indeed seemed striking while the iron was hot; for it appeared to me they never gave it time to get cold.

I started on the following morning for Ashton, to spend a few hours with my newly-found sister and her husband. During our conversation I learned that their circumstances were not very flourishing; I therefore made such arrangements as contributed towards the amelioration of their present condition: and as the day drew nigh to a close, took my leave of them. On regaining my lodging, I procured some refreshment and retired early; for as the morrow was the last day I purposed spending in Manchester, I determined to rise betimes, and visit those parts of the town I had not yet seen.

As the clock struck five I sallied forth, and visited the Peel Park, together with other places and buildings of note that were to be met with in my wanderings. Returning to breakfast, I saw a gentleman emerging from a Catholic church, whom I knew as having been formerly of Caius college. We recognised each other instantly. He told me that he was now manager of one of the large firms, the extensive premises of which he invited me to inspect, and also accompanied me to several others, where he courteously introduced me; amongst the number was that of Watts, then mayor of Manchester. Being desirous of seeing as much of this wonderful centre of trade as possible, I had nearly exhausted my powers; so much so, that partially overdone nature began to remind me it was time to pull in and slacken my pace. Availing myself of the gentle hint, I passed the remainder of the day in quiet: and after dining with my friend for the last time, bade him good-bye. I then paid my bill, packed up my things, and prepared to start for London on the morrow.

As I had taken a first-class ticket, the company on the journey was very agreeable. Nothing transpired to mar the happiness of our little party, until fatigued and nearly worn out by a week's incessant exertion and excitement, I dropped off to sleep; and my hand, falling over the elbow that divides the seat into compartments, came in contact with a lady who occupied the next place. This purely accidental circumstance gave umbrage to her male companion sitting opposite; not that he said more than (or quite so much as) *I* should have done, being in his place, and believing that an insult had been offered to a female rich or poor. But being perfectly unconscious of harm, and knowing that impropriety of conduct is foreign to my nature, I simply shifted my seat: feeling indeed sorry that any cause of complaint should have been given by me even accidentally.

On arriving at King's Cross station, I was suddenly seized with what appeared to me to be English cholera. A policeman on duty perceiving the painful state I was in, fetched a cab, in which I drove off to the abode of a relative in the City-road. Here I lay prostrate for more than a week, taking nothing but quinine and brandy. This malady I attributed to a filthy and poisonous nuisance: which, to the disgrace of the railway authorities, I had casually encountered on my journey. However that may be, I was by this time very weak, and hardly fit to undergo a journey of sixty miles; but I was determined to reach home if possible. I therefore caused myself to be driven to the Eastern Counties Railway, and after a most painful ride reached my own dwelling more dead than alive. For eight weeks more I continued in the doctor's hands: at the end of which period my legs were not much bigger than broomsticks; but at length nature struggling with the envious disease gained the mastery, and I was restored to my usual health and strength.

Nothing now occurred of any particular consequence. The term passed away as usual; and Christmas-day arrived in due course, which we spent in strict accordance with ancient custom, surrounded by such good things as generally deck the board at this festive season. The following day being generally considered a holiday, I proposed to visit a gentleman at a village about six miles distant; taking with me a nephew, for whom I thought the excursion would be a pleasant change, as he had been entirely brought up in London. We reached our destination in a very short time, having a good hackney and light trap, and were most hospitably entertained. Some friends of our host joined us after dinner, with whom we spent a most agreeable evening; nor was anything omitted that could conduce to our comfort. Thus, between good fare and excellent company, the minutes flew apace. The time having arrived for taking our departure, the horse was put-to: and, after taking leave of the party, we started on our homeward journey,—but had scarcely got half-way, when an accident of the most fearful description befel us. The horse, from some cause which I could never clearly divine, swerved suddenly from the road, bringing the wheel of our vehicle in contact with a stump-post. The concussion was of so sudden and violent a nature, that it threw us both into the air: my nephew's arm being broken by the fall. As for myself, I was completely stunned and incapable of rising for some time. The most marvellous part of the business was, that the horse (which was nearly thorough-bred) stood perfectly still. Being near some cottages, we called for help: when a churlish fellow put his head out of the window, and demanded to know, if he rendered us assistance whether we would pay him? In a short time three or four labourers came to our aid, and having procured a cart we rode home tolerably well jolted. The axle of the gig was twisted quite round, so that one wheel was brought to the back of the vehicle, which was thus rendered perfectly useless.

My unfortunate companion on our arrival rung up the doctor, and got his arm set; whilst I retired to bed, not feeling much pain at the time. But on awaking next morning, I found myself completely helpless: being unable to raise my body from the horizontal posture in which I was set fast. Thus I remained for nearly a week; until fairly wearied of this recumbent position I grew impatient, and determined by one desperate effort to regain my perpendicular. Having succeeded with great pain in drawing on my clothes, I managed to descend the stairs just as the family were sitting down to dinner. Quite surprised at my unexpected appearance, they jumped up and handed me a seat; and from this time I gradually recovered, although it was some weeks ere I could walk with a firm step: and even now the parts that were injured are very tender. This pulverising process would have sent most men of my age to their last account; but, thanks to a cast-iron frame and constitution to match, I am still in the land of the living, and as well as at any period of my existence.

Here then, in the sixty-third year of my mortal pilgrimage, I close these truthful (however humble) reminiscences of a life that, I would fain believe, has not been all misspent. Man proposes, and GOD disposes: but,—

> "Like the wanderer of the desert,
>   When, across the dreary sand,
> Breathes the perfume from the thickets
>   Bordering on the promised Land;
>
> When afar he sees the palm-trees
>   Cresting o'er the lonely well,
> When he hears the pleasant tinkle
>   Of the distant camel's bell,"—

I feel that I have well-nigh gained a secure haven: and may reasonably look to end my days in the enjoyment of ease and domestic tranquillity. It is indeed but the accident of an accident, that I was not born to competence: instead of having to battle for a bare livelihood during two-thirds of my career. But as the inheritor of broad acres, which, within the memory of living men, have been for ever lost to me and mine, it would hardly have been my lot to realise the 'sweet uses of adversity.'

I might never have imbibed that detestation of hypocrisy,—that hatred of oppression,—and that sympathy with my afflicted fellow-creatures, which have combined to form the ruling principle of my existence. I pray you, gentle reader, mock me not; but truly, I am vain enough to believe, that this same autobiography of mine, along with many 'trivial, fond records,' embodies also a tangible MORAL: one which, if rightly read, may be addressed, in turn, to friendless youth, to struggling manhood, and to prosperous old age. EVEN IN THIS WORLD, THERE IS SOMETIMES A REWARD VOUCHSAFED TO

Faith and Perseverance.

BROWN'S BILLIARD ROOMS, RACQUET COURTS, ETC.

14 JA 59

www.ingramcontent.com/pod-product-compliance
Lightning Source LLC
Chambersburg PA
CBHW080235170426
43192CB00014BA/2460